Fidel Castro & the Cuban Revolution

What the f**k was all that about?

J. Sheppard
Copyright © 2017

To Laura, my most favourite revolutionary in all the world, and to all my friends and family, who have politely suffered my constant blabbering about all things Cuba over the years.

Introduction

There is no shortage of books on Fidel Castro and the Cuban Revolution, but trying to get people to read them is another matter. Here in the UK there is, on the whole, an overwhelming sense of indifference when it comes to the subject.

The reason behind this lack of interest is understandable, not least because of the lack of shared history and trade links between the countries. But another possible reason is that many books about Fidel and the Cuban Revolution aren't really made for the layperson. As such, they usually require a certain amount of prior knowledge on the subject, often involving long tracts of socialist jargon that make you want to get on with the housework instead.

So with this in mind, I decided to write this book in the way that I talk to my friends down the pub – by which I mean informally, and with anecdotes, odd tangents and jokes that would make my partner roll her eyes. In this way, it will be accessible to those who have not come across the subject before, whilst offering a more engaging story to those already well-versed.

I must confess that none of this is new. I have merely read a great number of books on the subject, whose authors have already done all the hard work. They have done all the research, conducted all the interviews, looked at the documents and made the Freedom of Information requests. I am not standing on the shoulders of giants; at best I am stealing a cheeky piggy-back ride and peering over their shoulder.

What I hope to offer is a fresh perspective, where the story is not just about a man who was jailed for trying – and failing – to start an uprising, who fled to Mexico before returning with 82 men to oust a dictator. And it won't just be about the time he repelled an invasion which had been organised and financed by the biggest military superpower the world has ever seen even though his army had to learn how to drive their tanks on the way to the battlefield. And it won't just be about how he survived hundreds of assassination attempts, how he helped end apartheid and created one of the most enviable healthcare systems in the world.

Because what it will mainly be about is the ways in which one's life can be guided by the grandest ideas of equality and fraternity, and result in a surreal chaos in which boy scouts are held responsible for keeping the streets free from rioters, oranges are declared bourgeois, and the U.S. National Security Council discuss a plot to fake the resurrection of Jesus Christ.

3

I
A Rebellious Youth

"The first duty of a man is to think for himself."
José Martí

In August of 1927, in a small Cuban town called Birán, Fidel Castro was born. His father, Angel Castro, had come to the country as an illiterate Spanish soldier but ended up (sometimes by literally moving the fence-posts) controlling 26,000 acres of farmland. After Angel's first marriage ended in divorce he married his self-educated, spirited and determined sixteen year-old housekeeper, Lina Ruz.

Lina cared for the children almost single-handedly and the most notable account of Angel's personal involvement in Fidel's upbringing seems to be giving him his first cigar at the age of fourteen or fifteen. But as Fidel grew older – and more rebellious – his relationship with his father became more fractious, with reports that Fidel once challenged him to a duel (on horseback no less) and tried to get workers on the family farm to strike in demonstration at their exploitation.

When he was six Fidel was sent to stay with a teacher in the nearby city of Santiago de Cuba. Like most Cubans at the time, the schoolteacher was suffering from extreme poverty, and so instead of feeding and educating the children she pocketed the fees and did neither. Added to this, the schoolteacher made the children adhere to strict house rules that prohibited 'raising their voice' and 'asking for things' – with all transgressions punishable by a spanking. Any child would have found it hard to keep to these constraints and Fidel was no exception. For one thing, a child has no real concept of volume. And not being able to ask for things seems ludicrously strict, because children want *everything*, and most of the time they don't even know what it is, so you have to explain to them that "You can't have that, that's a lamppost.... no, no you don't want that, that's a cloud.... no put that down, that's Donald Rumsfeld."

Soon after, accompanied by his two brothers Ramón and Raúl, Fidel was sent to a prestigious Catholic school in Santiago. It proved a bad mistake. The Castro boys found it hard to integrate themselves with the snobby children of the elites and inevitably were involved in numerous scuffles. After Angel was informed of their bad grades and even worse behaviour, he informed them that they would not be returning. His brothers were fairly nonplussed by the news but Fidel was horrified and insisted he be sent to another school and threatened to burn the house down if he wasn't. Whether they thought the headstrong boy was capable of such an act, or whether they were impressed by his passion for learning, his parents acquiesced to his request and promised to find him a school.

They settled on the Jesuit-run Dolores School, and it was here that Fidel's behaviour – and grades – improved dramatically. The religious aspect of his schooling, however, was not readily absorbed. "When I was a young boy," Fidel explains, "my father taught me that to be a good Catholic, I had to confess at church if I ever had impure thoughts about a girl. That very evening, I had to rush and confess my sin, and the next night, and the next. After a week, I decided religion wasn't for me."

It was during his time at the school that Fidel made his first foray into world affairs by writing a letter to President Roosevelt to congratulate him on his triumph in the recent Presidential elections. In the letter he requested that he send him a ten dollar bill. This may have been cheeky, but at least he didn't end the letter with, "After all, you have exploited our nation for years, so it's the least you can do you capitalist worm." Incredibly, Fidel did actually receive a reply but sadly was left rather unimpressed. He said to one classmate "The Americans are ass-holes, I asked for ten dollars and they didn't send me a cent." It was possibly the most expensive ten dollars the U.S. never spent.

In high school – another Jesuit-run establishment – Fidel proved himself to be an outstanding athlete, breaking many of the school's records, and he showed true bravery when he saved a priest from a swollen river. He also developed an almost photographic memory, so refined that he could recite randomly chosen passages in books he had studied, which allowed him to spend his time playing basketball instead of studying. That is not to say he did not enjoy studying. Throughout his teens Fidel became enamoured with geography, physics and maths but his main passion was history, and it was there that he was to find arguably the most important influence of his life – José Martí.

*

The history of Cuba was one of romance and tragedy. Cuba had been subjected to Spanish rule since 1514[1], but by 1868 this status quo was strongly challenged as a landowner called Carlos Manuel de Céspedes freed his slaves and mobilised a large number of Cubans (including many of the slaves he had freed) to fight for their independence in what became

---

1   Apart from a ten-month period between 1762-63 where it fell under the control of the British Empire

known as the Ten Years War.

During the war a young sixteen year-old boy called José Martí became famous throughout the land for his politically charged poems and essays in which called for democracy, healthcare, educational reform, an end to racial divides and true national independence. He was decades ahead of his time and quite different from what me and my mates were doing at that age; namely getting drunk on cheap cider, hanging around bus stops and demonstrating a clear lack of grammatical knowledge with cans of spray paint.

The Spanish eventually crushed the rebels and sent Martí into exile, only to see him return a few years later with his own army to carry on the fight. Unfortunately for Martí, he would not see much of it as he was shot dead less than six months after the war began. Nevertheless, his writings and martyrdom had saturated the nation with revolutionary, nationalist passion and firmly entrenched his legendary status in the Cuban popular consciousness.

The war raged on for three more years until a U.S. battleship, the USS Maine, was blown up in Havana harbour killing 258 sailors in the process. To this day nobody knows the real cause of the explosion but the U.S. accused the Spanish of terrorism, declared war on them, and publicly backed the Cuban independence fighters.

Already a declining power, the Spanish were no match for the U.S. military and within three months they capitulated. In a further embarrassment the Spanish were then forced to sign over control of Cuba, Puerto Rico, Guam and the Philippines in reparations. The U.S. were hoping to hold out for Mayfair, Park Lane and a Get Out of Jail Free Card too, but no doubt sensed it best to quit whilst they were ahead.

Although some of the Cuban independence fighters had welcomed the U.S.' involvement, many remained cynical of their intentions. Martí himself had warned that he "Knew the monster" because he had "lived in its lair" and that the Latin Americans needed to unite to resist being colonised by their Goliath northern neighbour. And it appeared that the cynic's worst fears were well-founded, as when the Spanish left it was not the Cuban flag that flew from the Presidential palace but the Stars and Stripes of the U.S..

The U.S. had long since contemptuously considered Latin America to be 'their own backyard', as if it was nothing but a mere patch of turf with a shed in the corner to keep their power-tools and back issues of Penthouse. So it was not that surprising that with the Spanish gone they forced the Cubans to accept an amendment to the constitution which would give Washington the freedom to interfere in their affairs. The Platt Amendment, as it became known, also prohibited the acquisition of foreign debt or the signing of treaties with any other country other than the U.S., who also were bequeathed the right to establish a military base at Guantánamo Bay with a lease set at $1,000 a year for a thousand years.

The new constitution stipulated that elections be held every few years, but in practice they were so corrupt and fraudulent that they became little more than a charade. Meanwhile presidents came and went with remarkable speed as they struggled to contain a rebellious populace that were perpetually calling for an end to U.S. rule as well as more labour rights and land reform.

Then in 1933 the deeply unpopular Cuban President Gerardo Machado was ousted from power in a coup by a group headed by a sergeant called Fulgencio Batista. To try and pacify the domestic rebellion, Batista gave the presidency to Ramón Grau, a popular figure amongst the people. Yet Grau was to make the fateful mistake of doing what the Cuban people wanted and not what the U.S. government wanted. He ushered in stronger labour laws and nationalised various U.S. corporations. As was to be expected, the U.S. sent in the Marines. This left Batista to fill the power vacuum and rule through various puppet presidents before winning the 1940 election on his own ticket. Yet he would not have it all his own way. To his shock he lost the following 1944 election to Grau, who had returned to take back his position. But this time Grau was the antithesis of his former self, kowtowing to U.S. interests whilst presiding over a stark rise in political oppression. He had clearly learned his lesson.

During this period Cuba's capital city, Havana, was suffering from a serious outbreak of gang violence. There were two main rival gangs, the Socialist Revolutionary Movement (MSR) and the Insurrectional Revolutionary Union (UIR). The gangs may have sounded revolutionary but the only political ideology they espoused was violence and corruption.

To try and bring the gangs under control, Grau decided to not arrest them but instead gave them jobs in government. The tactic was obviously of dubious merit from the offset, but the positions to which the gangsters were allocated beggars belief. The leader of the MSR was made head of the Havana Police, while the leader of the UIR was given control of the National Police Academy. It was like giving the role of Health Minister to Harold Shipman and making Jimmy Saville head of social services. Unsurprisingly, far from alleviating the problem of armed violence in the capital, it exacerbated it as the two gangs fought each other, protected by their badges, and having their arsenals stocked by the government.

*

As all this was going on Fidel started studying law at Havana University. In a strange constitutional quirk, Havana University operated as a self-governing autonomous establishment where neither army nor police could trespass upon its grounds. This made it a haven for gangsters and gun fights and beatings on campus were common. Some lecturers were threatened with violence to ensure good grades were awarded to certain students and whereas normally students, seek out the local gangs to score drugs, at Havana University students had to seek them out just to get hold of textbooks as the gangs had almost complete control on their distribution. So this must have led to some awkward moments when young Cuban students approached dealers to buy some marijuana, only to be told, "Nah, none goin' mate. But I do have Graysmiff's Law of Torts. Guaranteed to give you a buzz that'll last till morning".

Fidel's first direct experience of politics was running as an independent for course delegate in 1946, the lowest position in the students union, the FEU. During the campaign Fidel strongly denounced the MSR gangsters, leading them to issue him with a stark ultimatum – shut up or die. Fidel took the message on board and asked if he could think about it and get back to them. Then once it had sunk in, he panicked, ran away to the beach, and wept. After much contemplation he pulled himself together and came to the conclusion that if he allowed himself to be intimidated now, he would be intimidated for the rest of his life. So, showing more balls than a Mecca bingo hall on a Saturday night he returned to face the music. As it turned out the gangsters were so surprised by this act of defiance that they left him alone – he had stood up to the bullies and come out unscathed. It was an invaluable life lesson.

It was not long before Fidel would again put himself in harm's way, as he decided to postpone his end of year exams and sign up (along with 1,200 others Cubans) for an armed expedition to depose the U.S.-backed Dominican Republic dictator, General Trujillo. During his rule Trujillo proved to be one of the most brutal and despotic rulers in the Caribbean, and had gained a reputation for feeding his enemies to sharks. He was only a hollowed-out volcano away from being the ultimate Bond villain.

Fidel had been excited about taking part in his first revolutionary adventure but to his immense frustration it was over before it had truly begun. The rebels had only just set off when the Cuban government – who had learnt about their plans – ordered the navy to intercept them. Realising the jig was up, Fidel jumped ship and and (incredibly) swam nine miles back to shores leaving those on board to be arrested. He had just learnt the first rule of revolution – you can't save everyone.

The following year Fidel found himself it yet more political turmoil, this time finding himself in the middle of a riot whilst attending a student conference in Bogotá, Columbia.

Leader of left-leaning Liberal Party and Mayor of Bogotá Jorge Eliëcer Gaitán had been favourite to win the upcoming Columbian presidential elections and had set aside time to meet various student groups, including Fidel's. Unfortunately, he was on his way to meet them when he was killed by a lone assassin. Bogotá, and the rest of the country immediately, erupted as people took to the streets to show their displeasure by looting shops and attacking government buildings.

Accompanied by another Cuban delegate Rafael del Pino, Fidel joined the wild rabble. First of all they spotted a man who was trying – and failing – to destroy a typewriter. It is not clear what significance the typewriter had to the downfall of Gaitán but eager to help in any way he could Fidel hurled it to the floor and smashed it to smithereens.

It was not long before things escalated from trying to smash typewriters into trying to smash the government, and shoot-outs with government troops broke out across the capital. Naturally Fidel was in the thick of things. It was his first real experience of a violent uprising and he was about to get a taste of exactly how surreal such situations can be. Later that night whilst on patrol with seven others, Fidel stopped a car which he believed to be suspicious, and to his disbelief found the red-faced occupant busily engaged with two prostitutes. But if nothing else it's nice to know that at least one man was getting some head whilst everyone around him were losing theirs.

After a tense night punctured by explosions and gunfire, the Liberal Party and the government signed an accord, upon which the rioters were asked to surrender their weapons or be arrested. This was a blow to Fidel, as notwithstanding the defeatism, during the course of events he had somehow managed to acquire a sabre and was very keen to keep hold of it. It probably wouldn't have been the most effective weapon during a gunfight with the army, but it was certainly a better souvenir than the conventional fridge magnet from Airport duty free.

*

Somehow, whilst studying, taking part in a botched revolution, a failed uprising, and being deeply engaged with national politics, Fidel also found the time to court a fellow student at Havana University, Mirta Diaz-Balart.

Mirta was a beautiful woman from a very wealthy and powerful family – her father was Batista's lawyer as well as the mayor of Banés, a town almost completely owned by the United Fruit Company.

After a whirlwind romance Fidel and Mirta were married in October 1948 and spent their honeymoon in the U.S., starting in Miami and from there travelling on to New York. Upon their return, however, Mirta found herself playing second fiddle to Fidel's political activism, and also to another woman as Fidel started having an affair with a beautiful socialite, Natalia Revuelta.

Fidel's political career had received a significant boost in 1947 when he was selected to lead the youth wing of the newly formed the Cuban People's Party which was more commonly known as the Ortodoxo Party. The party was led by a popular and eccentric politician called Eduardo Chibás who campaigned passionately on a platform of social justice and anti-corruption.

To Fidel's immense disappointment the Ortodoxo Party had performed badly in the 1948 general election, and Fidel had to watch Grau's successor Carlos Prío Socarras claim a convincing victory for the ruling Auténtico Party. But rather than fall into depression Fidel became more politically energetic than ever.

Despite Prío's clear electoral win, anti-government sentiment refused to dissipate and demonstrations continued to spill over into violent confrontations with the authorities. Even a demonstration against police brutality turned violent after one police chief really got into the spirit of things by darting up the university steps and pistol whipping a defenceless student.

In response Fidel called for a peaceful protest the next day, but just on the off-chance that it may turn violent – which it almost certainly would – some students mounted a machine gun on the top of the university steps. This does seem a bit over-the-top, but you just know there would still be one person in the group arguing that they hadn't gone far enough and that "their mate Fernando" knows someone who is "flogging tanks on the cheap out of a lock-up in Santiago". In the end the gun was not fired, but the protesters were attacked by riot police and Fidel was among those hit, leading to his bloodied portrait featuring on the front pages in the Havana newspapers the next day.

At the start of September the Castro household were blessed by the arrival of their first-born, Fidelito. With the baby born Mirta may have been hoping that Fidel would spend more time at home and act more responsibly. If so, it would not take long for her to be disappointed. Two months later Fidel gave a speech to five hundred students during which he denounced – by name – certain gangsters and government officials that he claimed were guilty of corruption. And he claimed to have the evidence to back it up. Then when the gangsters arrived to silence him he fled from the podium.

Realising he may have overstepped the mark Fidel decided to make his way to New York and wait for the dust to settle before returning. When he did return he kept a low profile and focused on his legal studies which he had so far badly neglected. Needing to play significant catch-up he launched himself into an intensive fifteen-hour a day revision schedule, and subsequently passed all his exams in September 1950, graduating as a Doctor of Law.

II
A Revolting Affair

"Every act of rebellion expresses a nostalgia for innocence and an appeal to the essence of being."
Albert Camus

Having graduated Fidel considered his options carefully. It is rumoured that he could have taken up an offer from U.S. baseball team the New York Giants. Fidel was certainly considered a very good baseball player, but there is no written record of any talks or offers, and Fidel also denies the approach. Still, there must be some Major League baseball players who secretly regret turning professional instead of launching a revolution and becoming supreme ruler of a tropical island.

Fidel had long considered looking for work in Europe or the U.S., though with such powerful in-laws a well-paid job could have been found for him in Cuba with very little effort. The first option would have pleased his in-laws, the latter option would have pleased his parents. True to form, Fidel chose neither; instead he decided to stay in Havana to pursue his promising political career and use his law degree to defend the poor for little or no cost.

Representing the poor and the dispossessed was one thing, but Fidel was also busy representing himself. During a student protest which turned particularly violent he was hit several times with rifle butts, arrested and then taken into custody and charged with inciting disorder – even though the more appropriate charge would of course been damaging police firearms. It's little wonder they didn't charge him for getting blood on their uniforms too[2]. Fidel represented himself in court and dominated proceedings from the outset, creating a significant amount of media attention with his erudite denunciations of the government. With the authorities quickly sensing that the case was becoming more hassle than it was worth, Fidel found he was soon acquitted.

Yet as Fidel's political stock was rising, the same could not be said for the leader of the Ortodoxo Party, Eduardo Chibás. His reputation was torn to shreds after he accused a government minister of corruption but then failed to come up with the proof he professed to possess. Feeling backed

---

2 This actually happened in the U.S. in 2009. Four policemen arrested an innocent man then beat him up and charged him with 'destruction of property' because some of his blood had fallen upon their uniforms.

into a corner, he gave an emotional speech on his weekly radio show in which he implored the Cuban people to fight for their economic independence, their political liberty and social justice, before shooting himself in the stomach. Such a political statement seemed almost fitting of the passionate and eccentric Chibás, but you are left wondering whether a nicely painted banner and catchy slogan might have sufficed!

Chibás was taken straight to hospital but died a few days later. If this was not bad enough, it later transpired that Chibás' last words were never actually broadcast because the show ran over the allotted time. The sound engineer didn't realise Chibás was still speaking and switched to a commercial break, leaving listeners bemused as they heard, "Comrades of Orthodoxy, move forward. For economic independence, political liberty and social justice. Let's sweep thieves out of the government. People of Cuba, rise and mo- ...*Café Pilón, the coffee that is tasty to the last drop!*"

Fidel regarded himself as the obvious successor to Chibás but the *Ortodoxo* leadership deemed him far too much of a live-wire. Instead, they elected Roberto Agramonte, a Dean at Havana University. With Agramonte in charge the party drifted to the political centre-ground, and Fidel was marginalised in case he scared off the middle-classes with his 'radical' views about national independence, healthcare and education. Unperturbed, Fidel decided to run as an independent in the elections scheduled for 1952, and looked certain to be elected intro the Chamber of Deputies.

Another person who was to partake in the presidential elections was former President Fulgencio Batista, but he had spent several years in semi-retirement in Miami and had lost much of his previous popular support – with the election looming he was languishing at the bottom of the polls.

Yet there was one segment of society from which Batista still received significant backing – the Cuban armed forces. They had been completely demoralised by the systematic corruption and nepotism of Prío's rule and were not especially keen to serve under an 'unpredictable' *Ortodoxo* government either. They wanted Batista in power, and Batista wanted Batista in power, but the only way that would happen was if they worked together and ousted the government by a coup d'etat. So that's what they did.

On March 10th all went according to plan and, after forcing Prío to flee, Batista took power without even a shot being fired. He tried to legitimise the coup, arguing that it was necessary so as to stop Prío clinging onto power by unconstitutional means – which is a bit rich considering his own power grab was both dishonest and unconstitutional. It was like going round to your neighbours and saying "Yeah I heard some kids talking about smashing all your windows tonight so I smashed them myself so they don't get the chance. Oh, and I urinated in your letterbox just in case they were thinking of doing that too." Yet for some reason everyone seemed to accept it.

To try and allay fears that he was about to install himself as a dictator, Batista announced that Presidential elections would be held in November of the following year[3]. Until then congress was to be dissolved, political parties banned and worker's rights rescinded. Going on strike was now considered an illegal offence.

The Unions protested against the measures – especially the one that made striking illegal – by calling a strike, but soon agreed to cut their losses and work with the new government. Other opposition groups also proved relatively feckless. Prio's Auténtico Party was hampered by infighting and its public reputation shattered by scandal. The *Ortodoxos* condemned the coup but did little else, whilst the Cuban Communist Party (PSP) – who at the time held nine seat in Parliament – managed only a half-hearted show of dismay.

With little popular support from the masses, Batista chose to rule by fear and force. Countless numbers of Cubans were subjected to brutal torture by Batista's regime. Women were raped, boys castrated, and an estimated 20,000 people were murdered – an average of around ten people for every day of his rule.

There are still apologists for Batista who point to figures that show Cuba becoming more prosperous during his rule than any other country in Latin America. At first glance it appears that they there is some justification in their claim. At $374, Cubans certainly had a higher per capita income than almost all other Latin America countries, but per capita income actually *decreased* under Batista's rule, with some of the poorest workers seeing their wages fall by up to 20%. Over a third of Cubans lived in severe poverty, a quarter were illiterate and the percentage of children attending primary school was actually lower than it was in the 1920s. And despite U.S investment increasing dramatically during Batista's rule (it rose 50% between 1950 and 1958), most of the wealth being created was being

---

3 Batista would keep his word and hold elections in November 1953. The problem was that all the opposition groups refused to participate until Batista resigned from his post so as to ensure a fair vote. This allowed Batista to romp home to victory in an election even Hilary Clinton would have been hard pressed to lose.

shipped straight out of the country. The economy was being sucked dry.

The situation was well summed up by philosopher Jean-Paul Sartre who made a visit to the island in the 1950s. "I had misunderstood everything, what I took to be signs of wealth were, in fact, signs of dependence and poverty. At each ringing of the telephone, at each twinkling of neon, a small piece of a dollar left the island and formed, on the American continent, a whole dollar with the other pieces which were waiting for it."

Meanwhile Arthur Schlesinger Jr., a historian who later became an advisor to President Kennedy remarked that during his visit to the island, he was "Enchanted by Havana – and appalled by the way the lovely city was being debased into a great casino and brothel for American businessmen over for a big weekend from Miami. My fellow countrymen reeled through the streets, picking up fourteen year-old Cuban girls and tossing coins to make men scramble in the gutter. One wondered how any Cuban – on the basis of this evidence – could regard the U.S. with anything but hatred." If Americans were living the dream, Cubans were living the nightmare.

*

Two weeks after Batista's coup Fidel filed papers to the courts calling for him to be thrown into prison for carrying out an unconstitutional power-grab. He argued that, "If, in the face of this series of flagrant crimes and confessions of treachery and sedition, [Batista is] not tried and punished, how will this court try later any citizen for sedition or rebelliousness against the illegal regime?"

Although Fidel lost the case, he actually got the answer he wanted as the judges ruled that Batista's claim was legitimate because 'revolution is the source of law', which was basically legalese for 'that guy has a much bigger balls than you'. So all Fidel had to do was grow much bigger balls – and start his own revolution.

So at the ripe young age of twenty-six Fidel started to concentrate on bringing about a *real* revolution. He went to work establishing a secret revolutionary group known as the Movement, the principle nucleus of which would contain ten loyal followers and friends.

Recruits were given training in the basements of university buildings and occasionally on the roofs. But there was a problem with supplies. Around 1,200 rebels had been signed up within just a few months but the Movement only had one gun – which couldn't fire. As a result training mostly entailed wafting pieces of wood around and shouting, "Bang! Ping!

Piow!" followed quickly by, "Hey, I got you. You gotta play dead. Oi Pedro.... I *so* got you... no, no you did *not* do that 'Matrix thing'."

To try and raise money for the Movement, some members sold furniture or other possessions, one donated his severance pay from General Motors of around 4,000 pesos, whilst several others mortgaged their homes, resulting in awkward meetings with the bank manager.

"So why do you want a mortgage?"

"I want to raise money to help bring about an armed revolution."

"Ri-ght. So how much profit are you expecting?"

"Oh, well... hmm... not *too* sure. But it does include a *very* good health care plan."

"Hmm I see... And what is the likelihood of the venture succeeding?"

"Oh, I'd bet my life on it."[4]

To kick-start his revolution Fidel planned to target the Moncada barracks in Santiago, Cuba's second largest military installation. The idea was to have a commando team discreetly disarm the guards at the gate then remove the iron chain from the entrance to allow the Movement's other cars to gain entry to the compound. Once inside, the rebels would fan out, storm the barracks, distribute the weapons to the populace and retreat into the mountains to carry on the struggle. To aid the rebels, other groups would be sent to take control of the nearby Palace of Justice (the Santiago courthouse) and civilian hospital, so as to provide substantial covering fire from the rooftops. A raid at the Bayamo barracks a few miles away was to also take place in the hope of diverting attention and resources from the army's inevitable counter-attack.

The date chosen for the attack was Sunday July 26th 1953, so as to coincide with a festival which was to be held that weekend. But things started going wrong from the beginning. Fidel's younger brother Raúl, who at the time was a member of the Cuban Communist Party and studying social sciences at Havana University, was tasked to be one of those who would help take over the Palace of Justice. Unfortunately he had been drinking the night before – despite strict instructions not to – and had a hangover. But that's students for you. It's a miracle he didn't walk in with a traffic cone on his head whilst haphazardly clutching onto a soggy kebab and declaring his love for a girl he'd just met and couldn't remember.

The next problem came when Fidel ordered the rebels to put on their

---

4 Somehow it would take nearly sixty years before the world saw how this type of blasé approach to money-lending probably wasn't a good idea and still do nothing about it.

Cuban Army uniforms which were to be worn over their regular clothes so that they could be discarded if necessary. Unfortunately it soon became evident that their disguises were not all that convincing. The clothes were ill-fitting, and one of the men was still wearing his civilian belt which was adorned with a large glittering 'J' buckle.

Riding in sixteen cars, the small force of rebels left the farm at 4:45am on 26th July 1953, and almost immediately found themselves in disarray. One car got a flat tyre which left four of its occupants forced to squeeze into another car and the other four stranded. Another car containing eight men – and most of the heavy weaponry – took a wrong turn and missed the fighting altogether, whilst a third car also made a wrong turn and by the time it arrived at Moncada it was too late to be of much use.

As the rebels with functioning cars and competent navigators arrived at Moncada, the commando unit leading the group quickly disarmed the guards at the entrance gate as planned, but the cavalcade of rebel cars ran into an unexpected foot patrol. The subsequent gunfire woke the barracks from its slumber and the soldiers quickly took their posts. Chaos turned into mayhem as the rebels took cover behind their cars and tried as best they could to counter the onslaught. The element of surprise had been lost and within half an hour of the first shot the rebels were forced into a hasty retreat.

The group of men (which included Raúl) who had occupied the Palace of Justice ran into problems too. Having made their way to the roof they found that a high retaining wall meant that there was no angle from which to shoot. It was, quintessentially, an unfortunate oversight. Deciding to abandon the mission they made their way to the ground floor where they were captured by five policemen who were lying in wait. However they soon escaped after some quick thinking by Raúl who managed to disarm one of the policemen, which is not bad considering he started the day with a sore head.

The rebel group in the civilian hospital – led by Fidel's second in command, Abel Santamaría – couldn't see the chaos outside the barracks and was oblivious to the fact that everyone had retreated. By the time they realised the danger they were in, they were surrounded and cut off from all escape. The two women in the group, Melba and Haydée, spent their time in the maternity ward helping to calm the new-borns as the nurses found the men beds in an effort to disguise them as patients. Their desperate efforts proved futile. One of the patients in the hospital worked at Moncada and when the government troops stormed the building he told them of the ruse – and of Melba and Haydée.

The twenty-seven rebels that were to launch the attack on the barracks at Bayamo fared no better. Climbing over a wall, one of the rebels blew their cover by knocking over some cans, leading to a fifteen minute gunfight and twelve rebels losing their lives.

As the government scrabbled around trying to capture the remaining rebels and find out who was behind the attack, the CIA-trained Cuban secret service, SIM, were given orders to show no restraint in order to gain information. This meant that most of the rebels who had been captured were subjected to the most brutal and horrific torture – of the sixty nine rebels who lost their lives that day, only half died in battle.

Despite meticulous planning aimed at ensuring that no innocent parties came to harm during the attack, the rebels could not have foreseen the death of one much-loved member of a sergeant's household who was tragically caught in the crossfire. A newspaper reported that when the initial battle began, a burst of gunfire, "Stitched a row of holes across the upper wooden wall of their living room, killing their parrot on its perch." The rebels may have gained much sympathy and support from the populace at large, but the RSPCA were *livid*.

After four days on the run a contingent of the Rural Guard captured Fidel and two other rebels after finding them asleep in a hut in the Sierra Maestre mountains. But this was the moment when the rebels' luck changed for the better, because although the Rural Guard were normally led by a bloodthirsty madman called Lieutenant Santiago Gamboa Alarcón who would have killed Fidel on the spot, on this particular day he was in bed with flu. As it was, the Rural Guard were led by Lieutenant Pedro Sarría, a professional, principled soldier who tried to calm down the trigger happy soldiers. "Don't shoot, don't shoot," he ordered, "Ideas can't be killed, ideas can't be killed."

At first Fidel claimed to be a farmer called Rafael Gonzalez, which as it happens turned out to be actually more believable than the truth because the government had announced that Fidel had already been killed during the attack at Moncada. If he had claimed he was Fidel Castro, the soldiers may have become more aggressive, shouting "Oi! You think I'm an idiot or something? If you're Fidel Castro I'm Julius Caesar!" Before adjusting their laurels and invading Britain.

*

Two months after the attack, the government put Fidel and his men on trial. Fidel chose to represent himself. He left the court spellbound with his powerful oratory, leaving his opposite number looking as if he wasn't a highly experienced legal professional at all but instead a wet-behind-the-ears university graduate who hadn't *actually* graduated, or even enrolled, but had walked past the university building a few times and watched a few episodes of Ally McBeal.

Of the hundred or so rebels being prosecuted, Fidel managed to secure the release of over seventy of them by personally declaring their innocence, even though it has been common practice in legal systems for the *authorities* to judge whether somebody should be charged with an offence, and not the person standing in the dock charged with trying to create a violent uprising.

Fidel's next feat was to turn the whole trial on its head and put the government in the dock instead by expertly cross-examining the soldiers and other witnesses. The courts – and the country – were left horrified as the stories of rebels being tortured and murdered came out. Having secured the damning evidence he needed, Fidel had the judges allow the evidence be recorded and collated so that later prosecutions could be brought.

When informed that he would be cross-examined by Fidel, the man in charge of Moncada at the time, Colonel Chaviano (who, it was rumoured, hid under his desk during the attack) panicked and ordered one of the doctors write a letter to the court stating that Fidel was not well enough to attend his trial.

It was not long before Fidel worked out what Chaviano was up to and took steps to scupper his plans. Using the clandestine communication channels he had established in prison while awaiting trial, he wrote a message to Melba using onion paper, alerting her to the conspiracy that was taking place. So as the falsified medical certificate from the prison doctors was being read to the court, she dramatically pulled the note out of her hair and exposed the ruse. The judges subsequently asked for an independent medical examination, which inevitably confirmed that there was nothing wrong with him. But the government, in all their maturity, staunchly refused to let him stand trial. A stalemate ensued until eventually a compromise was found whereby Fidel would be tried separately – after all the other rebels, and behind closed doors.

In the end, those in the top leadership, including Raúl, were given thirteen year prison terms, and the others received sentences ranging from three to ten years. Melba and Haydée received seven month sentences each.

Fidel's trial restarted – behind closed doors – on October 16th 1953.

Over thirty people squeezed into a small hospital room just 12ft square, sharing their space with a model skeleton which loomed ominously in the corner. The prosecutor's summary lasted just a couple of minutes, leading to Fidel quip, "Two minutes seem to me to be a very short moment to demand and justify that a man be locked up for a quarter of a century." Then Fidel gave *his* speech. It was to last a 'modest' two hours and became one of the most famous speeches in Cuban history. Speaking without any notes, he crammed in references to numerous luminaries including Saint Thomas Aquinas, Stephanus Junius Brutus of ancient Rome, John of Salisbury, Martin Luther, John Calvin, Montesquieu, Rousseau, John Milton, John Locke, Thomas Paine, Honoré de Balzac and the national hero José Martí whom he quoted no less than fifteen times.

He began by denouncing the trial itself before moving onto legitimising the actions of his Movement. He vehemently castigated Batista's unconstitutional power-grab and subsequent crimes with high-brow flourishes such as, "Dante divided his hell into 9 circles; he put the criminals in the 7th, the thieves in the 8th and the traitors in the 9th. What a hard dilemma the devil will face when he must choose the circle adequate for the soul of Batista." He then went on to discuss other justified uprisings such as the English Civil War, the American War of Independence, and the French Revolution. He spoke about the Movement's political beliefs, stating that the Revolution rejected the doctrine of "Absolute freedom for enterprise, the law of supply and demand, and guarantees to investment capital," and called for a programme of comprehensive education and healthcare, the nationalisation of utilities, more social housing and the introduction rent controls. Leading to a crescendo, he delivered his final and now immortal line, "Convict me; it doesn't matter. History will absolve me." As the last words fell from his lips, lightning split the sky outside, a thunderclap rattled the windows in their frames, and an old woman started cackling. Or at least it should have, but sometimes the weather has no respect for drama at all.

He was duly sentenced to fifteen years incarceration and sent to join his comrades at the prison on the Isle of Pines. Even though he was stuck in a cell, his passion and confidence remained relatively unscathed as he and the rebels busied themselves with establishing a clandestine communication network, a library, and a prison school.

That said, Fidel's morale did receive a blow when Mirta filed for divorce after his romantic affair with Natalie Revuelta was exposed. With his family life in tatters Fidel tried to lift his spirits in other ways, but sometimes they proved counter-productive. For example, when Batista made a visit to the Isle of Pines prison, Fidel and his fellow comrades broke out in song, belting out the newly written rebel anthem. Realising that the tune was not a complimentary one, Batista stormed off leaving the prison authorities to ensure the choir were duly punished. And punished they were. The rebel who had penned the anthem, Diaz Cartaya, was beaten and whipped every day for several days, whilst four prisoners were forced to spend two weeks in solitary confinement in rooms so small a man could not stand up straight. Fidel meanwhile was sent into solitary confinement indefinitely.

To keep himself busy he began transcribing his closing speech from the trial, using invisible ink made from lemons and paper made from onion skin. It would take him three months and approximately a 'shed-load' of lemons to transcribe the entire speech, which was then smuggled out in cigars before being transcribed and distributed to the Cuban public.

In August 1955 the prison authorities finally removed Fidel from his solitary confinement and put him into a larger cell which he shared with his brother, Raúl. Although it must have been a relief for Fidel to finally have some company, the arrangement was not entirely to Raúl's liking. Some years later when he was asked if he had watched Fidel's interview for an American TV show, Raúl replied, "I think I've heard Fidel talk enough to last me for the rest of my life. [During our time in prison] he didn't let me sleep for weeks. Having been alone all that time, he just talked day and night, day and night..."

As public pressure to release the rebels mounted, Fidel was also causing Batista some sleepless nights. Hoping to turn the situation into yesterday's news, in March 1956 Batista offered the rebel prisoners an amnesty on the condition that they refrained from any more revolutionary actions. The offer was staunchly rebuffed by Fidel, who said "They are trying to discredit us in the eyes of the people or find a pretext for keeping us in prison. I'm not at all interested in convincing the regime to grant the amnesty... The regime commits a crime against our people and then holds us hostages... For, today, we are more than political prisoners; we are hostages of the dictatorship... Our personal freedom is an inalienable right as citizens... We can be deprived of these and all other rights by force, but no one can ever make us agree to regain them by unworthy compromise. We can't give up one iota of our honour in return for our freedom." He just couldn't do anything by halves. A simple 'no' would probably have sufficed, maybe accompanied by a heart-felt 'V' sign. But that's Fidel for you. If ever there is a hard way...

His stubbornness earned him thirty days more of solitary confinement but this merely exerted more public pressure on the regime to release him. The newspapers were actively supporting the pro-amnesty campaign and in April demonstrations were held all over Cuba. Backed into a corner, in mid-May Batista caved and offered the rebels an unconditional amnesty.

Upon his release Fidel soon heard that the Cuban government were going to assassinate him. Some rebels, including his brother Raúl, had already escaped to Mexico so Fidel deemed it prudent to join them. He left a letter to the Cuban people ending with, "From trips such as this, one does not return or else one returns with the tyranny beheaded at one's feet."

III

If at First You Don't Succeed.... Flee to Mexico and Raise an Army

*"The masses are the decisive element, they are the rock on which
the final victory of the revolution will be built."*
Rosa Luxembourg

Whilst in prison Fidel had rebranded his movement and now called it the July 26th Movement (MR:26:7) in commemoration of the Moncada attack. Now, upon arriving in Mexico one of his first priorities was to find somebody who could train its as yet non-existent guerrilla army.

His prayers were soon answered in the form of a sixty-five year-old Spanish Army veteran named Alberto Bayo. Bayo had found himself on the losing side during the Spanish Civil War, and after being forced into exile after Franco's victory he ended up in Mexico where he set up a furniture factory. Fidel thought Bayo was perfect to help train his men in the art of guerilla warfare, but Bayo thought Fidel was mad and refused to encourage such a ridiculous suicide mission. However Fidel would not let it go and as he persisted Bayo became enamoured by his bravado, so he decided to humour him and agreed to his request on the condition he find the men and the money first. He never thought for a moment Fidel would manage to do it, but then he *had* only just met him.

Over the following months Fidel met with an array of political exiles from all over the Caribbean. The most notable of these was a young Argentinian doctor called Ernesto 'Che' Guevara, a remarkably honest and passionate man who would forever be known for his contribution to the novelty knick-knack industry.

Che was both charismatic and intelligent, and even though he suffered from chronic asthma, he was a keen player of sports, especially rugby. He revelled in keeping a filthy and unkempt appearance, often wearing the same clothes for weeks on end. Once in his twenties he bet his friends that if he took off his underpants – underpants that he had been wearing for the past two months – they would stand up on their own. He won the bet. Its not noted what he won, but it is hoped that it was a clean pair of underpants.

In the middle of his medical degree Che had decided to suspend his studies and embark on a journey through Latin America on a spluttering, clapped-out motorcycle ironically nicknamed La Poderosa (the Powerful).

Accompanied by his friend Alberto Grando he trundled and bungled his way up the continent, getting drunk, trying it on with women (occasionally successfully), shooting a man's dog thinking it was a panther, volunteering at a fire station only to sleep through his shift, and helping out at a leper colony. The expedition turned out to be the making of Che, as he witnessed first-hand the devastating effects that exploitative global corporations had on the lives of the Latin American population.

In 1954 he was living in Guatemala, mixing with like-minded left-wing revolutionaries when the country's president Jacarbo Árbenz Guzmán was deposed in a coup organised by the U.S.. Fearful of political persecution Che fled to Mexico, having first written a letter to his mother to reassure her of his safety, which said "I'm a little embarrassed to say but I had as much fun as a monkey." For those who prefer metric, that is equivalent to about 30 cubic litres.

Within a few weeks of arriving in Mexico he married his fiancée Hilda but it was far from the romantic stereotype of fiery Latin American love. Che had first proposed to Hilda by writing her a poem, but then somewhat ruined the moment by confessing to having slept with a nurse a few weeks before. As if the mood hadn't been ruined already, he then asked to see her medical records as he didn't want his offspring born with any health burdens. Even Dr. Crippen showed more romance than that. It made no difference anyway as she was already pregnant and would later give birth to a healthy baby girl, Hildita, whom they nicknamed 'Little Mao' because according to Che "She has come out exactly like Mao Tse-tung."

It was the Cubans with whom he had met in Mexico who assigned him the infamous nickname 'Che' which is an Argentinian expression that has no literal translation, but can be considered equivalent to 'hey' or 'mate'. He had heard them speak of Fidel and was eager to meet the man behind the myth, so was delighted when he struck up a friendship with Raúl who subsequently introduced him to Fidel. Upon meeting, their first conversation lasted over ten hours, albeit with Fidel doing most of the talking,[5] and by the end Che had agreed to join his army and help to liberate Cuba.

We've all had nights like this; drinking beer with a friend, putting

---

5 Fidel would become famous for his long, impromptu monologues which could be triggered by almost anything. During a meal with friends, Hilda asked Fidel "But why are you here, when you should be in Cuba?" and he answered with a four-hour lecture. They must have been scared of even asking him if he wanted anything from the shops, as there would be a high probability that the shops would be shut before he finished speaking. Your only hope would be that by the time he *had* finished, the shops had reopened.

the world to rights and planning a romantic revolution, but the difference in this instance is that these guys got up the next day and actually got on with it instead of drinking copious amounts of sugary tea and watching the Hollyoaks omnibus.

To train and arm a guerrilla army, the rebels needed money. If the revolution had happened a few decades later Fidel probably would have broadcast an TV advert showing glum rebels sitting on the floor and pleas such as; "For just $1 a week you can sponsor a rebel through basic training, giving them the tools they need to change their lives. We don't want to put any lame rebel down, and we know you don't either." And "Give a man a fish, he can eat for a day, but give these guerrilla fighters a gun, and they will take control of the fish stocks." As it was, Fidel had to make do with a word of mouth campaign to elicit weekly donations from supporters in Cuba. And it was never going to be enough.

In need of other revenue streams, in late 1955 Fidel travelled to the U.S. to gain support from the various Cuban-exile communities dotted around the country. It was a remarkable success, not only did he raise thousands of dollars for his cause but he also massively increasing his support base. One speech he gave in Tampa was reported in the local newspaper as being so well-received that, "The two members of the FBI present at the meeting seemed to be impressed by his passionate appeal and eloquence."

Upon his return Fidel went to meet with Bayo. Astounded that Fidel had actually managed to drum up both the men and money in such a short space of time, he begrudgingly agreed to train them for a maximum of three hours a day, as he also had to manage his factory and lecturing commitments. But Fidel had other ideas. Adamant that it was necessary Bayo take up the post full-time he set out to persuade him to change his mind with one of his long and impassioned monologues. Bayo himself recalled that he "Subjugated me, I became intoxicated with his enthusiasm and he conveyed his optimism to me," and so, "there and then I promised Fidel to resign from my classes here and to sell my business." Bayo refused to take any money, later writing books to help pay back the initial $195 Fidel had given him.

Just when he thought everything was going to plan, Fidel suffered a serious setback. The Mexican authorities had caught wind of his activities and arrested him along with two other comrades. They took them to the Interior Ministry jail to join twelve others who had been picked up the same day. The police then raided their headquarters and arrested another thirteen rebels, including Che. Of around forty rebels in Mexico, nearly thirty had been detained, and Raúl was the only member of the leadership still at large. Baying for blood, Batista immediately put in a request to have the prisoners extradited to Cuba, but his pleas were ignored and the rebels were eventually released – in no small part due to the intervention of ex-President Lázaro Cárdenas[6] who had intervened on their behalf.

Fidel and his comrades may have been free but he was now almost back at square one. He had to replace all the weapons that were seized and they still needed to find a boat. He needed a *lot* of cash, and he needed it quickly. Up to now he had been careful to distance himself from the ex-president Prío and had refused any offer of aid. But now he was desperate, which meant being pragmatic, so when Prío offered to donate $50,000 (with another $50,000 to follow) Fidel swam across the Rio Grande River and picked it up personally.

The money was enough to re-equip his army and buy a boat. At first they bought a decommissioned naval patrol torpedo boat in Delaware, U.S. which came stocked with torpedoes and a 40mm cannon. It was everything a young revolutionary could wish for. But inevitably they found themselves with the obvious problem that comes with buying a fully armed torpedo boat;: how do you get it home? Nothing attracts attention at customs like a fully armed torpedo boat, and the only thing you might realistically do to disguise a torpedo boat is to put up a sign saying 'this is not a torpedo boat'. And they had no money left for a sign.

Soon after, the rebels stumbled upon a replacement, a wooden yacht called the Granma. It was far too small, full of holes, and its engine didn't work. However on the plus side, it was afloat (just) and was within their budget (barely). Fidel thought it was perfect.

Then with the Mexican authorities again on their heels, in late November 1957 Fidel and 82 rebels stacked the boat with as much weaponry, food and supplies as they could carry, and set sail. Revolution was on its way to Cuba.

*

The rebels knew that their days would soon be filled with adversity and trauma, but they assumed it would begin when they were on dry land and fighting Batista's forces. As it turned out, Batista's forces were the least of their problems, as strong winds flooded the over-laden vessel and virtually

---

6 Lázaro Cárdenas was himself a genuine revolutionary and sympathised with Fidel's cause. He had been a general in the Mexican Revolution and also served as president between 1934 and 1940 during which time he nationalized the oil industry.

every single man aboard came down with seasickness. Describing the voyage in his diary Che writes that "The entire boat had a ridiculously tragic aspect: men with anguish reflected in their faces, grabbing their stomachs; some with their heads inside buckets, and others fallen in the strangest positions, motionless, their clothes filthy from vomit... except for the two or three sailors and four or five others, the rest of the contingent were seasick." This was certainly not how it had been described it in the brochure.

To make matters worse they had completely underestimated the weight of the men and their cargo and so were forced to endure an extra two days at sea – then to cap it all off the engines failed and the boat started taking on water.

Before their departure a message had been sent to Frank País, the rebel leader of the urban groups in Cuba, instructing him to launch an uprising on the same day Fidel and his men were due to land. However due to the unforeseen delays the rebels aboard the Granma floated helplessly in the ocean, powerless to do anything but listen to news reports on the radio as the uprising was brutally put down by Batista's forces.

Despite this setback, the Urban Underground would survive and go on to play an integral role in the Revolution. They set up cells throughout the country and established a strong civil-resistance movement, and as Fidel and his men fought Batista's forces from the countryside it was Pais and the urban underground that provided them with the necessary supplies.

On December 2nd, the rebels on the Granma finally saw the Cuban coastline, although by now they were completely lost and weren't sure which bit of coastline it was. The navigator was so disorientated he managed to fall overboard, whereupon Fidel barked at those on board, "We're not leaving until we save him," leading to a frantic search for the missing mariner in the dark expansive sea. It was an act which according to one rebel on board helped galvanise the fighters and instil a great sense of camaraderie between them. "People were really moved by that. Fidel's words aroused their fighting spirit. They thought, 'This man won't abandon anyone'...We found him [the navigator] but it nearly wrecked the expedition." Nevertheless it must also be remembered that Fidel was probably not wanting to lose the one man who could tell them where they were.

The boat ran aground in broad daylight, drifting onto a sandbank several hundred metres from shore. Rene Rodriguez, a man of slight build, jumped into the waters to test the terrain, and seemed satisfied that the sandbank on which they had run aground was not too boggy. Then in a scene that was more reminiscent of Groucho Marx than Karl Marx, Fidel jumped in after him only to find his more robust frame sinking straight up to his hips into the mud.

Having freed Fidel from his slapstick quagmire the rebels endured two harrowing hours navigating their way through a mangrove swamp[7] to reach dry land. A labyrinth of twisted tree roots that lay concealed beneath the water caused them to constantly stumble as leaves and vines ripped at their uniforms and mosquitoes swarmed above them feeding from any naked flesh available. Many of their weapons were either rendered useless or were lost.

Reaching Cuban soil they were still far from safety. Knowing it would not be long before their arrival was discovered, they only had a few minutes to catch their breath before they were forced to march onwards into the protection of the Sierra Maestre mountain range.

The government tried to downplay Fidel's arrival by stating that he had been killed upon landing, adding that they knew this because they had found Fidel's passport on a dead body near the landing site. Yet their claim was greeted with much scepticism by the Cuban populace, who, amongst other things, must surely have wondered why someone invading a country would bring their passport with them – he may have had a history for doing crazy things,[8] but he probably wouldn't have gone through immigration control and stood in the 'anything to declare' queue.

However Batista did nearly kill him just a few days later, after the rural guard received a tip off from a local peasant and ambushed the rebel camp. Fidel had been on the periphery of the camp and had to watch as his comrades ran in all directions in complete disarray *before* being wrestled away by his comrades before he did anything stupid.

Of the eighty-two rebels, two died in the ambush, forty were captured – twenty-one of whom were executed. Just forty rebels had managed to avoid detection, and nineteen of these decided to call an end to their revolutionary adventure and return home, leaving just twenty-one (including Fidel) to carry on the fight.

---

7 When asked by a Soviet film-maker to re-enact it, Fidel refused, saying once was enough for any man

8 When in high school Fidel would play a game with his fellow pupils whereby each had to ride their bicycle as fast as they could towards a brick wall, and the last to start braking wins. Inevitably, Fidel's competitive nature meant that he ended up spending quite a few days in the infirmary.

Along with Universo Sanchez (who had lost his boots) and Faustino Perez, (who had lost his rifle), Fidel (who was starting to lose the plot) managed to escape into a nearby sugar cane field. The three of them lay motionless for nearly four days, whispering to each other and watching flames licking through the crop as Batista's forces tried to smoke them out. All the while Fidel's inability to realistically evaluate the immediate circumstances continued unabated, as he spoke of his future plans and said to his companions "We are winning... Victory will be ours!"

Perez later gave his own account of the incident. "Personally, I was thinking at that moment that perhaps it would be possible to arrange a truce... But Fidel was already talking about the future combat actions which we must undertake in order to keep growing... To be able to speak, we had to put our heads together, to talk in whispers, because we were certain that the army surrounded us. And in this whisper, speaking with his usual enthusiasm, Fidel told us his future plans. But not only plans for the future. For the first time I heard him speak a lot about the meaning of life, about our struggle about history, about all these things... I remember that for the first time I heard him repeat the Martí phrase that 'all the glory of the world fits inside a grain of maize'. I'd known the quotation, but not in this context, in the context of what life means for a revolutionary, and how one should not fight for personal ambition, not even for ambition or glory... He said that a revolutionary feels an obligation, and gets satisfaction from it at the same time, to fight for others, to fight for his people, to fight for the humble... What I'm telling you is what struck me most, but there were many other things. About organising the country, about the people in Cuba, the history of Cuba, the future. And about the need to launch a revolution, a real revolution. We didn't speak of Marxism and Communism in those days, but a social revolution, a true revolution..." Meanwhile Universo Sanchez saw things differently – he thought Fidel had gone completely bonkers.

Eventually they managed to sneak out of the sugar-cane field and find the farmhouse of Mongo Perez, a loyal MR:26:7 member. Over the next few days the sorry remnants of the Rebel Army would reassemble, causing equal scenes of rapture and remorse as they celebrated being reunited with their comrades and mourned those who had fallen.

Among the rebels who managed to find their way to Mongo's was Raúl, who after embracing his brother revealed his group had five rifles between them, Fidel was delighted, shouting, "And with the two I have, this makes seven! Now, yes, we have won the war!" Which makes you wonder what his reaction would have been if Raúl's group had only had four guns. "And with the two I have, this makes six… Well we can't win a war with just six guns! Sack this off for a pile of donkeys; I'm going to invest in the property market."

By the end of 1956 the Rebel Army had just twenty-nine men but over the following year a steady increase in numbers ensued, mainly recruited from the peasantry and working classes. Before signing up, recruits were informed that they would have to act under strict discipline at all times. Acts which could cause the rebels army harm, including desertion, not obeying orders, and even acts of defeatism, could result in the death sentence.

The rebel army also had to act with the greatest integrity, treating everyone with the utmost respect. This was the only kind of revolution Fidel wanted to lead, and was essential for building trusts among the public. At first the rural peasantry knew nothing of Fidel, and were wary of him and his rugged band of brothers. Most had never heard his speeches, nor had they the literacy skills to read his articles. Nevertheless, the rebels quickly won their trust and support as they paid handsomely for the food they were given, helped with local harvests, and took an interest in their well-bring – something nobody had done previously.

This principle was also extended to prisoners, and this had its own particular benefits. Not only was it the *right* thing to do, it meant that the enemy soldiers knowing that they would not be mistreated, surrendered much more quickly, resulting in fewer fatalities on both sides. Some of the Cuban soldiers were captured so many times they should have qualified for a free coffee and a muffin. The best example though, was when the rebels in the cities – known as the urban underground – managed to kidnap Argentinian Formula 1 driver Juan Manuel Fangio and treated him so well he proceeded to write to them every year until he died in thirty-five years later.

This humanist philosophy contrasted starkly with Batista's. In an effort to dissuade the peasants from helping the rebels, Batista informed them that unless they moved from their lands they would become victims of napalm bombing. Other acts of repression included physical violence and torture. In one instance, the army burst into a house to discover a 17 year-old girl breast-feeding her baby. After discovering that her husband was with the rebels they shot the baby in the head, with the bullet travelling through into the woman's breast. Acts such as these – and there were many –understandably terrified the peasantry, making some less inclined to aid the Rebel Army or, worse, persuaded to betray them. But on the whole it consolidated support for the rebels and made Batista even more unpopular. Nobody wants to support a dickhead.

*

The rebels' first attack was on a garrison at La Plata, which contained just five soldiers from the Rural Guard and five sailors serving under a sergeant.

Nearing the barracks the rebels came across a very inebriated man riding a mule. Discovering it to be Chico Osorio – one of the regions infamously brutal overseers – they pretended to be from the Rural Guard and ordered him to stop. According to Che, "We must have looked like a bunch of pirates, but Chico was so drunk we were able to fool him." Fidel then came forward and told Chico that he was investigating why the rebels had not yet been liquidated, and asked for details of the loyalties of the local populace. This intelligence, which was very forthcoming from the unsuspecting drunkard, proved extremely helpful in quickly finding those in the area who were sympathetic to the rebel cause. When Fidel had garnered all the intelligence he could about the barracks and the local populace, he asked Chico what he would do if he came across Fidel Castro. Chico replied that he would chop off his penis, bragged about how he had slapped a couple of peasants for being 'bad-mannered', and how he had taken the shoes he was wearing from a dead rebel. His trial was swift, as was his execution.

The rebels surrounded the barracks on the night of January 16th, calling for the soldiers to surrender. When they refused the rebels started firing, but the soldiers still refused to surrender so the rebels threw in two grenades – which failed to detonate. Unperturbed the rebels threw in some dynamite, but that didn't detonate either, so rebels set alight to a building next to the barracks, only to find it was in fact a storehouse full of coconuts. However their persistence paid off and the soldiers surrendered soon after: The rebels had tasted their first victory, suffered no losses and gleefully made off with a bounty of weapons and ammunition.

Although now being in the rare and encouraging situation of having more weapons than men, the rebels were becoming physical wrecks as life as guerrilla soldiers took its toll. Over the following few weeks one collapsed of dehydration, another become violently sick after drinking putrid water, and Che, forever at the forefront of medical ailments, suffered an attack of malaria. All the while they were being hounded by Batista's forces, including one Major Joaquin Casillas who was renowned for collecting the ears of his victims.

Soon after the victory at El Plata Fidel met with the leading figures of his rebel organisation. One of those present was a remarkable woman called Celia Sanchez, the daughter of a highly respected doctor who offered his services free of charge to the poor. Celia efficiently managed her father's medical practice – and household – whilst also running a charity that gave out presents to the town's impoverished children. Over the past few years she had become one of the most committed members of the MR:26:7 and had worked strenuously on the campaign to free Fidel from jail after the Moncada attack.

It did not take long before Fidel recognized how important Celia was to the success of the Revolution. She soon came to be his confidante, bodyguard, best friend and personal assistant. She was the rebel army's treasurer, recruiter and trainer. She organised Fidel's base camp and headquarters, installed a telephony system and established a radio station, *Radio Rebelde,* which disseminated news and music to the masses. She became, in essence, second in command and arguably the most important cog in the Revolutionary machine.

Celia was not the only woman to play a key role in the Revolution. Women fought side by side with the male rebels, there was a women-only battalion called the Mariana Grayeles,[9] and many other women risked their lives delivering supplies and messages between the Sierra Maestre and the urban underground in the cities. According to Celia, the women ensured messages were not intercepted by putting them "in a place where nobody can find them." Which presumably means down the back of the sofa.

As Batista was censoring most of the Cuban media, Fidel organised meetings with various foreign journalists. The most famous of these was with an experienced journalist from the *New York Times* called Herbert Matthews. Keen to make a good impression Fidel ordered the rebels to keep a clean and smart appearance at all times. This was easier said than done, as one man had no back on his shirt and so had to walk sideways like a crab whenever Matthews was present..

Not wanting Matthews to realise the true size of the rebel army which at that time was still so small it would struggle to fill a Ford Transit, Fidel came up with a plan. He arranged for Matthews to interview him in a windowless hut where their only view would be out of the door which he

---

9 Not all rebels were happy women being allowed to join the rebel army. But they quickly learned to come to terms with it. On one occasion, when one of the men complained that the women were being assigned the best weapons Fidel instantly rebuked him, saying "Listen, you know why [we're using women]? I'll tell you – because they're better soldiers than you are."

purposefully left open. He then had Raúl come and interrupt them to announce the arrival of the 'second front' whilst rebel fighters marched past before sneaking back around the hut and marching past again to make it look like there were dozens of them.

Incredibly this simple schoolboy trick worked, as did Fidel's charm. The veteran war journalist lavished praise on Fidel and his motley crew of revolutionaries, writing that "The personality of the man is overpowering." and "It was easy to see that his men adored him and also to see why he has caught the imagination of the youth of Cuba all over the island. Here was an educated, dedicated fanatic, a man of ideals, of courage, and of remarkable qualities of leadership."

Due to their distinct lack of facial grooming the rebels soon found themselves being nicknamed the *Barburdos* (Bearded Ones) and according to Fidel, "It had its positive side: In order for a spy to infiltrate us, he had to start preparing months ahead of time." So taken was he by the virtues of pogonotomy Fidel insisted the rebels should not shave at all.

That said, he tended to take this time-saving 'virtue' too far by also prohibiting the rebels from brushing their teeth. It was a massive mistake; fighting a guerrilla war is not the time to fall behind on dental hygiene. Many men fell victim to toothache and within six-months the rebel doctor, Che, was nicknamed the 'tooth-puller'. Why brushing your teeth should be prohibited is unclear – toothbrushes were not decreed as bourgeois or counter-revolutionary in any of Karl Marx's books, or Lenin's. I checked. Twice. It is true that Chairman Mao never used a toothbrush, but rotten green teeth are hardly something to aspire to no matter what your political creed.

A few months after, on May 28th, the Rebel Army attacked the garrison at El Uvero. The plan was to take the garrison with little fuss, but the soldiers in the barracks had other ideas and managed to hold out for three long hours.

By the end fifteen rebels were injured, and six lay dead. They had also nearly run out of bullets and the supplies captured from the barracks barely covered the outlay. As a result Fidel decided to focus on smaller outposts and ambushing troop columns and a year would pass before he felt confident enough to launch an attack on a major military installation.

Fidel's Rebel Army were not the only ones trying to depose Batista by force. The other major rebel group at this time were a centre-right group called the Revolutionary Directorate (DR). Despite not sharing the same political beliefs, both shared a keenness to prevent inter-rebel warfare, and so agreed a pact of mutual respect. Nothing should distract them from the toppling of Batista.

But the DR suffered a setback on March 13th 1957 when around fifty DR rebels, including their enigmatic leader José Antonio Echeverría, made an audacious attack on the Presidential palace. Having made their way in they found Batista had escaped up his office in a concealed lift. Few DR rebels made it out alive. Echeverría, along with forty of his comrades, lay dead whilst many more DR members were rounded up in the aftermath and subjected to horrendous torture and brutality before being executed.

With Fidel seeming to be enjoying a certain level of success in the Sierra Maestre the DR came to realise that suicide raids may not be the best idea and in late in 1957 they established a guerrilla front in the Escambray mountains, located in central Cuba. The DR would go on to play an important role in the war, but remained in the shadow of Fidel's MR:26:7.

By the middle of 1957 Fidel's Rebel Army had grown to around 200 strong and he had assembled a permanent base in the heart of the Sierra Maestre. Now able to attack on more than one front, he promoted Che to Commandante and assigned him a column. It was an incredible honour for Che, as he was the only non Cuban in the group and it even placed him above Fidel's brother, Raúl, who himself had shown himself as one of the most respected guerrilla fighters and tacticians.

Notwithstanding his impressive leadership skills Che was so reckless it is a miracle he survived five minutes. During one of his first raids, on the garrison at Bueycito, his men did not arrive at their positions on time so he decided to start the attack by himself anyway. Walking up to the entrance Che aimed his gun at a passing sentry and ordered him to halt. When the sentry did not heed his call Che went to shoot him only for his gun to jam, forcing him to run away under heavy gunfire, "With a speed I have never matched since..." Fortunately the other soldiers soon turned up and after a short skirmish the garrison fell.

Soon after this his column took another small garrison at El Hombrito and Che laid the foundations of a base, later relocated to La Mesa, which grew to include a bakery, armoury, and a basic printing-press for their newspaper *El Cubano Libre.*

Then disaster struck. On July 30th 1957 the authorities captured the leader of the urban underground, Frank País, and executed him in the street. The loss could not be overstated. País had been a popular leader, an incredible tactician, and undeniably cheeky. Having amazed everyone by managing to somehow supply the Rebel Army with $20,000 worth of weapons, he wrote to Celia saying, "The very meritorious and valuable American embassy came to us and offered any kind of help in exchange for our ceasing to loot arms from their base [at Guantánamo]. We promised this in exchange for a two-year visa for El Gordito and for them to get him out of the country. Today they fulfilled their promise... Good service... In exchange we won't take any more weapons from their base... So we will only take ammunition (they didn't mention that)."

Frank Pais was also loved by the masses, evidenced by the sixty thousand Cubans who defied police intimidation to attend his funeral the next day. Unfortunately scenes turned ugly when two hundred women began to chant anti-Batista slogans and the police reacted with water-cannon and truncheon.

*

Over the next several months the Rebel Army's numbers continued to grow and by February 1958 Fidel felt confident enough to open up a new front. Raúl had by this point proven himself as a disciplined and brave soldier, as well as a strong leader and organiser and so Fidel promoted him to *Commandante* and gave him a column of sixty-five men to lead a second front in the nearby mountains of Sierra Cristal.

Raúl and Fidel were so different that they barely came across as brothers at all. Whereas Fidel was tall, stocky and bombastic, Raúl was small, thin, and reserved. Fidel gained loyalty from his men by acting like a visionary and father figure, but Raúl acted like a friend and formed close bonds with his men and their families. Fidel issued orders, Raúl asked for suggestions. Fidel was intolerant of error, whilst Raúl was understanding and patient. But as different as they were, they somehow worked together in perfect harmony.

In April 1958 a national strike was scheduled and the urban underground, still eager to prove their worth, wanted to be responsible for organising it. It was a tense time for Fidel, for neither of the potential outcomes of the planned strike seemed particularly appealing. If the urban underground deposed Batista, Fidel's role as heroic conqueror would clearly be diminished, and he would be destined to make a living from opening local supermarkets and appearing in the Christmas pantomimes of small provincial towns. But if the strike failed, Batista may have more confidence and resources to send into the Sierra to try and eradicate him. Nevertheless he gave them his full support.

In preparation for the well-publicised strike Batista had drafted in seven thousand extra troops. They moved quickly to suppress the protesters, murdering one hundred and arresting hundreds more. With the strike quickly beaten and the resistance groups in the cities almost completely eradicated, Batista turned all his attention on the rebels in the Sierra Maestre [just as Fidel had feared]. Batista's plan, imaginatively called 'Finale Fidel' (End of Fidel), involved ten thousand Cuban soldiers moving on three fronts, backed by tanks and naval units which were ordered to fire on rebel positions from the coast. Villages were burnt whilst civilians (including children) who were suspected of collaborating with the rebels were murdered. One State Department official wrote to his colleague, "The tragedy of Cuba is that its youth is fighting and dying against Batista. If an Army officer or soldier is killed, three, four or more youths are found shot to death the next morning beside a road outside the locality where the attack against the soldiers occurred. This had become standard procedure."

Just a few months prior to the summer offensive, the U.S. had bowed to political pressure and suspended arms shipments to Batista's government[10], however it only took Fidel a couple of months to uncover documents that proved Cuban aircraft were being refuelled and rearmed at the U.S. base at Guantánamo Bay. Faced with a public scandal Eisenhower, argued that they were replacement weapons for defective ones sold earlier. As excuses go it was pretty weak.

"Hi. Is that the U.S. government? It's Batista here... umm.. can I have some more bombs please?"

"Uh... No. We placed an arms embargo on you, you nutter. I mean, if the ones we sold you were in some way defective there is a small loophole that would allow us t-"

"Yeah all the bombs you sold us are faulty."

"All of them?"

"All of them. However many you ever sold us. Ever."

"Well what was wrong with them."

"They blew up shortly after we fired them."

Raúl meanwhile decided to deal with the issue in his own way. Showing initiative, cunning and a complete disregard for international relations he kidnapped twenty-five U.S. civilians who had been working at

---

10 Washington had been reluctant to place an arms embargo on such a good and loyal customer, but were left with no other option after the testimony of U.S. representative Adam Clayton Powell who reported seeing thee Cubans "mutilated beyond recognition and in a crude crib a child about 3 or 4 years old with a bayonet pinning it down through the stomach.

a nearby nickel mine, as well as twenty-four U.S. Marines who had been travelling on a bus to Guantánamo. As usual the prisoners were given remarkable treatment and were even treated to a 4th July party, though inevitably the kidnappings caused a public outcry in the U.S.. Fidel had not been consulted about Raúl's plan, and, scared the U.S. would send in the Marines he made a television announcement calling for them to be released.

Despite the controversy Raúl's actions did have the desired effect as aerial bombardments and U.S. military supplies to Batista were soon stopped. This gave the Rebel Army a brief respite to reorganise themselves, and two weeks later the prisoners were freed no worse for wear after their ordeal. According to Ruby Hart Phillips from the *New York Times*, "Almost all the kidnapped men returned as confirmed *Fidelistas*."

With no more military aid from the U.S., Batista started to look elsewhere, and found the British government were more than happy to oblige, agreeing to sell him seventeen Sea Fury fighter jets along with fifteen Comet tanks. Despite this support Batista continued to struggle to break down the rebel defences and instead soon found his own forces under pressure. In late June, and with less than three hundred rebels at his command, Fidel's column had surrounded and defeated a battalion of over one thousand soldiers. When more government troops were sent to rescue them, they were surrounded and captured too.

Indeed Fidel proved extremely cunning on the battlefield and constantly outwitted and outmanoeuvred Batista's forces. For example when Fidel had discovered that a government spy had given away the location of their camp, he ordered a clump of trees that acted as the principle landmark to be uprooted and moved. Just a few hours later Batista's air force swooped over and bombed the wrong location. On another occasion Fidel managed to obtain the Cuban Army's radio codes and not only tricked them into dropping supplies into rebel controlled territory, but made Batista's air-force drop bombs on their own troops.

Overall the Rebel Army scored many successes and proved themselves incredibly disciplined and motivated on the battlefield. Nevertheless they still had moments of stupidity. One night half a dozen rebels were on patrol when they came across an army patrol. Neither side realised that they were on opposing sides and they stood talking to each other for a while. When their contrasting loyalties were revealed they both rolled down the hill in a ball of fists, boots and curses for a whole ten minutes.

By mid August Batista was out of ideas and he was forced to admit defeat and ordered the Cuban Army to retreat; His offensive had failed. Now Fidel would launch an offensive of his own, and his would not fail. The Rebel Army finally left the safety of the Sierra Maestre. Che was sent to take the city of Santa Clara[11], whilst Fidel headed towards Cuba's second biggest city, Santiago.

*

With the country engulfed by revolution and the army on the edge of defeat, Batista decided that November would be a fantastic time to hold an election. As all the main political parties believed Batista was going to rig the vote anyway, they refused to take part. So apart from Batista's chosen successor, Andrés Rivero Agüero, the only candidate was an independent candidate called Márquez Sterling, a man who had been jailed many times due to his opposition to Batista's rule. Despite his numerous bouts in prison nobody had ever heard of him, but not being known at all was still much better than being known as Batista's lapdog and on the day of the election he looked certain to win. So Batista rigged the vote and Andrés Rivero Agüero was declared the winner.

Taking little notice of this electoral charade, in late December Fidel took a break from being a romantic revolutionary and went home for Christmas to see his mother and siblings. Arriving in time for Christmas Eve, Fidel received a hero's welcome, although he was given a stern reprimand by his mother for burning their sugar-cane that they had just spent $26,000 having weeded. He may have been old enough to start a revolution, but he was not too old to be put in his place.

By the end of 1958 Batista saw no hope of averting his own downfall so on New Years Eve, as the cities of Santa Clara and Santiago fell under rebel control, he fled to the Dominican Republic leaving General Cantillo to take power as head of a military junta. When Fidel found out Batista had escaped he immediately made a radio announcement calling for a general strike whilst ordering Che to march on Havana. Cantillo may have been in charge, but he would not be in charge for long. The revolution was coming to town.

Hearing of Batista's departure, Colonel Barquin (who had led an uprising of Cuban army officers against Batista in 1956 and who had

---

11 Confidence in Che's group was at an all time high. When told by a local that there were 5,000 of Batista's troops in the city of Santa Clara, thus outnumbering them by nearly 15 to 1, one plucky rebel replied "Good, with our *Jefe* [leader] that's no problem." Unfortunately Che remained as calamitous as ever, and when running to cover during an air raid, he fell off a wall and broke his arm.

recently been broken out of prison) headed straight to Cuba's biggest military barracks, Camp Columbia. Upon arriving he took control by simply walking in and ordering Cantillo to be placed under house arrest. Fidel must have been kicking himself for not thinking of that first – that would have been so much easier than two years of gruelling warfare. In the end Cantillo's reign had lasted less than a day.

Appreciative of his efforts but not yet able to trust Barquin's loyalty or motives, Fidel instructed Camilo Cienfuegos (a popular guerrilla leader who commanded alongside Che) to take charge at Camp Columbia whilst Che was sent to occupy the nearby La Cabana fortress in Havana. Then he went on the airwaves and declared victory for his rebel army. "The Revolution will be a very difficult undertaking.... [But] It will not be like 1898, when the North Americans came and made themselves masters of our country... for the first time the republic will really be entirely free and the people will have what they deserve..."

IV
How to Win Friends and Alienate People

"The battlefield is a scene of constant chaos. The winner will be the one who controls that chaos, both his own, and the enemies."
Napoleon Bonaparte

Now that victory had been declared Fidel faced the risk that, like with many revolutions, anarchy and violence would explode as the people took vengeance on the fallen regime. With this in mind he enlisted the help of the boy scouts. This does seem like a rather naive plan but as it turned out, instead of widespread rioting the nation submerged itself in vibrant Caribbean beats as people took to the streets to party like it was 1959. The scouts meanwhile were actually quite helpful in aiding the many drunken revellers safely back to their homes. In fact everyone was having such a nice time that it was decided to extend the partying – that is, the general strike – to three days instead of one. The scene was summed up beautifully by a *New York Times* correspondent who reported that "One had the feeling that they would not hesitate to shoot a Batista supporter, but he would be shot with the greatest courtesy."

Fidel meandered his way to Havana, savouring every moment of his triumph by stopping in every provincial capital along the way. One person who travelled with Fidel recalls that "Elderly ladies embraced him," and at "every intersection of the highway, women stopped him, the old women kissed him, telling him he was greater than Jesus Christ."

He rode into the capital on a Sherman tank on January 8th where he was mobbed by the adoring crowds, leading to a journalist from the Chicago Tribune to write, "In all my years of reporting in Latin America never had I seen a similar tribute to one man."

That evening Fidel made his way to Camp Columbia to give the most important speech of his life so far. Thousands upon thousands had crammed into the barracks to hear him. After a somewhat nervy opening he turned to Camilo and asked if he was doing okay, causing a ripple of laughter to flow through the crowd. He soon gained confidence though, and whipped the crowd into a frenzy. Even foreign observers were becoming bewitched by him, with the British Ambassador describing Fidel as a "Mixture of José Martí, Robin Hood... and Jesus Christ."

Fidel then touched on what people could expect from the new government. He did not paint a picture of a communist utopia, but instead warned of a long, arduous struggle. He pleaded for unity to ensure divisions did not kill the new-born Revolution whilst it was still young and fragile. Nobody was to be anti-Protestant, anti-Catholic, or anti-Communist. Everyone now had to work together to create a better future and more prosperous Cuba for all. He was also cautious not to convey an image of perfection, or infallibility. He warned that the Revolution would make many errors on the path, they were not special men, not Gods nor Saints, and were as prone to mistakes as anyone. But all mistakes would be *honest* mistakes.

Near the end a few doves were released as a symbol of peace and when all of a sudden one fluttered back and landed on Fidel's shoulder, causing a collective gasp from the crowd. The moment cemented his messiah-like status among the people as most Cubans followed the African-influenced Santería religion, in which white doves were seen as the messengers of Oshun to indicate the anointed one.

Some of his critics alleged that the scene with the doves was staged, though this seems unlikely. Taking over a country with just a few thousand men is quite time consuming in itself; training doves would be somewhat low on the priority list. Also, the TV footage of the speech shows Fidel looked as shocked as everyone to see the unexpected guest appear on his shoulder, and momentarily paralysed by perplexity as one of the other doves took advantage of the diversion by washing its head in Fidel's cup of water just before he picked it up and had a big gulp.

*

At the beginning of his quest Fidel had thought that all he needed to do was to throw out the corrupt parliamentarians and install honest ones. But during the latter stages of the war in the Sierra he realised that it wasn't just politics that he needed to change, he also needed to change the economic order. After all, you can have all the political power in the world, but if the money is controlled by a few wealthy elites you won't achieve much.

Although both Che and Raúl were known to be communists at this stage, Fidel, and the MR:26:7 as a whole were not. At the beginning Fidel had talked about turning Cuba into a social democracy (like that in Britain, France and the Scandinavian countries), but during the latter stages of the war his ideological conviction moved swiftly leftwards.

He was cynical of the model used in the USSR and he wasn't not too enamoured with the Chinese one either. He wanted something different, something that mixed the nationalism of Martí and the romanticism of French philosopher Jean-Jaques Rousseau, a path that allowed for equality but didn't hamper people's freedoms.

Many years later he reflected that "Toward the end of my university studies, I was no longer a utopian communist but rather an atypical communist who was acting independently. I based myself on a realistic analysis of our country's situation…"

Obviously Fidel knew that no matter what form of communism he was going to implement, U.S. interests were going to be threatened. He also knew that whenever that happens the U.S. sends in the Marines, and if they sent in the Marines his Revolution would be over before it had truly begun. He needed to tread very carefully.

To keep Washington in the dark, Fidel performed a clever piece of political slight-of-hand. He remained 'neutral' as head of the Rebel Army, and offered the post of provincial president to the distinguished liberal, anti-communist judge, Manuel Urrutia. Urrutia's government was made up of centre right politicians from the MR:26, Auténticos and Ortodoxos who unknowingly acted as a fig leaf to hide Fidel's real, radical government that really pulled the strings. As Urrutia later lamented, "I had only nominal power, all real power, political and military, was in the hands of Fidel... He was supported not only by his personal prestige but by his revolutionary organisation, the rebel army, and by popular fervour."

The secret government included half a dozen of Fidel's most trusted comrades, including his brother Raúl, Celia Sanchez, and Che Guevara. They quickly realised few people in the MR:26:7, especially those in the Rebel Army, had the skills or knowledge to implement a communist overhaul of the economy, so they were forced to look further afield.

They decided to enlist the help of the Cuban Communist Party (PSP), having brokered a friendly relationship with some of its leading members since middle of 1958. The PSP had experience in government (having served in a coalition with Batista in the early 50s), a solid organisational network across the country, and were a major influence within the trade union movement.

Their help would make the move to a socialism much easier, but it was not going to be a bed of red roses. The PSP were notoriously opportunistic and Fidel knew it would be hard to keep them from trying to grab power for themselves. He intended to keep them on a tight rein.

The other problem was that when the PSP involvement became public knowledge the other opposition groups were going to be outraged that a party which only offered support to the MR:26:7 halfway through 1958 – when the rebels looked certain to win – were being given such a prominent position in government. Especially when it was at their expense. But when they came, Fidel, confident he enjoyed the support of the masses, brushed such criticisms aside and accused critics of seeding division.

This secret government clandestinely incorporated itself into a newly formed government department, the National Institute of Agrarian Reform (INRA), and Fidel ensured it was given more and more power until it was able to bypass the government completely.

From the very start INRA was to be responsible for many (soon to be) nationalised industries, the redistribution of land, and 100,000 militiamen. It was also in charge of organising social projects including healthcare, education provision and the construction of houses, highways and electricity supplies.

Obviously running a country via two governments was incredibly difficult to manage, and it certainly didn't help that the secret government had no experience of how to do it. One member of the secret government, Alfredo Guevara, described the chaos and confusion that abounded during the early stages; "[We] had to become specialists in the craziest things; for example, we began to work in the National Bank. Castro wanted us to start going to the bank, and we went there once a week... Fidel kept saying, 'We don't know what a bank is, and we must know what a bank is.'" Fifty years later and the world is still dumbfounded as to what a bank is, but there is some suggestion that it may have something to do with money and old rope.

*

Celia had proven herself as the most important member of the MR:26:7 and she was popular amongst the masses – in some cities people were more eager to meet her than Fidel. She now began to work alongside him as the Revolution's First Lady.

Fidel and Celia were not lovers but their bond was so great they were almost inseparable. They lived together in a small austere concrete house in Havana which was expanded to make room for six adopted children whose parents had died fighting for the Revolution. Although Fidel was surrounded by numerous other intelligent and strong willed people, it was still Celia who had the most influence over him. Just as she had in the Sierra Maestre, Celia made everything happen. Fidel would finalise the plans, but it would be Celia who ensured they were carried out. If Fidel was its brain and Che its spirit, then Celia was its heart, and with the Revolutionary War won she showed no signs of forgetting her roots. On January 6th 1959 she found time to organise a plane to parachute presents to children in Santiago for the Kings Day festivities and she sent presents to mothers who had lost children during the Revolutionary War in time for Mother' s Day.

The first laws that Fidel personally enacted were extremely well received. He nationalised assets owned by Batista cronies, forced the reinstatement of workers sacked for striking at the Cuban Electric Company, reduced rents, reduced telephone charges and electricity rates, and introduced a minimum wage. To add to the revolutionary romance it was announced that getting married would be free, including the ceremony, the reception, the cake, some refreshments, and a few nights in one of the county's most illustrious hotels.

Of course the new policies were not welcomed by everyone. The ministers in Urrutia's cabinet were still unaware that they were being used as a smokescreen by Fidel, and were thus more than aggrieved at not even being consulted about policies that were supposed to be under their jurisdiction. Middle-class landlords were also extremely disgruntled. They had previously received substantial incomes from their rental properties, and were furious to discover that not only was it was to be forbidden for anyone to own more than two houses at any one time, tenants were now to be given first refusal to buy the properties they lived in and allowed to pay in instalments.

But whilst a small number of wealthy people decried the new laws, millions benefited. The lowest 40% of earners saw their share of national income rise from 6.5% to 17% by 1962. The percentage of owner-occupiers soared. By 1972 75% of households were owner-occupied, and at the time of writing the figure is around 85%. Those who do not own their own property find that rental costs only take up between 6 – 8% of income because of rent cap laws. In comparison, in Britain the percentage of home-owners as of 2015 was around 64% (from a high of 71% in 2003), whilst rents took upon average 40% of a worker's income.

It soon became apparent that despite these policies being popular, and in many ways successful in their aims, there was one big problem that the Revolutionaries had overlooked. In their rush to push through their policies as quickly as possible, they had neglected to work out how much they were all going to cost. At Fidel's own admission, "Our accounts weren't particularly 'economics based.'" And due to their rather blasé approach to accountancy it took some time for anybody to notice that Batista had taken off with the treasury's coffers.

In case that wasn't enough to contend with, in the Batista years preceding the revolution the budget deficit had increased from 177 million to 788 million pesos, the net monetary reserves of the country had fallen from $534 million to $111 million, and public debt stood at $1.2 billion. Batista had left the country bankrupt.

Along with sorting out the nations finances, the new government had to deal with the prominent figures from the previous regime. It was essential that the people saw that justice was done but Fidel wanted to ensure that the Cubans kept their humanist image. With this in mind it was decided that those responsible for the most heinous crimes should be held accountable using the model of the Nuremberg Trials held after World War II. Each trial was overseen by two or three members of the Rebel Army, an assessor, a defence counsel, a prosecutor, and on occasion, a member of the local community. On the whole the trials were seen to be well run; the British Foreign Minister stated that there was a "Genuine effort to establish guilt and follow due process," whilst the U.S. consulate in Santiago stated that, "There is little doubt but that a number would have faced the possibility of capital punishment in any state having… war crimes trials."

However not everyone was impressed. In public the U.S. vehemently denounced both the trials and the resulting executions. This was a little bit rich given the U.S.'s own involvement in Cuban state violence. The CIA had been closely involved in some of the repressive activities of the Batista regime, including the creation of the Bureau for the Repression of Communist Activities which tortured thousands of Cubans in the preceding decade. Phillip Agee, a former CIA agent, says in one documentary, "A lot of the CIA's people, well some of them at least, were on trial for having been murderers and torturers of Batista." Indeed, one U.S. journalist, Andrew St. George, who attests to having been asked by the CIA to plead clemency on behalf of José Castaño who had been the second-in-command of the Bureau for the Repression of Communist Activities.[12] The U.S. were, at best, extreme latecomers to the cause of Cuban political tolerance.

Annoyed by the amount of outside criticism, Fidel went on the offensive. He attacked the world's media whom he accused of creating a false narrative by describing those on trial as merely 'Batista supporters', saying, "We are not executing innocent people or political opponents. We

12 When the journalist came back from his meeting with Che, he reported to the CIA station chief that "Che said to tell you that if he didn't shoot him for a Batista thug he would shoot him for being an American agent." Gentle diplomacy was never going to be Che's strong-point.

are executing murderers." His wrath then turned to the U.S. whom he lambasted for their hypocrisy; "When Cuba was governed by thieves, there were no campaigns in the U.S.. When Cubans were being killed every night, when young men were found murdered with a bullet in the head, when barracks were heaped with corpses, when women were violated, there were no campaigns. Nor did congress, with rare exception, speak out to condemn the dictator." The trials eventually ended after six months, with five-hundred and fifty men executed.

*

With his standing amongst the people stronger than ever, it was not long before Fidel started to manoeuvre himself into a position of official power. First, in mid-February, he publicly criticised Prime Minister Miro Cardona for his handling of anti gambling and prostitution prohibition measures. Then he 'reluctantly' accepted the offer to take his place.

Fidel may have taken direct control but his problems were mounting. As the revolutionary government's ideology became apparent more and more of the educated middle-classes were leaving, causing the economy to suffer a cataclysmic 'brain drain'. After two years, 270 of the 300 agronomists on the island had left, along with half the teachers and doctors, and 80% of the technicians.

The massive exodus of qualified personnel meant that many workers were assigned to posts for which they had no prior experience or training. This ushered in a new mantra declaring that everyone should overcome problems 'sobre la marcha' (on the move). As admirable as the project was, it must have made a trip to the dentist an incredibly nerve-wracking experience.

One of the administrators who worked closely with Che explains the chaos of the times; "We'd go to the library or we sent for books and we spent an entire night arguing. There would be one person here, two over there, everyone reading, and soon someone would exclaim 'Oh it's here, I've got it!' And another would reply 'No, look what I've got here!' we would have a tremendous discussion all night. We didn't sleep and then carried on with our work the next day. When we had a problem we grappled with it until we knew how to resolve it. We found a solution and afterwards we continued reading and we went on improving."

On the plus side this meant social mobility was at an all time high, and that in itself helped to persuade some skilled workers to stay. For instance, one technician who worked at the Cuban subsidiary of Proctor & Gamble had been offered a lucrative contract at its parent company in the U.S.. At first amiable to the offer, he then turned it down because the people at the U.S embassy had sneered at him and asked for proof of his University Degree, despite him having a signed letter from the vice-president of the company. He explained, "I said... 'Go to hell!' and I left. My wife was waiting at home: 'What happened?' She said. 'We are going to stay and see what happens', I told her. The next day I had responsibility for five or six different posts, because other people had left." He later became vice-president of the petroleum industry.

At first the country's business leaders had been quite happy with Fidel's revolution, with one U.S. embassy official noting how "The government was much better than they had dared hope." But as the rights of workers increased and radically left-wing policies were announced the business leaders became. They started to hoard wares and run-down their operations, resulting in lower productivity, more unemployment and a shortage of goods. Yet in the end such business leaders were hoisted by their own petard as it merely made the new government more eager to nationalise them.

In once case it was discovered that stocks of belaying pins – essential for the construction of buildings – were to run dry within two months. An architect working closely with Che at the time recalls that, "I took the information on one page to Che in the National Bank. It was evening. Che was hurrying out and said 'Don't give me bits of paper now – I am going to the Council of Ministers.' I said 'This is for the Council of Ministers' and he replied 'Well then, do give me bits of paper.' It read: 'Commandante, here is the number of belaying pins that will be produced in Cuba and how many we need to consume. Greetings Jorge.' And below that was a table showing the figures. The next morning my secretary threw me the newspaper. The headline said 'Nationalised – the Steel and Iron Industry in Cuba!'" If the capitalists didn't want to run the companies, then the state would.

One of the most romantic of the government's new policies – almost certainly influenced by Che – was the attempt to build and mould a 'new man' whose outlook was that of mutual cooperation and respect. Che's theory was that to truly achieve communism, moral incentives such as social praise should be seen as the most important, as this would create strong fraternity between worker and state whilst increasing competition and thus production. He pointed out that there was little point in offering more material rewards anyway, because if the worker wanted money he could make his way to the U.S. and be given a salary astronomically higher than Cuba could ever afford.

It wasn't just Fidel and Che who were making big changes to the way the country was run. Vilma Espin, who was married to Raúl Castro, established The Federation of Cuban Women. Comprising over 85% of Cuban women over 14 years of age, it would become one of the most effective and powerful civic institutions in the country. It provided women with essential job training, helped to educate the public about issues affecting women and ensured their voices were heard in government.

Trying to eradicate ingrained sexist attitudes in a country that exuded *machismo* culture from every pore (and still does) was not an easy task, making their achievements all the more impressive. In the 2013 Global Gender Gap Report Cuba was ranked 15th out of 136 countries for gender equality. Britain was ranked 18th and the U.S. 23rd.

Before the revolution, women made up just 19% of the workforce, and they were mostly employed in low-paid menial jobs. Today they make up 38% of the workforce, and hold 70% of the professional positions, 45% of the science and technical positions, and over 60% of university places. They have a higher life expectancy than their counterparts in the U.S. and even managed to have a law passed that required husbands to do an equal share of the housework!

Yet for all their progress there is still work to be done. Although men nowadays contribute much more to household chores, women still find themselves shouldering most of the burden, and although women hold 50% of the positions in the National Assembly (compared with 29% in the UK, this drops to only 22% representation in the Council of Ministers.

Another central plank of the Revolution's plan for a new Cuba was the eradication of racism. Within the first few months, Fidel announced the introduction of a raft of anti-racism laws as part of the 'Proclamation against Discrimination'. Racism was implied to be both counter-revolutionary and anti-Cuban. Cuba was for everyone.

Giving a speech in March 1959 he spoke frankly about the problem, and how he felt it could be solved. "In all fairness," he said, "I must say that it is not only the aristocracy who practice discrimination. There are very humble people who also discriminate. There are workers who hold the same prejudices as any wealthy person, and this is what is most absurd and sad and should compel people to meditate on the problem. Why do we not tackle this problem radically and with love, not in a spirit of division and hate? Why not educate and destroy the prejudice of centuries, the prejudice handed down to us from such an odious institution as slavery?"

Black Cubans would become – on average – the best-off black people in the world in terms of employment opportunities and infant mortality. By 1985 the gap between the life expectancy of black and white Cubans narrowed to just one year, while the gap in the U.S. at that time stood at 6.3 years. By 2004 black and *mulatto* Cubans, despite the economic hardships of the Special Period, had still enjoyed an infant mortality rate of less than half that of their U.S. counterparts.

Racial inequalities were certainly dealt a severe blow, but, as with gender equality, the issues were not solved completely and problems still persists today. Afro-Cubans are still unrepresented in almost every higher-level profession, especially the political leadership.

*

In April 1959 Fidel threw himself head-first into what Martí once described as the 'belly of the beast' – New York – after accepting an invitation to meet with the American Society of Newspaper Editors at their annual meeting. Upon arrival he was greeted by a cheering American public who came out in droves to see him. Standing outside the United Nations building he gave out cigars to the crowd before speaking to a gathering of 35,000 people in Central Park. Clearly in his element Fidel seemed to have no concern about his own safety. He happily mingled amongst the crowds and even decided to jump the guard rail at The Bronx Zoo to taunt the tigers by sticking his hand through the bars.

But he didn't have it all his own way. A group of rich Cuban businessmen had outsourced their political activism and hired people to hold an anti-Castro protest. No doubt they had the gall to write off the expense against tax as well.

When the U.S. had denied Cuba its independence after defeating the Spanish at the turn of the century, it had taken its dignity and pride as well. One of Fidel's principle aims of the Revolution was to restore it, so when meeting with U.S. officials Fidel made sure he showed no deference. When somebody introduced him to the State Department official in charge of Cuban Affairs, Fidel replied dryly "I thought I was in charge of Cuban affairs."

Not wanting to give this cocksure upstart the honour of meeting with the 'leader of the free world', President Eisenhower made himself unavailable during Fidel's visit and sent Vice-President Richard 'Tricky Dicky' Nixon to greet him instead. Nixon appeared severely dismayed at Fidel's talk of national health care and education, and was horrified at his "almost slavish subservience to the prevailing majority opinion" (A puzzling comment from the future president of the 'world's biggest democracy'). He concluded that Fidel was either ignorant about the dangers of communism, or a communist himself, saying, "Whatever we may think of him he is going to be a great factor in the development of Cuba and very possibly in Latin American affairs generally." He may have been mad, paranoid and extremely tricky, but on this occasion at least, Tricky Dicky was right.[13]

During his stay Fidel gave many speeches but at one gathering he unexpectedly announced that there would be no elections in Cuba for four years, stating 'Revolution First, Elections Later'. Yet, although the U.S. government became increasingly concerned (and rightly so) that Fidel intended to make himself dictator, it was generally accepted by the Cuban people with a shrug of the shoulders. Such affable acquiescence was, in part, due to their past experience of western-style 'democracy' which had brought a tyrant to power, created an oligarchy, inflicted poverty on the populace and proved useless when confronted by their imperialist neighbour. They had no faith in western democracy, but they did have faith in Fidel.

Fidel made sure that their faith was not taken for granted. He had promised them the earth, and he was determined to deliver, so in May 1959 the Agrarian Reform Act was passed. It distributed much more land and wealth than he had previously implied, which was a miraculous thing in itself. If your average politician promised to distribute land to the people they wouldn't then distribute *more* than what was promised. That would be ridiculous. What would actually happen is that they would delay the policy for as long as possible and in the end give all the land to a faceless corporation registered in a tax haven who would turn it into luxury flats for the wealthy.

By the end of Batista's reign around 9% of landowners had owned nearly 75% of all land, with 70% of farms tilled by workers indentured on a quasi-feudal basis. This arrangement now changed dramatically. The Agrarian Reform Act stated that no person could own more than 966 acres of land (although larger plots of up to 3,300 acres were allowed to operate as cooperatives if it made economic sense). The expropriated land handed was those over who worked it.

The law also contained a list of companies that were to be nationalised, including the U.S.-based, United Fruit Company. At the time

---

13 Nixon was not the only person showing impressive prescience. After meeting Fidel during a reception at Princeton University, former Secretary of State Dean Acheson noted "This fellow Castro really knows what he is doing... He is going to cause us problems down the road."

the United Fruit Company[14] was arguably the most hated company throughout Latin America. They were regarded as 'untouchable', a company who if threatened, would call upon the strength of the U.S. military to bend national governments to their will – hence the term, 'Banana Republic'. Considering all the effort Fidel had made to reduce the chances of any U.S. intervention, this was clearly a bold move.

The nationalisations, as well as being done by popular consent, were actually very fair. All those affected were offered generous compensation, although rather amusingly the amount paid was linked to the land value figures supplied by the companies in their previous tax returns. Some were therefore left in the rather difficult position of wanting to argue against the government's valuation, but not wanting to admit to massive tax fraud.

The next vital step in the Revolutionary programme was to create a free, open-access healthcare system. But they had a major problem to contend with – two-thirds of the medical professionals had left the country soon after Fidel took power. Incredibly, the Cuban government managed to replace them all within the decade, and create the infrastructure to ensure they could train thousands more. At the time of writing, Cuba has 8 doctors per 1000 people, whereas the UK has just 2.7 and the U.S. 2.5.

British paediatrician Imti Choonara, who led many delegations to the island, reported that, "Healthcare in Cuba is phenomenal... The irony is that Cubans came to the UK after the Revolution to see how the NHS worked. They took back what they saw, refined it and developed it further; meanwhile we are moving towards the US model."

One of the reasons for Cuba's success is the philosophy underpinning their system – prevention is better than cure. Along with an extensive vaccination programme, everyone is visited by a doctor at home at least once a year and given a full check-up, whilst those with serious health problems, such as heart attacks, angina, diabetes, stroke and cancer are seen daily.

Cuba became the first country in the world to eradicate polio, pertussis, rubella, mumps, measles, tetanus, and diphtheria. Mortality rates dropped year upon year until they rivalled – and in some cases even bettered – those in developed nations. At the time of writing, infant mortality the figure stands at 4.2 per 100,000 births, down from 120 before

14 The United Fruit Company is now known as Chiquitta, and still find themselves embroiled in controversy. In recent years they have been found guilty of helping to finance terrorist paramilitary groups in Columbia and have been accused of various human-rights and labour transgressions

1959. In 1959 the average life span was just fifty-eight, today it is seventy-nine – so Cubans can enjoy over twenty more years of life, and the pleasure of retirement.

Amazingly, as well as being among the best healthcare systems in the world, Cuba is also one of the cheapest. According to figures from the World Health Organisation in 2010, Britain's medical costs per person were £2,815. In the U.S. this was £6,719, but in Cuba it was just £674.

A report in the Oxford International Journal of Epidemiology in 2006 gives its own frank assessment of the Cuban system; "If the accomplishments of Cuba could be reproduced across a broad range of poor and middle-income countries the health of the world's population would be transformed." This was echoed by Secretary General of the UN Kofi Annan, who stated in 2000 that "Cuba should be the envy of many other nations," and that "Cuba demonstrates how much nations can do with the resources they have if they focus on the right priorities – health, education, and literacy."

*

Despite the extremely long hours Fidel put into his socialist project, he still made time for more personal pleasures. He would sometimes turn up at the Cerro sports stadium to play baseball with the Sugar Kings, and was known to ride around the island in his Jeep asking people their opinions on government policy, good or bad.

One area of his life where Fidel showed a chink in the armour, was his family life. Fidel saw little of his child, Fidelito, and after his brief affair with Naty Revuelta led to the birth of a girl called Alina, Fidel remained emotionally distant from them too.

There were a couple of reasons for this. One was that like many 1950s fathers, he saw his main role as that of breadwinner, though in Fidel's case this was taken to an unusually grand scale. The other main reason was that Fidel was determined not to allow nepotism to rear its ugly head. His children would stand on their own two feet and be judged on their own merits.

Fidel's other family relationships were also rather rocky. His older brother Ramón had publicly criticised Fidel's agrarian reform which had redistributed the wealth their father had moved so many fence posts to accumulate. Fidel upset his sister Emma by turning up to her wedding late and covered in mud having come straight from working on a farm. Meanwhile his other sister Juanita was already vehemently hostile to her rebellious brothers' leftist vision and was soon aiding counter-revolutionaries and the CIA. She defected in 1964 and still lives in the U.S..

After being reduced to a mere figurehead, President Urrutia had become demoralised. He rarely attended cabinet meetings, regularly delayed rubber stamping new laws, and refused to halve his $100,000 salary as his ministers had done. In protest at such obstinate behaviour, Fidel resigned live on television, leading to a public outcry. Urrutia took the hint and resigned his own position before fleeing to the Venezuela Embassy. Later that day Fidel held a mass public meeting in Revolution Square where an estimated one million people gathered to listen to his long bombastic speech, by the end of which – and 'at their insistence' – he agreed to resume the role of Prime Minister of Cuba.

Hüber Matos, a popular and talented officer in the Rebel Army, was dismayed at they way Urrutia was pushed out. He wrote a stinging rebuke to Fidel and offered his resignation, claiming twenty others were willing to resign along with him.

Fidel was incensed. Having long suspected it, Fidel now accused Matos of working for the CIA (which declassified CIA records later revealed to be true) and despatched one of the Rebel Army's most admired leaders, Camilo Cienfuegos, to arrest him.

Having taken Matos safely into custody Camilo travelled back in a light aircraft, but the plane mysteriously crashed and he was never seen again. Numerous theories evolved as to what had happened; he was assassinated by Fidel for being a threat to his rule; or the counter-revolutionaries in retaliation for Matos' arrest; or the CIA did it (to be fair, that is usually the right answer). The truth is, a little less exciting. Various investigations – and broad consensus – suggest that there was no foul play and that the most likely cause was that his plane developed a fault and crashed into the sea.

No matter what the reason it was a bitter blow to the Revolution. Camilo, possibly even more than even Fidel or Che, embodied the romantic revolutionary image. He was a charismatic soul who looked like he'd been borne from a genetic experiment to cross Jim Morrison with Russell Brand, and he had proven himself to be a fantastic military commander and a selfless countryman.

Matos was not on the plane with Camilo and arrived safely in Havana where he was given a public trial. Keen to show off his dazzling courtroom skills again, Fidel himself gave the summing up. Well actually, summing up isn't really the correct phrase as it implies a short evaluation of the key points that proved the defendant's guilt or innocence. Fidel was summing up for seven long hours. You have to have some sympathy for Matos, who not only had to sit through it but then had to attempt to better it and hope the judge was awake enough to hear it. He was sentenced to twenty years in prison.

V
Banking on Progress

"Human progress is neither automatic nor inevitable... Every step toward the goal of justice requires sacrifice, suffering, and struggle; the tireless exertions and passionate concern of dedicated individuals."
Martin Luther King, Jr.

Whilst many sectors of the economy were undergoing a socialist transformation, the rebels knew that they would never be able to complete the task without taking control of the money supply. The Bank of Cuba was still serving the capitalists it had been created to support – it was still they, not the government, who ultimately decided which industries would receive investment. To solve this problem, in November 1959 Felipe Pazos, a liberal member of the government, was removed from his post as President of the National Bank and replaced by Che who was charged with making Cuba's financial system work under socialism.

At the time, capital flight was presenting a big headache for the country's new economic planners. Upon Che's appointment, investors looked at this bearded revolutionary and panicked, causing a run on the banks and a huge draining of bank reserves. It was to be expected. Financial institutions rely on long-established, conservative indicators of competence. What they were facing now was a rugged Argentinian who, the story goes, was given the job because during a meeting of the secret government Fidel asked if anyone was a good economist and Che, half-asleep, raised his hand. Astonished, Fidel said to him "Che, I didn't know you were a good economist."

"Oh" he replied, "I though you asked for a good communist!"

Che's economic qualifications may have been lacking, but he was in good company – his support staff were also completely out of their depth. One new bank administrator recalls, "I was scared... I had never been in a bank and I didn't possess an account. I said 'I don't know anything about banks.' Che replied 'Me neither and I am the President [of the bank], but when the Revolution assigns you to a post the only thing to do is accept, get studying and work to perform as you should'" So it's probably a good job they didn't have any nuclear power stations.

Che was immediately beset by a series of problems. He needed to stop the flight of capital and regain control of the money supply. He also needed to recapitalise the banks and reduce the national debt. Of course what they *could* have done was to cut the Child Tax Credits and increase the pension age whilst making the youth into a pool of slave labour for *Poundland*, but instead they decided to make the rich pay.

First Che took all the gold they held in the U.S., then withdrew from the IMF and World Bank. He then announced that all banknotes were to be replaced with a new range (which included his personal signature scrawl, 'Che'). People had four days in which to exchange all their money but that any sum over 1,000 pesos would be placed in an account offering 3% interest with withdrawals limited to 100 pesos a month. Any amounts over 10,000 pesos were unchangeable – they were now the government's pesos to invest in public projects.

*

With a new socialist economy in full -swing, Fidel turned his attention back to creating a socialism-only political sphere. In early 1960 in a move that would forever detract from the purity of the Cuban Revolution, Fidel began neutralising all forms of political opposition. The once treasured independence of the Havana University was rescinded and staff who did not support government policies were dismissed and replaced.

A more innovative approach was used with the media. To counter anti-communist articles in the capitalist press, a law was passed whereby all articles critical of government policy had to end with a *caletilla* (tail-piece) by the printers union to counter-argue the main points. This was an interesting piece of policy, as although it clearly permitted government interference in the press, it did not actually limit what could be said. And in many ways it would be rather pleasing if it were introduced in the UK so that Daily Mail articles could all end with, "The union would like to remind its readership that the Daily Mail is owned and run by a bunch of tax-dodging, fascist-loving, small-minded racists. Please stop buying it, you only encourage them."

Notwithstanding the new media balance law Cuba's newspapers were already close to collapse. Most found their readers deserting them in their droves as evidence of the media's complicity with Batista's corrupt regime came to light. Also advertising revenue had collapsed as many private businesses deliberately cut back on their operations or had already been nationalised by the state.

But being in control of the nation's media could not totally prevent embarrassing footage from being broadcast. During a live television interview Fidel made some contentious allegations against the Spanish Ambassador Marques de Vellisca, whom he charged with aiding and abetting counter-revolutionaries. The Ambassador, who happened to be watching, jumped into his car and raced to the studio. Storming passed the surprised (and evidently crap) guards and officials, he marched over to Fidel and angrily confronted him live on air.

The Ambassador turned to the moderator to ask if he could make a statement, to which a slightly bewildered but nevertheless furious Fidel suggested that he instead, "Ask permission from the Prime Minister of the Republic." The Ambassador was not so easily intimidated and wryly pointed out to Fidel that, as a man who supported freedom, he would surely not mind at all. For once it was Fidel who was on the back foot. With millions of Cubans watching at home, Fidel and the Ambassador began furiously arguing with each other until eventually somebody finally had the mental capacity to stop the cameras. Quickly expelled from the country, when the Ambassador arrived back in Madrid he was met by General Franco who said, "As a Spaniard, you did well, as a diplomat, very badly."

The Dominican Republic dictator President Trujillo was similarly keen to bring Fidel down. Trujillo was a good friend of Batista, and he shared the U.S. fears that his revolutionary example would spread. And he no doubt knew that Fidel had joined the anti-Trujillo expedition whilst at university.

Trujillo started to arm and support counter-revolutionary groups soon after the *Fidelistas* triumphed, but his attempts proved disastrous. The most memorable was when two Cuban Rebel Army commanders travelled to the Dominican Republic pretending to be defectors and persuaded Trujillo to give them a million dollars to start a counter-revolution. Returning with half of the money they sent a message to Trujillo to inform him that they had taken the town of Trinidad and needed reinforcements (and the rest of the money). Trujillo was delighted and immediately flew over an array of arms as well as nine Batista cronies. Upon their arrival they were given passage to a 'safe house', where they were greeted by Fidel who arrested them all personally. Enjoying himself immensely Fidel then paraded the captives on television and broadcast the telephone conversations between his men and the Dominican government. Trujillo was a laughing stock. An article in the Washington post quotes one of the men involved as saying, "I should not be judged as a conspirator, but as an imbecile."

Yet the biggest external threat to Fidel's rule of course came from the U.S. government who were not too happy to see their puppet president deposed and their country's businesses nationalised. But possibly the main reason they wanted Fidel gone was that people might just start to think that he had the right idea. In 1959 J.C Hall from the State Department's Bureau of Inter-American Affairs said that the U.S., "Must insure that a successor government comports itself in our interests,". He also warned of 'the impact that real honesty' was having on the Cuban masses, who had "Awakened enthusiastically to the need for social and economic reform." The real danger was that "If the Cuban Revolution is successful other countries in Latin America and perhaps elsewhere will use it as a model," and that "we should decide whether or not we wish to have the Cuban Revolution succeed."

This sentiment was shared by the subsequent U.S. administration. At one National Security meeting in 1961, Kennedy and his advisers discussed how Fidel was dangerous and must be overthrown not because he was a threat militarily, but because he "Provided a working example of a communist state in the Americas, successfully defying the U.S.," and that "his survival, in the face of persistent U.S. efforts to unseat him, has unquestionably lowered the prestige of the U.S.". The following year, Director of Central Intelligence John McConnell remarked to President Kennedy that, "If Cuba succeeds, we can expect most of Latin America to fall."

They were not scared of Fidel because they thought him a communist, or even a dictator. What scared them was that he might be able to show that there *was* another way of doing things – possibly a better way, but not *their* way. *And* if he did, other people might get the same idea – and that was the scariest thought of all.

Their worries were not unfounded. In November 1959 the U.S. State Department noted how "In the eleven months that Castro has been in power the standard of living of low-income groups appears, on the basis of available statistics, to have improved." Clearly something had to be done to stop him.

Not long after Fidel took power, the CIA began funding Cuban-based counter-revolutionary guerrillas who established themselves in the Escambray Mountains, hoping to topple Fidel in the way he toppled Batista. But the CIA's support could not offset the support they lacked from the Cuban people. Ultimately by 1966 all the guerrilla groups were extinguished, but not before having claimed hundreds of lives and cost the Cuban economy a whopping $1 billion.

Records show that for decades CIA supported groups – inside Cuba and in the U.S. – carried out terrorist attacks on schools, hospitals, factories, farms, oil refineries, sugar mills, plantations, lumber yards, water systems, warehouses, chemical plants, communication facilities, trains and rail-road bridges. These attacks saw hundreds of innocent people killed, and many more scarred for life. In one incident in November 1962 a six-man CIA squad blew up an industrial facility killing four-hundred workers.

As time went on the CIA did everything their little minds could think of to bring Fidel and his Revolution to an end. But every time they tried, they failed. And every time they failed, they became even more desperate. And as they became more desperate, the more ludicrous were their plans.

When the U.S. put their first astronaut into space, the CIA planned to blame Fidel should anything go wrong. Their cover story was to claim that Fidel had used a magnetic ray to zap the module, and then use that as a way of justifying an invasion of Cuba. As it turned out, astronaut John Glenn arrived back in one piece. Although if he hadn't, it would have been interesting to see how the U.S. government were going to manage to convince the world that Cuba had a massive death-ray gun. It is said that if you are going to lie, lie *big*, but there has to be a line drawn in the sand doesn't there? You *may* be able to convince a *really* gullible person that old photographs are all in black and white because the world was only coloured in halfway through the twentieth century, but you probably couldn't convince someone that ducks have four legs when you are looking at a duck and both of you are, in fact, ducks.

Nevertheless, imaginary death rays were not to be the limit of the U.S. government's audacity. In 1962 General Lansdale, a high ranking member of the Department of Defence suggested they fake the 'Second Coming', whereupon the 'Messiah' would walk out of the sea onto a Cuban beach and declare Fidel to be the Anti-Christ. Who would be playing the part of Jesus wasn't mentioned, nor was any detailed plan to convince everyone that he *was* Jesus Christ. CIA technology is great at killing people but not so good at bringing them back from the dead, and pretending to levitate would only get you so far before someone says "Hang on, he's just got his feet at an odd angle and standing on tip-toe."

Another plan involved putting a powder in Fidel's shoes to make his beard fall out, which, it was assumed, would break the spell he cast over the Cuban people. This really is a compelling illustration of how baffled the CIA became over the Cuba situation. They just couldn't understand *why* Fidel and his cohorts were so popular. They completely overlooked the fact that he had overthrown a brutal dictator, given the people the land upon which they worked and the homes in which they lived. Ignoring all of this they instead came to the conclusion that the reason Fidel was so popular was because he had a really good beard.

Former Chief Security Officer for Cuba Fabio Escalante claims that his team identified 637 plots to assassinate Fidel between 1959 and 1999, the vast majority of which were linked with the CIA in some way. If the figures are correct, this averages around one plot every three weeks for forty years.

Finding no luck in assassinating Fidel themselves, in the summer of 1960 the CIA turned to the The Mafia for assistance. (Brief rundown of which mafia) The Mafia were all too happy to oblige as they were eager to settle a score and return to their 'business' in Cuba. But they failed too.[15]

Arguably the closest the CIA came to success was when they recruited one of Fidel's lovers, Marita Lorenz. Marita had fallen out with Fidel after asking her to visit Fidel in his hotel room and slip a poisoned pill into his drink. The pill would dissolve instantly and remain colourless, odourless and tasteless. The poison was highly lethal and he would be dead in seconds. According to Marita, she "Went to the Hilton [Havana Libre]. Just simply walked in, said hi to the personnel at the desk, went upstairs to the suite... I was scared to death." She had smuggled the pills in a jar of cold cream, only to discover that they had partially dissolved and were covered in goo. Forced to abandon the plan she flushed the offending items down the bidet and tried to act naturally. But by now Fidel was starting to show a sixth sense when it came to assassination attempts, and asked if she had come back to kill him. When she admitted that she had, he leaned forward and gave her his gun. She recalls that when she pointed the gun at him and cocked the trigger, 'He didn't even flinch.' After a tense few seconds she lowered the gun and gave it back to him, saying that she couldn't do it. Chewing thoughtfully on his cigar Fidel leaned back, smiled and replied "Of course you can't kill me. Nobody can kill me."

Marita would later have an affair with ex-Venezuelan dictator Marcos Evangelista Pérez Jiménez, who, she claims, used to sometimes "make abusive telephone calls to Fidel in Havana in which he began boasting that he now had Fidel's girlfriend and he had made her pregnant. Such calls became so frequent that one day secret agents approached me and asked me to urge Marcos to stop making calls to Cuba."

---

15 When asked in an interview in 1994 if he was really the devil that the western powers described him as, he replied, When asked in 1994 if he was the devil, Fidel replied, "If that is the case, then I am a devil who has been protected by the gods."

With the threat of outside aggression growing by the day Fidel needed to muster up some troops. But instead of creating a professional army he opted for a militia made up of volunteer workers, peasants and students. They were to be the first line of defence against any invasion and would assist with rooting out possible counter-revolutionaries. They may not have been as good as a standing army, but they were much cheaper to maintain, more mobile, and arguably more impassioned.

The government also ordered rifles and ammunition from Belgium, but deliveries stopped in March 1960 when a ship delivering arms was blown up in Havana harbour. The terrorists had also planted a second bomb timed to explode as people ran to the aid of those injured by the initial blast. Eighty-one people were killed, and three-hundred more injured. A state funeral was held for those killed during which Fidel gave a passionate, four-hour speech which ended with the maxim, "Homeland or death, we shall prevail!"

Although no culprit was ever found, most people – especially Fidel – suspected the U.S.. However there are also suspicions that it was the handiwork of the French secret service (the guns were being delivered by a French ship) in retaliation for Cuba giving arms to Algerian independence fighters, the FLN, who would claim victory and throw off the French colonial yolk in 1962. Despite the length of time that has passed, at the time of writing neither the French nor the CIA have declassified their files on the event.

Fidel was also thwarted when trying to restore his air-force. The British were due to deliver some fighter jets that they had sold to Batista the previous year (despite knowing they were being used to suppress the domestic population), but the U.S. asked them to cancel the order. And as ever the British government slavishly agreed.

In the beginning Fidel was quite determined to remain neutral in the Cold War, but as time went on it was becoming harder and harder to maintain this stance.[16] With Europe and the U.S. giving him nothing but grief, Fidel turned to the only realistic option left open to him and began negotiating trade links with the Soviet Union.

---

16 It is suggested that the U.S. actually wanted Fidel to side with the Soviets so they could have a 'justifiable' reason to remove him. According to one British ambassador at the time, CIA director Allen Dulles asked the UK government to refuse to supply the Cubans with the military aircraft because he "hoped that any refusal [to supply arms] would directly lead to a Soviet bloc offer to supply. Then he might be able to do something."

After the agrarian reform was passed, the U.S. had retaliated by reducing the amount of sugar that could be bought from Cuba. This had caused an enormous economic headache (which was of course the intention) but the Soviets were happy to step in and soon agreed to take *twice* what the Americans were refusing (albeit, at below market rates) every year until 1965.

As part of the trade deal the Cubans were also given vast quantities of oil and as the first batches of supplies arrived Che ordered the three oil refineries on the island to process it. Only it wasn't that easy. Not least because the government had little control over the oil refineries – two were owned by the U.S.-based companies ESSO and Texaco, whilst the other was owned by the British company BP.

The refineries were already slightly irked at having a new tax of five cents a gallon placed on them to finance a minimum wage for the workers in the garage forecourts, as well as seeing 60% of their profits redirected to the public purse. Nevertheless the refineries were inclined to acquiesce to the request, but decided to wait until they received advice from their respective governments.

A stand off ensued for several weeks until finally, in early June, the U.S. and British governments told the refinery owners not to process the Soviet crude. Just a couple of weeks later Fidel responded by nationalising them. Within a week the U.S. announced that all imports of Cuban sugar would be banned. So Fidel set about nationalising all U.S businesses operating in the country – and stipulated that compensation would be paid via a fund linked to U.S. purchases of Cuban sugar. So if the U.S. didn't buy any sugar, it wouldn't receive any compensation. Needless to say this left a bitter taste in the mouths of the U.S. government.

This caused further retaliation from the U.S., who despite being champions of the free-market, placed an almost blanket trade embargo (referred to by Cubans as 'the blockade') on the island, prohibiting any U.S. company or citizen to trade with the island except a limited range of medicine and foodstuffs (they would be banned a few years later) and banned all travel to the island. Always keen to have the last word, Fidel then nationalised every last inch of U.S property on the island.[17]

The trade blockade had a devastating effect on the Cuban economy

---

17 The brusqueness in which this measure was implemented is summed up by the owner of the Hotel Capri who laments who that not only was his hotel, apartment, and belongings confiscated, but because he was not able to travel back to the U.S. until the following day he was charged $30 for staying in his own hotel.

which had been extremely reliant on U.S. for almost everything, from food to machines. Factories and businesses were forced to close, consumer goods became harder to find, and various foodstuffs became scarce.

Although the USSR were more than willing to help try and plug the trade gap, the restructuring required would hit the country hard. Whilst previously goods from the U.S could be shipped quickly and in small quantities, those from the Soviet Union had to be ordered weeks if not months beforehand in large-scale shipments, which meant that bigger warehouses and ports needed to be constructed in Cuba to receive them.

Not only that, the entire nation needed to be re-plumbed and rewired because as Lars Schoultz notes in his book *That Infernal Little Cuban Republic;* "the island's measurements were taken in U.S.-standard inches and feet, its plumbing used U.S.-standard threaded pipe (to screw a metric-standard fitting onto a U.S.-standard pipe is to ruin both), and its electrical system was based on the U.S-standard 110 volts, not the European 220. Even the simplest electrical devices were generally of the type used by the U.S. but not by the world's other principal suppliers."

A UN study into the effects of the trade blockade carried out in 2008 showed that dairy products had to be imported from Canada or Europe, and rice from China or Vietnam. Had they been able to buy those goods from the U.S. they would have paid just one third of the price, and instead of taking forty-five days for the goods to arrive it would have only taken two.

Meanwhile the speed of the nationalisations caused considerable upheaval all over the country. A man called Borrego, who worked closely with Che during this period, recalls that he received a telephone call from Che in the early hours of the morning declaring that they had to find managers for 140 factories and eighty sugar-mills. "I nearly had a heart attack! Where were we going to find them? I only knew about three people with any accountancy experience. Half an hour later Che called me again and said 'Fidel had an idea...' There was a boarding school with 200 youngsters aged between fifteen and twenty years old, training to be voluntary teachers for the Sierra Maestre. Fidel said 'We will nominate them as managers of the factories.' I was shocked! Minutes later Fidel called to tell me to go to the school to wake them up even though it was the middle of the night. He arrived at 4am. The students went mad with joy, throwing their things up in the air. They were very happy to be told they would be managers." They may have found their managers but it's a miracle the country wasn't besieged by administrators proffering notes from their mothers in order to get out of meetings, or claiming their dog ate the end of year accounts.

Meanwhile, with no obvious way of bringing Fidel under control, the U.S. had set about organising a military invasion of Cuba. To aid their quest they began vastly increasing their support of counter-revolutionary groups and planning thousands of terrorist and sabotage attacks including; hijackings, derailments, fire bombs, white phosphorous being thrown into theatres, and teachers murdered to try and prevent the government succeeding in its quest to eradicate illiteracy.

*

This was probably not the best time for Fidel to make *another* trip to the U.S., but he was invited to speak at the United Nations General Assembly in New York and you don't turn offers like that down. Besides, it would be a good opportunity to tread on Uncle Sam's toes.

The U.S. authorities were on orders to keep Fidel safe from hostile anti-Castro groups, causing some disgruntlement within the ranks. Upon receiving their instructions, Kevin Tierney of the U.S. army's counter intelligence corps made his frustration known "You're telling me I gotta take a bullet to keep that son of a bitch alive so he can go back to Cuba and have them [the CIA] kill him?"

The Cuban delegation had reserved accommodation at the Shelburne Hotel but they were turned away upon arrival because the hotel manager did not want the bad publicity. Another version has it that the Cubans left when Fidel became indignant as the hotelier demanded the money up-front, whilst yet another account attests that they were turfed out because of their reputation for uncouth behaviour. This latter reason is certainly at least plausible. One person from the group, Carlos Rodriguez says "The place where the Cuban delegation arrived, was where the greater disorder I have ever seen would be installed. We could even bring disorder to the Palace of Versailles." In reality it was probably a mixture of all three.

Upon hearing about the fiasco the manager of the Theresa Hotel in Harlem offered them free accommodation. This was a somewhat different type of establishment from the Shelburne and served a very different type of clientèle. The Shelburne was elegant, exclusive, and frequented by the very wealthy white elites whereas the Theresa Hotel was run-down, shabby, and visited almost solely by the disenfranchised black community, pimps and prostitutes.

Fidel accepted at once, and in a gesture of goodwill invited the entire staff of the Hotel to dinner. He then entertained many of the world's leading politicians and intellectuals including Soviet Premier Nikita Khrushchev, Egyptian Prime Minister Gamal Abdel Nasser[18] Indian Prime Minister Jawaharlal Nehru, poet Allen Ginsberg and civil rights campaigner Malcolm X.

Of all the people Fidel met, Khrushchev was arguably the most enraptured. Shortly after coming to power in 1953 Khrushchev delivered a bone-shattering speech at the 20th Party Conference in which he had denounced Stalin so vehemently that some Soviet delegates were reduced to tears, others became nauseous, and one person had a heart attack. Instead of ruling with an iron fist, Khrushchev hoped to win the hearts and minds of the world's people by showing that the Soviet Union – and communism – was truly superior to capitalism. And in Fidel, he saw a glistening hope.

After the meeting a reporter asked Khrushchev if he thought Fidel was a communist, and he replied, "I don't know if Fidel is a communist, what I do know is that I'm a Fidelist." Which is a not so subtle way of saying yes.

Having considered their visit a success, the Cubans left the hotel and were smiling all the way to the airport when their smiles turned to grimaces as they were told that their plane had been impounded by the U.S. authorities. Not looking forward to a long swim home in shark infested waters, Fidel and his entourage gratefully accepted the offer of a Soviet replacement. As he eventually boarded, a thoroughly cheesed off Fidel summed up Cuba's feelings clearly as he remarked to one reporter, "Here you take our planes... Soviets give us planes."

*

To try and root out counter-revolutionary behaviour, 'Committees for the Defence of the Revolution' (CDR's) were established in every village, on every block. Made up of local residents, they were tasked with reporting any suspicious behaviour, organising community projects, promoting government policies, helping organise elections, running immunisation campaigns, and acting as grass-roots social services. Anyone over fourteen could become a CDR member and in the first year they would attract almost 800,000 members.

Critics of Fidel and the Revolution claim the CDRs are nothing but a tool of oppression, but others see things rather differently. For instance Mark Kruger, Director of the Criminal Justice Programme at St Louis

---

18 The CIA had previously channelled millions of dollars to Nasser in the hope of gaining his loyalty, only for Nasser to spend $3m of it on a Minaret that he called 'Roosevelt's Erection'. He then placed it outside the Nile Hilton. The U.S. were not best pleased.

University writes that the low crime rate in Cuba is due to a strong sense of community, fostered by the CDR system which 'provides the glue that attaches individual community members to the larger community.'

One man I spoke to in a square in Havana, whose support for Fidel and the Revolution dissipated in the late 1960s, remarked that CDRs were important when the U.S. aggression was at its peak, but that in modern times it is no more than a Neighbourhood Watch. When asked if he took part, he replied that he couldn't be bothered looking after other people's houses, but would give them money for local projects – as long as he didn't actually have to do anything himself!

*

Along with increasing security, Cuba's other main task was to raise productivity. Tasked with making the economy as efficient as possible, Che was keen to make full use of modern technology in factories and farms, and recognized the huge advantage of utilising computers to help with analysis. It was therefore rather unfortunate that the only computer on the island in 1959 was used at the racing track for calculating betting odds. It couldn't even run *Tetris*.[19]

In late October 1960 Che flew to Moscow to discuss more trade agreements[20] and attend the anniversary of the Bolshevik Revolution festivities. It would be his first visit to the country, and he did not like what he saw. Not only concerned about the low standard of living he was aghast to discover that the USSR were light years behind the U.S in developing computers. Visiting factories, Che was left frustrated that Soviet technology was often incompatible with existing U.S.-made machinery in Cuba, and was largely inferior. As one Cuban put it, "The technology they brought was... sturdy, but also wasteful and unviable [sic], heavy and ostentatious; in other words, just *too* Russian." Nevertheless, they had little option but to make use of what the Soviets had to offer.

Needless to say, Cuban production levels suffered massively. Some factories were closed and disassembled, allowing spare parts to be

---

19 Tetris was actually released in 1984. It was invented by Alexey Pajitnov while working for the Soviet Academy of Sciences at their Computer Centre in Moscow, and it is said that the Moscow officials had to lock it away because the game was so addictive and was distracting all the staff.

20 His visit would bring him up close and personal with the true egalitarian nature of the Soviet Union. Whilst waiting to catch an elevator he was told it was for members of the Comintern, leading him to reply curtly "Yes, already I see there are as many privileges here as in capitalist countries."

distributed to the areas most in need or working most efficiently. Within a few years only eighteen of 106 pharmaceutical factories were still operational, the number of textile plants fell by over 60%, a quarter of buses were out of action, as were half of the passenger rail carriages and three quarters of the *Caterpillar* tractors.

In an attempt to keep the country running, Cubans were encouraged to come up with inventions and contraptions themselves, resulting in an explosion of exciting ideas. So great was the enthusiasm for ad-hoc invention and adaptation that it quickly became incorporated into the country's culture. As one U.S. anthropologist states, "*Inventando* is not only material wizardry, it is also a mental process and a state of mind." As there were no domestic copyright laws protecting these inventions, they could be easily adopted – or improved – by others and used around the island.

The stress was clearly starting to take its toll on Fidel. According to the philosopher Jean-Paul Sartre, Fidel was due to make a speech at a baseball game in Holguín but looked haggard and exhausted – and still had two more speeches to make that day.

Uncharacteristically Fidel spoke for just a couple of minutes before sitting down, causing a sense of disappointment around the ground. Some children in the front row to start crying, two of whom jumped on stage and started tugging at his ankles. Picking one of them up Fidel asked what the problem was, to which the boy said he wanted him to visit their village. Becoming concerned, Fidel asked if anything was wrong. "Everything is fine, Fidel," the boy replied, "But come over to our place!" Fidel reassured him that he would come but the boy continued to wail, and was soon joined on stage by all the other children in the front row who wanted Fidel to come to *their* homes too. Sartre described Fidel as overwhelmed and intimidated, at first unable to leave the stage before literally running through the crowd to sanctuary.

Speaking to Simone de Beauvoir, Fidel admitted that, "I am happy that they surround me and jostle me. But I know that they are going to demand what they have the right to receive and what I don't have the means of giving them."

*

It is striking that at this time, as Fidel was struggling with the burden of actually *trying* to meet the utopian demands of the young children in the audience, the CIA were involved in a nefarious plot to kidnap them.

In alliance with the Catholic Church, ex-Batista supporters, Pan

American Airlines, Esso Standard Oil and the British Embassy, the CIA launched Operation Peter Pan (also referred to as Operation Pedro Pan). Propaganda was spread throughout the island via leaflets, radio and hearsay, with one rather tasteless piece stating that Cuban children were to be sent to Soviet work camps and would be brought home as canned meat.

Having created an atmosphere of fear and uncertainty the plotters then approached parents and offered to spirit their children away to safety in the U.S.. Between 1960 and 1962 around 14,000 Cuban children were given away by their parents and placed in foster homes, orphanages, juvenile delinquent institutions, boarding schools, and homes of U.S. citizens who had become empathetic to their plight. It was to leave thousands of families ripped apart, many never to be reunited again.

The Cuban children were given private schooling paid for by U.S. taxpayers and given access to student and business loans at rates below market price, few of which were ever repaid. Indeed, Cubans have become one of the most privileged immigrants in U.S history, receiving more government support than any other group.

That said, for many of the children life apart from their families was a horrific ordeal and far from comfortable. One child, Carlos Eire, later recorded his experience in his autobiography, *Waiting for Snow in Havana*. As the son of a judge, Carlos' family were part of the Cuban elite who were horrified to see their wealth and privilege dissipate at an alarming speed. Fearing the U.S. propaganda to be true, they sent Carlos to the 'safety' of the U.S.. As it turned, out he probably would have been better off in Cuba. For the first three and a half years he was sent to live in a foster home where he was fed only one meal a day. He shared his living quarters with twelve other children in a dismal three bedroom house "infested with roaches, mice and scorpions, [and was] under the care of two adults who didn't really care for us."

*

Inaugurated by Fidel on January 1st, 1961 was to be the Year of Education. Nearly a quarter of the population were illiterate, but in the rural areas the figure was much higher at 41.7%. Less than half of Cuban children aged six to fourteen years had ever been to school, whilst some teachers complained that they had not seen any new textbooks for ten years.

Mirroring the low literacy levels, books were not big business in Cuba, with less than one million books printed each year prior to the Revolution. By 1980 around fifty million were printed annually, and sold below cost price. School textbooks were (of course) free.

68

The National Literacy Campaign, launched in March, saw 271,000 volunteers, trade unionists and professional teachers travelling to stay with rural communities and teach over 700,000 people how to read and write.[21] Around 100,000 of the volunteers were teenagers – some as young as fourteen – who had left the comforts of town life behind and were sent with only an oil lamp and the New Teachers Literacy Guide to get them through. It wasn't a walk in the park for the volunteers – they were harassed, attacked and forty of them were killed by the CIA and counter-revolutionary groups. The use of youths during the campaign also had an unintended and unforeseen consequence. Away from the watchful eye of their parents, many of the teenagers returned from the countryside pregnant, causing a mini baby-boom.

The National Literacy Campaign proved extremely successful, with literacy rates soaring from 76% to 96% within two years. The figure soon reached 99%, where it remains to this day.

Education was seen as the bedrock of the revolution, with everyone encouraged to fulfil their potential, learn new skills and trades, and even new languages. The education drive saw an explosion in school attendance and in just one generation the children of illiterate peasants and the urban poor were graduating from university. And there were plenty of new universities to choose from. Prior to 1959 there had been just three universities, but today Cuba has 47.

The new revolutionary government couldn't resist the temptation to tweak the school curriculum to try and teach the population more about the nature of Cuban communism, which sometimes spilled out into outright propaganda. For instance, it has been claimed that there was a maths problem in a Cuban textbook that went; "Before our great Revolution Ramiro Gómez used to pay his scumbag capitalist landlord thirty pesos a month for rent. Now that our Maximum leader Fidel Castro has made the Urban Reform possible Comrade Gómez only has to pay twenty-five pesos. What percent reduction in rent has the Revolution gained him?"

Yet this is still arguably more tasteful than the exam question set by the elite British private school Eton College in 2013: "There have been riots in the streets of London after Britain has run out of petrol because of an oil crisis in the Middle East. Protesters have attacked public buildings. Several policemen have died. Consequently, the Government has deployed

---

21 It was not just teachers who were being sent to the country, projectionists were also sent so as to allow peasants to see films and TV shows for the first time in their lives. This service was, of course, free of charge.

the Army to curb the protests. After two days the protests have been stopped but twenty-five protesters have been killed by the Army. You are the Prime Minister. Write the script for a speech to be broadcast to the nation in which you explain why employing the Army against violent protesters was the only option available to you and one which was both *necessary* and *moral*."

Overall the Revolution's achievements in education have been mind-blowing, and have led to startling statistics. For example whilst Cuba today houses 11% of all Latin American scientists but comprises just 2% of its population; they have more doctors per capita than almost any other country in the world. A 1998 study by UNICEF showed that Cuban children in the third and fourth grade (equivalent to years 4 and 5 in the British education system) scored one hundred points above the regional average in tests of basic language and mathematics skills, but most incredibly, even the test results of the lower-scoring Cuban pupils were higher than those of the higher-scoring pupils from other Central and South American countries.

Even the World Bank, hardly an entity that could be said to have communist sympathies, admitted in a 2014 report that not only does Cuba have the best education system in Latin American and the Caribbean, they were the only country on the continent to have a high-level teaching faculty.

Today the Cuban state spends over 13% of its GDP on education, whereas the UK and U.S. governments both allocate just 5.5%. But another possible reason for Cuba's educational success is the way the schools are run. They are run by the community; parents, teachers, and students. Everyone has a significant input. This structure helps to draw communities together rather than alienating them, and has enabled Cuba's schools to become some of the most cooperative and innovative in the world.

Students are expected to take responsibility for their own school and education, a policy which is described by the World Bank as being 'lost in western schools'. Cuban students are asked their opinion. Interestingly they are also responsible for cleaning, fixing facilities, working in the school gardens, suggesting ways of localising the curriculum, and helping their peers who are struggling. Education is not regarded as a competition – it is a team effort.

VI
Pigs, Jesus Christ, and Some Nuclear Weapons

"If you want to make God laugh, tell him about your plans."
Woody Allen

Towards the end of 1960 Fidel alleged that eighty percent of the staff at the U.S. Embassy were spies (and to be fair, he wasn't far wrong) and ordered them to reduce their numbers from sixty to eighteen, in line with numbers at the Cuban Embassy in Washington. Eisenhower responded by closing down the Embassy and cutting off all diplomatic relations, whilst also imposing sanctions on any country buying Cuban sugar if they also received U.S. loans. With this done, Eisenhower then handed over power to John F Kennedy who had just won the Presidential elections.

Having only just wiped his shoes on the welcome mat, in early 1961 Kennedy gave the go ahead for a CIA plan to remove Fidel from power and 'restore democracy' through directly indirect means. The plan called for a military invasion fronted by Cuban exiles, whilst the organising and support was to be the left solely in the hands of the U.S. government.

Far from 'heroic revolutionaries', the Cuban exiles in the invasion force were described by one of the mission's leading planners Howard Hunt, as "shallow thinkers and opportunists" and that "For Latin American males their calibre was about average; they displayed most Latin faults and few Latin virtues."

To soften up the Cuban regime, another large wave of terrorism was carried out and acts of economic warfare (dubbed by the U.S. as 'economic denial') were expanded and enhanced. "We wanted to keep bread out of the stores so people were hungry," explains one CIA officer, "We wanted to keep rationing in effect and keep leather out, so people got only one pair of shoes every eighteen months." One method was to deliberately buy up all the products the Cubans wanted. According to Frank Sturbits of the CIA, "If there was a single source of supply for a particular good, we would go in and buy it to deny the Cubans the market."

To further cripple the Cuban economy Kennedy tightened the trade blockade by prohibiting the import of any goods that originated in Cuba, thus ensuring businesses could not flout the existing ban by sending imports via third parties in foreign countries. Coincidentally, the ban was implemented just after Kennedy received his extremely large order of his favourite Cuban cigars. But like the cigars he would see his hopes of toppling Fidel go up in smoke.

The invasion force of around fifteen hundred counter-revolutionary fighters were trained for the mission by the CIA; some in Louisiana; some at a disused zoo in Miami; but the vast majority were sent to camps in Guatemala, which were equipped with everything the recruits would need, including their own brothel. So they were screwed even before they started.

The operation began late at night on April 14th 1961, as a ship made its way from Florida to the coast of Oriente province as part of a diversionary attack. Following this, just after midnight a squadron of B-26 light bombers set off from Nicaragua to attack Cuba's military airports and the Cuban air-force.

Cuba's new home-grown militias saw one group of teenagers triumphantly shoot down one of the B-26 bombers but overall the attack was devastating. The Cuban air-force was reduced to just four operational Sea Furies fighter jets, one B-26 bomber and three T-33 trainer planes. The attack killed seven Cubans and left over fifty wounded. The people were outraged. To rub salt into the wounds, the U.S. claimed that the bombings had been carried out by Cuban pilots who had afterwards defected to the U.S. after being ordered by Fidel to attack the Cuban people. And to make these outrageous accusations seem plausible they paraded a 'Cuban' plane – with pre-made bullet holes – around the national media.

Appearing on television the morning after the attacks, Fidel categorically denied that any defections had taken place. He also produced photographs showing that the aircraft was actually an American jet painted with the Cuban FAR (Revolutionary Air Force) colours, which demonstrated a clear breach of international law[22]. Later that day at the funeral of those killed in the air-strikes Fidel gave another powerful and emotional speech in which he likened the bombing raid to Pearl Harbour, except being, "twice as treacherous and a thousand times more cowardly." Then with the crowd in the palm of his hand, he dropped a bombshell. He suddenly bellowed "Do you agree with the Agrarian Reform?" The people roared back, YES! "Do you agree with the Revolution's changes in education and health?" YES! "This is called socialism." The people went wild. "What the imperialists cannot forgive us," he continued, "is that we

_____

22 Acts of aggression made under the insignia of the enemy are deemed illegal by the Geneva Convention of 1949

have made a Socialist revolution under the noses of the U.S.. And that we shall defend with these rifles this socialist revolution." The gloves were off.

The U.S.'s main invasion began just after midnight on April 17th. Having set sail in boats donated by the ever benevolent United Fruit Company, the counter-revolutionary forces landed at Playa Girón (more commonly referred to as the Bay of Pigs) in Cuba. With the country already on high alert it was not long before they were spotted by a party of militia, but with no working telephones nearby it took over an hour for the news to reach Fidel.

Fidel knew that the military force had to be dealt with expediently. If the invaders could 'conquer' enough territory they would declare themselves the official government and be recognized by the U.S. who could then legitimise more serious and direct military intervention.

With reports filtering in of paratroopers landing elsewhere on the island, Fidel sprang into action. His first step was to ensure the invasion force did not have time to gain much territory. Ordering ground troops to advance to the beachhead, he assembled what was left of his air-force and instructed them to take out the ships anchored offshore in order to cut off any reinforcements.

Just after 6am two Cuban Sea Furies and a B-26 bomber went on the offensive and attacked two enemy ships lying off the coast. The two ships in question were the *Houston*, and the *J.*, which, on a side note, really makes you wonder just how serious the CIA were listening to Kennedy's demand that U.S involvement be kept low key. The Cuban air attack proved very effective, which is all the more remarkable considering some of the pilots had never even fired the machine guns on their planes before. Both ships took direct hits.

After returning to rearm and refuel, the Cuban air-force launched their second attack, this time hitting a large freighter that was still unloading supplies. Exploding into a massive fireball, the freighter sank rapidly, along with what was left of its cargo. The remaining ships had seen enough and sped off as fast as they could, promising those still ashore that they would return at nightfall. They didn't.

This left 1,350 counter-revolutionary troops ashore with no chance of reinforcements and nowhere to retreat to. Three Cuban T-33 planes, fitted with two .50-calibre machine guns managed to shoot down four of the U.S.'s fifteen B-26 bombers which had flown in from Nicaragua. Cuba's effectiveness surprised the CIA, who had thought they were unarmed, which seems a little naïve considering that the planes had been purchased from the U.S. just a few years prior. All they had to do was check the invoice.

Yet Fidel did not have it all his own way. Knowing time was of the essence Captain José Ramon had to break down a door to retrieve some maps because the man with the key was miles away in another province. But as it turned out he probably shouldn't have bothered. The maps were from a different era and not only were some towns not on there, those that were often had different names. It was like invading Britain with a map from the 1800's, and when marching between London and Birmingham suddenly becoming bemused by the appearance of Milton Keynes. So when Fidel ordered him to attack Pálpite, Fernandez had no idea where he meant. Which meant he was even further delayed. The issue was finally resolved when an officer looked over Fernandez's shoulder and noticed the discrepancy.

Cementing his image as a warrior-philosopher, Fidel left his office in Havana to join the troops on the front-line. Reinforcements had begun to arrive, including some Soviet tanks whose crews had to learn how to use them en route. This must have been absolutely terrifying for the soldiers, especially if they had to negotiate a roundabout or parallel park.

By noon of April 18th the U.S. invasion force looked all but doomed. Only direct intervention by the U.S. military forces could have turned the tide but Khrushchev had already sent a message to Kennedy to affirm that the Soviet Union would help defend Cuba if they suffered any external aggression, and Kennedy was not willing to risk a nuclear war. His aides and advisers, however, did not share his concern. According to Arleigh Burke, Chief of Naval Operations at the time, when the request for U.S. military assistance was denied on grounds that the U.S could not be seen to be involved he replied, "Hell, Mr President, but we are involved. Can I not send in an airstrike?"

"No."

"Can we send a few planes?"

"No, because they could be identified as U.S.."

"Can we paint out their numbers or any of this?"

"No."

"If you'll let me have two destroyers, we'll give gunfire support and we can hold that beachhead with two ships forever."

"No."

"One destroyer, Mr President?"

"No."

It was like a child trying to stay up past their bedtime, pleading for even the most minuscule of concessions. "Oh please just let me watch the end of this film. Look it's almost finished. Oh at least wait till the end of the credits... oh come on, I want to know who operated the boom mic..." And like every parent, Kennedy caved. At three o'clock in the morning he gave the order for six unmarked U.S. military planes to provide cover for the beleaguered B-26 bombers.

The U.S. planes could have turned the tide of the war if it wasn't for one tiny detail – they had forgotten about the time difference between Nicaragua and Cuba so as the B-26 bombers arrived over Cuba the U.S. planes were still on the aircraft carrier. With no air support, the B-26 bombers were all either shot down or forced into a hasty retreat.

By late-afternoon on April 19th, having lasted around seventy-two hours, the battle was over and the CIA sent a message to the leader of the counter-revolutionaries. It said, "Sorry... you've done everything you could. You've fought well. Break off and scatter. Good luck. Don't call me again." All things considered, this was a bit of a kick in the teeth. It was the equivalent of sending a text message saying 'Run4 it. Gd Lk. LOL!'

The attack resulted in over 150 Cubans losing their lives and hundreds more wounded – including Che Guevara, when in a somewhat embarrassing moment he managed to shoot himself in the face. The incident occurred when he accidentally dropped his pistol causing it to discharge a bullet which flew up and grazed his cheek (leaving an impressive scar). To make matter worse he suffered an allergic reaction to the subsequent tetanus injection and had to be rushed to hospital before he died of anaphylactic shock.

The battle saw nearly 1,200 counter-revolutionary troops captured, and 120 killed in action.[23] Those taken prisoner experienced the same humane treatment meted out to Cuban soldiers during the war against Batista. All prisoners were given medical treatment and were neither tortured nor abused. The same could not be said from the other side. Late on April 19th, with the battle all but over, the *Houston* managed to capture two militiamen (whilst killing four others) who had ventured near in a patrol boat. According to the CIA observer who was aboard the ship, the

---

23 Despite Kennedy insisting no direct U.S. involvement, four members of the Alabama National Guard were later found piloting some of the B-26 bombers. They had been killed in combat but their families were never to know the truth for many years. Their grief became a security issue.

prisoners were quickly executed because of the "logistical problems they made for the survivors."

That is not to say that all of the counter-revolutionaries fared well. In a tragic accident, eight prisoners asphyxiated when being taken to Havana because the officers forgot the vans were airtight. No foul-play was suspected; if war has taught us anything it is that at times all military forces show signs of fatal incompetence.

Kennedy's assertion that the U.S. had not been involved in the invasion was becoming harder and harder to explain. The entire world could see U.S warships stationed off the Cuban coast and they knew they weren't there for the fishing opportunities. Finally, on April 22nd, Kennedy came clean and took full responsibility for its failure. "Victory has a thousand fathers," he said, "but defeat is an orphan."

However this confession put Kennedy in an awkward position. U.S. law dictates that it is a criminal offence for the government to instigate a military invasion from the U.S. against a country with which the U.S. is not officially at war. Fortunately for Kennedy the 'free press' were too incensed about all the other aspects of the débâcle to linger on this point too long and the issue was brushed under the carpet.

*

Basking in his victory Fidel could not have been more popular. He had not just beaten off the 'yolk of imperialism', he had made an omelette and served it up in time for breakfast. The entire nation celebrated, drunk on pride, comradeship and gallons of rum. He spent many hours being interviewed by the media, taking people on tours of the battle sites and giving minute by minute accounts of the most important moments.

Fidel then gave a speech which, although it might not have been his most important, it was certainly his most sarcastic. "We are going to give them all a medal and say thanks to [Nicaragua's dictator] Somoza [for allowing the use of his country as a base for counter-revolutionary force], to the State Department, Mr. Kennedy, and Mr. Dulles for being so noble and democratic and respectful of international laws and human rights, for preparing the group to liberate us from agrarian reform and urban reform and from all these teachers and literacy workers. Come again to bring the Yankee administrators; come again to close the beaches, to form aristocratic clubs, to give us unemployment, to bring back the soldiers for the barracks which have been transformed into schools, to bring lower wages and higher prices. Come again to exploit and rape."

The prisoners were taken to the Havana Sports Palace where

journalists asked them questions in front of a highly entertained audience. On the whole the prisoners remained steadfast in their anti-Castro convictions and criticised Fidel for not holding elections, yet they also accepted that they had been treated well and some even apologised for the attack. Under more questioning, fourteen admitted being culpable of murder and other crimes during Batista's era and were subsequently arrested, five of whom were later executed and the other nine were given thirty year prison sentences.

During the trials Fidel himself took over questioning, walking among the men like a chat show-host. "Be honest," he said to one prisoner, "Surely you recognize that you are the first prisoners in history who are allowed to argue with the head of government you came to overthrow, in front of the whole country and of the whole world!" Meanwhile, the crowds were acting like they were watching an episode of *The Jerry Springer Show*, cheering, jeering and chanting 'Fidel! Fidel!' Such was the atmosphere that at one point one of the prisoners seemed to forget which side he was on and started applauding Fidel too.

The prisoners were used as a bargaining chip as Cuba sought reparations from the U.S. in the form of $30 million, five-hundred tractors and an apology. The U.S. dragged out the negotiations for a year and a half until eventually, on December 23rd 1962, the U.S. agreed to give the Cubans medicine and food to the value of $50 million, along with a further two million dollars in cash. They still refused to apologise but as a sign of goodwill they presented Fidel with a wetsuit, which when analysed was found to be full of poisonous spores.

Fidel would later forgive Kennedy for the attack, explaining that, "I am convinced that he had doubts... but he did not decide to cancel it because many forces were committed... And even though he launched the invasion, I think that Kennedy had great merit. If it had been Nixon, he would not have resigned himself to the defeat of the invasion, and I am convinced that there would have been an escalation and that in this country we would have been trapped in a very serious war between North American troops and the Cuban people, because the people, without any doubt, would have fought... There would have erupted in our country a war that would have cost us tens of thousands, hundreds of thousands of lives. And I think that the man who had the personal qualities, who had the personal courage to recognize that a great error had been committed...."

The Bay of Pigs had made Fidel a hero and Kennedy a major embarrassment. On April 22nd 1961, just three days after the defeat at the

Bay of Pigs, Kennedy started planning his revenge.

*

Having successfully protected his country from U.S. interference Fidel turned his attentions to domestic affairs once again. Having already nationalised the media he moved to nullify dissent in other cultural art-forms. In a two-hour speech to the country's top cultural figures (later titled 'Words to Intellectuals'), Fidel explained that whilst the country was under attack it was essential to show unity and not criticise the regime. "Within the Revolution, everything; against the Revolution, nothing."

Despite this cultural constraint the nation still enjoyed a fantastic cultural scene, with an enormous array of artists, musicians and writers, and producing some of the world's finest folk, jazz, blues, salsa, art, ballet, and poetry. In fact Lee Lockwood, a U.S. journalist, remarks of the Cuban cultural scene in the mid 1960's, "Under the loosely administered patronage of the Revolution, the arts have flourished in Cuba and remained refreshingly free of the ideological influence and restraint common to other socialist structures."

In fact, the socialist nature of the Revolution *ensured* that art and culture not only remained, but thrived. One common characteristic of capitalist nations is that people are often denied the opportunity to participate in cultural and sporting activities, not because there are no facilities, but because they cannot afford them. In a socialist society, the only prevention should be the provision of the facilities and your personal time. The Cuban philosophy was that nobody should be prevented from bettering themselves, their community and their country, or realising their true potential. This approach also created an added bonus in that by allowing everyone to participate talent can be drawn from a much bigger pool. This increased the odds of discovering and producing some of the best athletes and cultural works which might otherwise have been lost. And there is no better example of this than the Cuban ballet.

Prior to 1959 ballet was considered the culture of the elites, and only the wealthy could ever dream about watching or performing in the ballet. Not any more. Now everyone had the opportunity to learn ballet and it was not long before Cuba gained an international reputation for producing some of the best dancers in the world. Yet the success came at a price. And that price, was the audience.

According to a recent book by Aviva Chomsky, as the working classes were able to access what had been considered to be high-brow culture, they brought their own culture from the sports grounds with them. As a result when people go and watch a ballet performance they are liable to clap when they are not supposed to, shout when they should never do, and break out in brawls like nobody has ever done at the ballet ever. One Cuban performer even describes how dancers are forced to break from their routine because the noise of the crowd drowns out the orchestra and the stage is bombarded with flowers.

So whereas usually at a ballet you might see people in their finest attire, desperately trying to avoid any faux pas such as forgetting their snuff box, in Cuba there might be a load of people fighting about which performer performed the best Balançoire, before bursting out with a few chants of 'the swan in black's a wanker!' before kissing the person next to them as their favourite ballet star scores a complex manoeuvre to put their team 1-0 up before the interval.

Cuban culture had its low points however, such as the few years where *The Beatles* were banned for having a corrupting influence on the youth. Luckily sharing a view with Bible Belt America evidently made Fidel uncomfortable, and it was not long before the ban was overturned. He later remarked that it was "One of the greatest cultural errors of the Revolution." Today a statue of John Lennon stands in a park in Havana, but for reasons unknown the sculptor decided to use real glasses which could be removed. This short-sightedness inevitably resulted in people stealing them and now an attendant is tasked with guarding them every day. Only in a socialist society could a man be employed to prevent the theft of a statue's spectacles. And they don't even have lenses. Clearly they should have gone to Specsavers.

Another cultural error was the 'moral crusade' that aimed to eradicate 'social ills'. In the mid-1960s police trained in Moscow started to arrest pimps, prostitutes and homosexuals in a flurry of raids. Some members of the government protested the action, especially the degrading treatment of homosexuals, pointing out that many of them had supported the Revolution and remained loyal to it.

After a few years Fidel belatedly acknowledged their concerns and ordered that homosexuals should not be tried or jailed. However this was not the progressive step it initially appears.

Instead homosexuals (along with religious followers and counter-revolutionaries) were sent to serve in Units to Aid Military Production, which were ostensibly agricultural work camps whose entrances were displayed with the frightfully Orwellian slogan, 'Work Makes You Free'. From the outset there were allegations of torture and abuse at the camps, yet it took nearly three years for the government to launch a serious investigation. Horrified to find the allegations to be well founded they closed the camps with immediate effect.

The ongoing poor treatment of homosexuals would cast a dark cloud over the Revolution's more progressive achievements. All the way through the 60s and early 70s, people who were found to be gay would lose their jobs, be banned from having contact with children, were thrown of university, and expelled from the Party.

But in 1975 there was an unexpected breakthrough when a group of gay artists took the government to the country's Supreme Court, who duly awarded them compensation for their persecution and ordered the government to let them return to their places of work. This landmark decision would turn the tide of gay rights, but the current would still be agonisingly slow.

Same-sex relationships were eventually decriminalised in 1979, and the government started to take a more anti-homophobic line, with Fidel declaring homophobia to be anti-revolutionary. Unfortunately he didn't seem to tell the police, who continued to subject homosexuals to house raids and 'round-ups'. Incredibly it was not until 1988 that the government finally repealed the [pre-Revolution] 1938 law that criminalised those who 'flaunted' their homosexuality in public.

By the 1990s however the anti-homophobic message had started to take hold, both institutionally and culturally. In 1993 a Cuban film was released called Strawberries and Chocolate which discussed the persecution of the LGBT community, winning many awards both domestically and internationally. Two years later, drag queens were leading the biggest event in the socialist calendar, the May Day procession.

Fidel would later publicly, and profusely apologise for the Revolution's actions, calling them a 'great injustice' whilst blaming it on the culture of Cuban machismo, the misguided zeal for Soviet Puritanism, and his own ignorance. "If someone is responsible," he said, "it's me."

*

By the end of 1961, Fidel found the Soviets making too many demands, the U.S. still trying to kill him, and the economy was in chaos. He was stressed, depressed and disillusioned. He needed a break. For the following months he withdrew from public life, and delegated more of his powers.

Because of the huge wealth redistribution from the rich to the poor, demand for food, clothes, and luxuries soared and the country could not cope. National beef consumption increased 50% in the first year of the revolution alone as more and more people were able to afford it, whilst fish consumption increased from an average of 10.6 pounds per person in 1958, to 33 pounds in 1978. This inevitably resulted in shortages and in March 1962 a rationing system was introduced so as to make sure those with higher incomes could not buy up all of the food. It was a similar system as used by Britain during World War II, and ensured that every citizen had access to the necessities of life. It wasn't much, but there was enough for everybody. Pregnant women and families with children received extra rations, as did those who were due to be married or celebrate their birthday.

At first it involved just staple foodstuffs such as milk and rice, but as the people's demands increased, so did the ration list. Even oranges were added to the growing list of rationed goods, leading to President Dorticós declaring them to be a bourgeois fruit. This was plainly ridiculous; everyone knows that the only bourgeois fruit is the avocado. But such was the chaos of the times...

Meanwhile, in the Ministry of Industry, Che was at his wits end trying to deal with the effects of the U.S.-imposed trade blockade and the legions of educated workers leaving the country. So when complaints started being received about the insecticide being produced, Che wrote to the man responsible, "The sad reality is that this product to kill cockroaches is coming out with terrible quality, and I am receiving many complaints from all over. I think we will have to produce this with a label that explains that to kill cockroaches we have to tie them together, submerge them in a bottle of insecticide... so that if they don't die from the poisoning, they will die from the drowning." If only Che came with an 'extreme sarcasm' warning.

Another issue to contend with was trying to change attitudes In the workplace. Before the Revolution, workers were told what to do, when to do it, when they could eat, when they could urinate... For centuries the workers, peasants, and general populace had been forced to be submissive to their 'betters', to show deference to those wealthier or more powerful. Their opinions meant nothing. Now this culture was so ingrained that it was a struggle for many to break free. Now they were being asked to take responsibility themselves and contribute to debates about how things should be done..

It was going to be a hard slog. When one director of a textile factory asked Che for his opinion on the new women's range, he received a stinging rebuke. "Do you believe that I should be in charge of deciding how the women of this country should dress? I refuse to give my opinion about this design. It is up to specialists and designers to decide this issue. The worst thing that could happen to the women in Cuba is that a minister decides what clothes they wear."

*

After a few months of quiet introspection, Fidel returned to political scene to discover that Anibal Escalante, a member of the Cuban Communist Party (PSP), had been torturing people and plotting with the Soviets to wrestle control of the country and turn it into a satellite state of the USSR. Armed with the evidence Fidel made a televised announcement warning of a sectarian plot to oust him, whilst also promising to end the to the "transgressions of power, the arbitrary arrests, the wilfulness, the excesses, the whole policy of contempt towards a people" that Escalante had unleashed.

For his role in the affair, Escalante was removed from the government and sent to Czechoslovakia for an 'extended vacation', remaining there until 1964 when he returned to take up a minor administration position. But what was Fidel to do about the USSR involvement in the affair? Fidel was dependent on the Soviets for political backing, military support, and trade. He could hardly break off relations now. So putting on his pragmatic hat, he brushed the affair under the carpet. Which was just as well because the U.S. were about to make their next move. And it was a big one.

Over the pond in Washington, battered, bruised, and eager to claw back some pride after the Bay of Pigs debacle, JFK allocated $100m to a project known as Operation Mongoose, the aim of which was to destroy Fidel's Revolution by October 1962. Meanwhile Secretary of State Robert Kennedy informed the Special Group that toppling Fidel was "the top priority of the U.S. Government – all else is secondary – no time, money, effort, or manpower is to be spared."

It was a serious operation; 600 CIA officers, 5,000 contractors and so many submarines, patrol boats and seaplanes that it became the third biggest navy in the Caribbean. In the first eight months of the year they would be involved in 5,780 terrorist attacks on Cuban soil, hitting over 700 'major economic and social targets'. According to Noam Chomsky, such attacks included speedboats firing upon Cuban seaside hotels "killing a score of Russians and Cubans."

The gloves were well and truly off. The U.S. establishment was clearly not afraid to circumvent international law, with one document brazenly declaring that, "Although the U.S. cannot defend this action as justified under international law, we can stress the morality of the action on the basis that a chaotic, near civil war situation exists just off our shores where millions of Cubans are seeking freedom by throwing off the Communist yoke and have requested our assistance."

The problem they had was that nobody in Cuba seemed to want their help. One State-CIA joint report noted that, "Every key national figure in Cuban society, with the notable exception of the Catholic hierarchy, is by now either a dedicated supporter of communism and the Castro regime or a non-Communist so deeply committed to the regime as to be unlikely to turn against it." The following year a National Intelligence Estimate noted that, "On balance Castro is in a stronger position now than appeared likely a few months ago." It also added that "Unless the U.S. was willing to send in the marines – lots of marines – physical force was not going to solve Washington's problem."

After a few months of nefarious brainstorming thirty-three plans were placed on Kennedy's desk for approval. Many of the documents are now declassified, but some documents were shredded in 1967 lest they incriminate the government. Considering the nature of the information that did survive, it is unsettling to wonder just what the more incriminating documents contained.

The plans ranged from mad to bad, and all the way to dangerous. For example one of the most wacky plans involved firing "star-shells from a submarine to illuminate the Havana area at night" in the hope of creating "a rumour inside Cuba about portents signifying the downfall of the regime." It's not known how many Cubans were astrologists, but the plan didn't work. Another suggested Photoshopping Fidel into pictures to make it look like he was living a life of greed and debauchery, but that was never going to work because *Photoshop* hadn't yet been invented.

Arguably the most sinister of these was the plan to develop a 'Cuban' terror campaign in Miami and Washington in order to give the U.S. pretext to start a military invasion. They also suggested blowing up a U.S. passenger plane, with the Pentagon even going as far as suggesting 'the passengers could be a group of college students.'

Not content with killing its own people it adds that the terror campaign could also be pointed at Cuban refugees seeking haven in the U.S.. It suggests they sink a boatload of Cubans en route to Florida 'real or simulated.'

The levels of espionage between the superpowers at this time meant that the USSR soon knew about Operation Mongoose, and duly informed their Cuban allies, who duly panicked. Defeating a bunch of ex-Cubans supplied by the U.S. was one thing, but the only way Fidel was going to survive a direct U.S. invasion was if it didn't happen. With this in mind the USSR offered the Cuban government the ultimate deterrence – nuclear weapons.

The Soviet offer appeared to be an extremely generous one yet it was not an entirely altruistic act. Despite their bluster the Soviets knew they could not compete with the U.S militarily. At the time the U.S. had hundreds of nuclear missiles, many of which hugged the borders of the USSR in countries such as Turkey, Italy and Japan. In an attempt to keep the threat at bay the Soviets boasted that they were churning nuclear missiles out wholesale – but in reality they had just a few dozen, and they were mainly made out of cardboard, PVA glue and glitter. So as Khrushchev saw it, installing a few nuclear missiles ninety miles off the coast of Miami seemed an ideal way to counter the Yankee threat, he remarked, "It was high time America learned what it feels like to have her own land and her own people threatened."

Getting the missiles over the pond without being spotted was going to be a challenge, but as it turned out, hiding the weapons was only the start of their problems. One ship got caught in a storm – not what you want when travelling with a cargo of the most deadly bombs the world had ever seen. It resulted in one death, and half of those on board fell down with seasickness. When it finally arrived in Cuba, one of the crew was heard muttering, "You're not going to get me on that mother-fucking barge. Until they build a bridge to Russia, I'm not going over the ocean for anything." So presumably he's still there.

It was always going to be impossible to keep the installation of nuclear missiles secret from the U.S., especially as it was happening right on their doorstep, but for some reason the Soviets intended to do just that. Upon hearing this the Cuban leadership pleaded with Khrushchev to reconsider, pointing out that apart from it being impossible to achieve, all the Soviets needed to do was copy the wording from the same missile contract that the U.S had with its allies. That way, they U.S. couldn't complain. There was no need for subterfuge. Subterfuge suggests they were doing something naughty – which they weren't. Unfortunately Khrushchev did not heed their advice, and it would push the world to the precipice of nuclear Armageddon.

Cuban fears were realised in mid-October as an American spy-plane uncovered the prepared nuclear missiles sites. The U.S. military was instantly assembled and placed on high alert. Calling together an executive committee, Kennedy questioned why the Soviets would do something so stupid, remarking that, "It's just as if we suddenly began to put a major number of MRBMs [medium-range ballistic missiles] in Turkey. Now that'd be goddam dangerous, I would think." This was followed by a short, uncomfortable silence, which was broken as one of his advisers tentatively replied "Well, we did, Mr President."

Moving swiftly on before anyone had a chance to consider the moral ramifications of what had just been said, some of the advisers called for an immediate air-strike. At first Kennedy was in agreement, but in the end they opted for the plan suggested by Secretary of State Robert McNamara which was to establish a naval blockade of the island to prevent the missiles from arriving. What he didn't know, however, was that some of the missiles were already there and operational.

So it was that on October 22th 1962 180 U.S. warships containing forty-thousand marines encircled the island, while 579 fighter jets and 300,000 troops assembled in Florida as Kennedy made a televised broadcast. Sitting in the Oval Office he explained the events so far and demanded the Soviets remove the missiles. No Soviet ship would be allowed to break the naval blockade without first being stopped and searched.

In Havana Fidel responded with his own announcement the following day which (naturally) went on for much longer than Kennedy's. He was incensed by the U.S response to the missiles, arguing that Cuba need not ask them permission for anything. He also laughed off claims they were offensive weapons, pointing out (correctly) that Cuba would be wiped off the map were they to declare war. "What have we done? We have defended ourselves. This is all." In another speech he attacked the U.S. with all the sarcasm he could muster, "If the U.S. desires disarmament, magnificent! Let us all support a policy of the dismantling of bases, of troops throughout the world." Surprisingly the U.S. declined to take him up on the offer.

The USSR meanwhile were still insisting that there were no nuclear weapons in Cuba at all, but they didn't fool anyone. This deceit left Fidel furious. Speaking about the incident years later he remarked that, "In a political battle, you can't afford to lose the moral high ground by employing ruses and lies and half-truths."

The situation clearly called for calm and carefully considered actions, but what instead happened was that the Cubans shot down a spy plane near Guantánamo Bay, killing its pilot Major Rudolf Anderson.

The event caused a massive diplomatic commotion and, as is so often the case, it turned into an episode of Hercule Poirot as different accounts of the incident emerged. One story attests that after receiving intelligence via the Brazilian government that suggested an invasion was imminent, Fidel ordered all unauthorised aircraft in Cuban airspace to be fired upon, saying, "Well, now we'll see if there's a war or not." Another version has Fidel visiting the SAM site when the spy-plane was spotted and asked which button would fire a missile at it, and then went ahead and pressed it. Yet another, less exciting version, which most people have accepted as the official version, states responsibility lay with Soviet General Stepan Naumovich Grechko, the Soviet air force's head of military plans in Cuba, who ordered the strike because he figured that if the U.S. *were* going to attack, it was prudent to prevent them from receiving any more reconnaissance.

Washington had already agreed that if the Soviets did not dismantle the missile sites by the 29th they would start air-strikes, followed by an outright invasion the following day. But now there was pressure from the U.S. military to launch an immediate attack.

Interestingly, whilst all over the planet people looked on, terrified of the possible scenarios that could unfold from this very precarious and volatile affair, the majority of the Cuban people were in almost carnival cheer, albeit with some macabre undertones. After Fidel's numerous successes they considered him unbeatable. In the end however, Fidel would have no part to play. Much to his annoyance, he had been written out of the final scene.

Things came to a head when Fidel sent a letter to Khrushchev in which he implied that the USSR should not shy away from nuclear retaliation if the U.S were to attack (even if it wasn't a nuclear attack) adding that he understood that it would mean sacrificing himself and his people.

His reasoning was that having nuclear weapons weren't going to stop you being attacked if you didn't use them when you were being attacked. But Khrushchev and his colleagues read it and looked at each other in disbelief. Had Fidel lost his mind? Had he not realised that the nuclear weapons were for *deterrence*? They had given Fidel enough power to create 4,000 Hiroshimas but he was not supposed to actually go and *do it* – the missiles were strictly for display purposes only. Like Star Wars action figures, you're not supposed to take nuclear weapons out of the box and start playing with them.

Fearing that he was losing control of the situation, on the 28th

Khrushchev moved to end it and sent Kennedy an offer in which he promised to remove the missiles from Cuba in return for the U.S. removing their own nuclear missiles in Italy and Turkey, and 'promising' not to invade Cuba. Kennedy readily agreed.

The world breathed a huge sigh of relief that Armageddon had been cancelled, or at least postponed, but the news was not well-received by many in the U.S. establishment. Admiral George Anderson, Chief of Naval Operations told Kennedy that they, "Make a strike on Monday anyway."

Khrushchev had hoped that as it was his proposal which had ended the stand-off, public opinion, both home and abroad, would paint him as a pragmatic, mature and peaceful leader, but all it achieved was to make him look weak. One of the main criticisms was that for some reason that cannot be found outside a bottle of high strength vodka, he accepted the American request that the missile withdrawals be kept secret which allowed Kennedy to pretend to the wider world that the USSR had left the negotiation table with nothing but their tail between their legs.

The other major failing was that the oral promise to leave Cuba alone was quite literally not worth the paper it wasn't written on. Why Khrushchev didn't insist on a formal signed agreement beggars belief. If the U.S. were to be true to their word then it can be assumed that putting pen to paper wouldn't be that difficult a proposition.

'That's very nice of you, but you wouldn't mind writing that down would you?'

'Oh we don't need to go through all that formal stuff, we are friends after all.'

'No, we're not.'

'Well, my word is my honour.'

'All the same, I really would prefer to have it in writing,. I have a pen if y-'

'Just take my word for it. We are honest guys. Honest... Do you want a wetsuit?'

According to the editor of the Cuban newspaper Revolución, it was he who had to break the news to Fidel that the affair had been settled without him. Apparently Fidel's immediate reaction was to call Khrushchev a "Son of a bitch! Bastard! Asshole!" and apparently he, "went on in that vein for quite some time."

He was not a happy bunny. Having not even been invited to the negotiating table – or even told negotiations were taking place – Fidel refused to comply with some of the agreement stipulations, such as giving the UN permission to oversee the dismantling of the missiles and allowing low-flying reconnaissance planes until Cuba's conditions were met, which were namely:

1. An end to the economic trade blockade on Cuba
2. An end to sabotage, assassinations and other subversive   activities
3. An end to hit and run military attacks by exile groups based in Florida
4.   An end to the violation of Cuban territorial waters and airspace   by U.S. ships and aircraft
5. U.S. withdrawal from Guantánamo Bay

Rousing his people, Fidel made a speech in which he stated his refusal to submit the country to the international humiliation that was being thrust upon them by their enemies, and their so-called friends. "We have not violated anyone's rights. We have not attacked anyone. All our actions have been based on international law. We are the victims of a trade blockade, which is an illegal act, and of an attack by another country... The U.S. has repeatedly violated our air space. The business of inspections is just another attempt to humiliate our country. Therefore we will not accept it." With no way of making the Cubans capitulate, a compromise was agreed between the U.S. and the USSR to have the missiles inspected at sea.

Needless to say, the U.S. pledge not to invade Cuba was never registered at the UN and Kennedy privately told his advisors that, "Our objective is to preserve our right to invade Cuba." It was to be business as usual as Washington was concerned. And business as usual when Washington is concerned meant a whole new wave of sabotage, propaganda and terrorism.

With no nuclear missiles to prevent the U.S. from invading, it was announced that every Cuban between sixteen and twenty-seven years of age would have to complete at least two years service in the military or police force. The Revolution was to be defended to the last man. Homeland or Death.

VII
Could Everyone Please Stop Getting Shot?

"Demoralise the enemy from within by surprise, terror, sabotage, and assassination. This is the war of the future."
Adolf Hitler

With their Soviet sugar-daddies only wanting sugar for their vast volumes of aid, in 1963 Cuba's hopes of diversifying the economy were put on hold. Sugar was again to be the lifeblood of the Cuban economy and targets were set to double the harvest by 1970. Reasoning that to increase yields they would need more land, the government passed another Agrarian Reform Act limiting private land to 168 acres, down from 966. These measures gained the state five million acres, increasing its share of agricultural land to 70%.

Along with the agrarian reform, a raft of plans were put into practice in order to increase agricultural production: Canadian bulls were imported to increase the quality of Cuban beef, and tracts of land outside Havana were turned into coffee plantations and citrus orchards (to help satisfy the need for bourgeois oranges!)

Production levels became such a hot topic on the island that certain high producing livestock started to become national celebrities. The most famous of these was *Ubre Blanca* ('White Udder'), a dairy cow who managed to produce twenty-four gallons of milk in one day – a world record and four times the average.[24] When she died in 1985, she was mummified then put on display in a museum, received a full obituary in the newspapers and even had a song dedicated to her.

As should be the case in any authentic attempt at socialism, the government was committed to reducing inequality and ensuring that ordinary working people received a decent share of the national wealth. The responsibility for creating and implementing the new national salary scale was given to Che, who subsequently devised a system comprised of eight pay grades, the highest pay being 'merely' three times that of the

---

24 Sadly the agricultural results fell well below the government's lofty expectations. High producers like White Udder needed special conditions which it was difficult and expensive to replicate on a massive scale, and many of the imported cattle failed to adapt to the Cuban climate.

lowest.[25]

Under the new pay structure production and worker satisfaction rose dramatically whilst inequality decreased drastically. In 1958, before the Revolution, the poorest 40% received an average per capital income of $182, whilst the richest 5% enjoyed $5,947 but by 1978 the disparity in incomes fell dramatically, with each group receiving $865 and $3,068 respectively. In fact, when you consider that everyone also had almost free healthcare, education, utilities, food and transport, money was becoming more and more meaningless.

Efforts at raising production levels weren't helped when, in November 1963, Hurricane Flora hit the island sweeping away towns, killing 4,000 people and caused $500 million worth of damage. In the aftermath the government were again on the front lines, with Fidel and other government officials helping out in the fields, rebuilding schools, and helping with rescue efforts.

If during this trying time the Cubans were hoping for more leniency from the U.S., they were sorely mistaken. The U.S. blocked shipments of aid which had been collected by American citizens, claiming it was 'contrary to the national interests'. This was not a time for humanitarian sentiment, this was the time to drive the Cuban people into the ground. They continued their propaganda and terrorist campaigns, more bombs were detonated, more sabotage attempts made, and more innocent civilians killed.

Then something big happened. In a macabre twist, on November 22nd 1963 as CIA operatives met with a man in Paris to collude in yet another plot to assassinate Fidel, Kennedy was assassinated whilst sitting in his motorcade during a Presidential parade in Dallas. As the world struggled to catch its breath a whirlwind of events saw the supposed 'lone assassin' Lee Harvey Oswald; accused, caught, assassinated by a nightclub owner, and then posthumously found guilty by a commission set up by the new President Lyndon Johnson – despite admitting not being able to prove his motive.

Everyone seems to have their own theory as to who was involved in the plot; it was the CIA, the Cuban Exiles, the Mafia, the USSR, the Israelis... Some people blamed Kennedy's bodyguards, some blamed the

---

25 Those on the large incomes of the previous regime saw their contracts respected, as Fidel remarked, "The revolution cannot equalise incomes overnight. The Revolution's aspiration is to arrive at equal incomes starting from the bottom up, not from the top down. It would be incorrect to do it the other way."

driver, whilst others pointed the finger at the bankers. It seemed the only person not accused was the one man who actually 'admitted' carrying it out, the mad Haitian dictator President Duvalier, who said it was all his doing as he had placed a voodoo curse on Kennedy in May.

Sceptics of the official line were given significantly more ammunition in 2010 when the son of ex-CIA agent Howard Hunt released a recorded confession his father had given to him before he died. In the tapes Hunt admits to the true role of the CIA and Cuban exiles in the assassination of Kennedy, in what he claims was referred to as 'The Big Plan'. He implicated the future President Lyndon Johnson, J. Edgar Hoover, CIA agents Cord Meyer, David Atlee Phillips, David Morales, Williams Harvey and Cuban exiles including Antonia Veciana (founder of terrorist group Alpha 66), and Frank Sturgis (who later became embroiled in the Watergate scandal). He also mentioned a Corsican assassin called Lucien Sarti, whom he claimed was the second shooter on the grassy knoll.

To add further muddy the waters, in her autobiography, *'The Spy Who Loved Castro,'* Marita Lorenz claims she met Lee Harvey Oswald and Frank Sturgis at the house of a prominent Cuba exile called Orlando Bosch (we will hear a lot more about him later). And she also links the mafia don Jack Ruby to the plot along with CIA operative Gerry Patrick Hemming.

Some pointed the finger of blame at Fidel, but the accusation has little credence. Despite his shortcomings Fidel had always spoken out against assassination philosophically and morally.

Also, despite the increasing numbers of CIA terrorist attacks on the island, the relations between Havana and Washington were actually beginning to improve. The two governments had established an open dialogue using French magazine editor Jean Daniel as a go-between. According to Daniel, Kennedy had become more sympathetic to the Cuban situation and had told him that; "I believe that we created, built and manufactured the Castro movement out of whole cloth and without realizing it. I have understood the Cubans. I approved the proclamation which Fidel Castro made in the Sierra Maestre... to some extent it is as though Batista was the incarnation of a number of sins on the part of the U.S.. Now we shall have to pay for those sins."

For his part, Fidel was optimistic about repairing ties, saying to Daniel "maybe he has changed. Maybe things are possible with this man... [who] may at last understand that there can be coexistence between capitalists and socialists, even in the Americas..." And asked Daniel to take back a message to Kennedy "So far as we are concerned everything can be restored to normalcy on the basis of mutual respect of sovereignty."

It was in fact during one of these meetings with Daniel that Fidel learnt of Kennedy's assassination. "This is terrible" Fidel said, "They are going to say we did it." Turning to Daniel he added, "This is the end of your mission of peace."

Over the years Fidel was to retain a rather romantic view of Kennedy, saying in the 1980's that "He was, simply, very new, you might say – besides, very inexperienced in politics although very intelligent, very wise, very well prepared, with magnificent personal qualities. I can speak of experience and inexperience in politics because when we compare ourselves now with what we knew then about politics – the experience we had in 1959, 1960, 1961 – we are really ashamed of our ignorance at that time."

Under Kennedy the CIA had been authorised to give financial support (to the tune of $5 million a year) to Cuban-exile terrorist groups based in the U.S., but added a safeguard whereby the groups targets had to be authorised by the CIA first. After coming to power President Lyndon Johnson removed the safeguard. This was in spite of the U.S. Department admitting in private that, "Our support of exile organisations has probably produced more problems than results. Our experience in supporting clandestine and commando activities by autonomous exile groups has been especially negative, and such activities are at the heart of the RECE proposals." The policy of economic denial was maintained, and terrorist attacks continued.

At this time Fidel was constantly reaching out to the U.S. searching for an end to the hostilities, even going as far as offering to halt his aid to Latin American revolutionaries, release political prisoners, and negotiate payment for all the property he nationalised. He sent a message to President Johnson, stating that "I seriously hope that Cuba and the U.S. can eventually sit down in an atmosphere of good will and of mutual respect and negotiate our differences. I believe that there are *no* areas of contention between us that cannot be discussed and settled within a climate of mutual understanding..."

Unfortunately President Johnson was not interested. According to Leogrande and Kornbluh in their book *Back Channel to Cuba* the Johnson administration were of the opinion that 'relaxation would reduce pressures on Cuban to break with the USSR, give Cuba political and economic respectability, and demonstrate to Latin American nations that the Cuban model was worthwhile...'

At the beginning of 1964, the Year of the Economy, the Cubans signed another trade agreement with the Soviets. This time it was much more lucrative to Cuba, but it came with a conditions; Cuba would be forced to follow the Soviet economic model. Fidel would later lament the amount of Soviet intervention, and Cuba's deference to them, saying in one speech in 2005. "Among the many errors... the most important was the belief that someone knew something about socialism, or knew how to build socialism. As if it were an exact science, as well known as an electrical system conceived by those who considered themselves experts in electrical systems. When they said 'Here is the formula,' we thought they knew."

With economic diversity on the back-burner Che was no longer needed at the Ministry of Industry so was instead given the position of rebel statesman and would represent Cuba around the world at international gatherings.

His first undertaking in his new role was to attend a UN conference in New York in December 1964 and somewhat unsurprisingly his arrival was met with a cavalcade of chaos and hostility. Angry protesters stood shouting outside, one woman wielding a knife tried to run inside and stab him, whilst a group of Cuban exiles were detained after firing a bazooka at the building. As unnerving as it was for the bulk of the delegates, Che remained nonplussed and spent his time playing chess with the New York City police guards who had been stationed outside his room. When a reporter asked if he was worried about the assassination attempts he smiled and said "If only all dangers were of that sort."

Che's used his one and a half hour speech at the UN to lambaste many of the countries attending for exploiting developing nations and meddling in their affairs. Having said his piece he continued to pursue his dream of international socialism and set off on a three month diplomatic tour, visiting several African and socialist bloc countries.

It may have been a diplomatic tour, but Che was in no mood to be diplomatic. In his last public speech at the end of the trip he openly condemned the USSR[26] for their weak support for the Developing World, and castigated them for being 'accomplices of imperialist exploitation'. Then he essentially told the entire socialist world to stop behaving like children and grow up and unite against the capitalist enemy, hoping that

---

26 Che was disgusted at the Soviets, and had asserted his belief that they would revert to capitalism. He would be proven right, and it would take Fidel another two decades to truly understand his reasoning.

they would realise what was at stake before it was all too late. The socialist world responded by blowing a big fat raspberry.

Ever since initially agreeing to join Fidel's expedition Che had asserted his desire to continue the revolution throughout Latin America and the wider world. After the triumph of 1959, when asked what he was to do with his medical career he told his father that "[I don't] even know in which land I will leave my bones."

Ideally he wanted to help the anti-colonial fight in Latin America but the leftist movements in many countries were fractured, weak, and uninterested in guerrilla war. Africa, on the other hand, seemed extremely fertile for revolution as almost all of the countries were at the time seeking to rid themselves of their colonialist masters and regain their independence.

The current hotbed of rebel action was resource-rich Congo, a country that causes cartographers to break out in hives by sharing its borders with another country called Congo. The Congo where Che went was historically ruled by the Belgians and called the Republic of the Congo or Congo-Léopoldville. In 1964 it was renamed the Democratic Republic of the Congo which everyone was happy with until the early 1970s when a re-branding was deemed in order and the country became known as Zaire. The other Congo next door was historically ruled by the French and known as the Republic of the Congo, and sometimes referred to Congo-Brazzaville, apart from a period of Marxist rule between 1970-1991 where it was referred to as the People's Democratic of Congo. Today it was again called the Republic of the Congo (DRC). And if that isn't confusing you haven't read it properly. So to avoid any further confusion, from this point on the Belgian Congo will be referred to as DRC and the French Congo referred to as Congo-Brazzaville. Just to be clear...

DRC gained independence from Belgium in 1960 and in the subsequent democratic elections Patrice Lumumba's left-leaning MNC party came to power. Soon after the election the U.S., Belgian and British governments worked together to bring him down. The fact that he was democratic seemed inconsequential. He wasn't amiable to their interests.

The following September Prime Minster Lumumba was ousted after a power grab from the President, Kasavubu, which started a violent civil war. Having been given support and funding by Western powers, the leader of the army, Colonel Joseph Mobutu, took the side of President Kasavubu and arrested Lumumba. Soon after Lumumba was shot and, in a horrifying spectacle, his body dissolved in acid.

It transpired that the U.S. had sponsored Lumumba's capture but the Belgians admitted to giving the order to kill him. In 2013 a new twist was added as British politician Lord Lea claimed that the British were highly involved too. The U.S. may have caught him, the Belgians may have shot him, but it was the British who organised it. According to Lord Lea, Baroness Daphne Park, who had been the British consul and first secretary in Leopoldville between 1959 and 1961, once told him over tea that she organised it. A Foreign Office document from September 1960 also lends weight to the claim. In the document a top ranking official, who later became the head of MI5, Britain's domestic intelligence agency, noted that he could "See only two possible solutions to the [Lumumba] problem. The first is the simple one of ensuring [his] removal from the scene by killing him." The fact that he was a popular democratically elected leader appeared completely irrelevant.

Those loyal to Lumumba fought against Kasavubu's rule and in 1964 were beginning to pose a real threat. Fearing a rebel triumph the U.S. put pressure on European countries, mainly Britain, France and Belgium, to intervene. This time they refused, leading the U.S. to turn to Ethiopia, Nigeria and Senegal. They also refused. With few options left the CIA recruited mercenaries, putting aside $300,000 per month to cover the payroll. Most of the mercenaries were from Europe (including the UK) and displayed all the moral stature of a syphilitic Viking warlord on an overdose of steroids. Perpetually involved in thievery, murder, rape, and torture, their only claim of decency was to kill virtually everyone they came across so as to put them out of their newly inflicted misery.

At the UN in 1964 Che had declared that, "All the free men of the world must prepare to avenge the crime of the Congo." Now, in April 1965 he was to do just that. Though he would have to do so secretly because being on the CIA's most wanted list does nothing to ease one's passage through customs. Not even the Cuban people could know.

Before he left Che wrote Fidel a personal, farewell letter;

'Fidel:

At this moment I remember many things – when I met you in the house of Mária Antonia, when you proposed I come along, all the tensions involved in the preparations. One day they came by and asked who should be notified in case of death, and the real possibility of it struck us all. Later we knew it was true, that in a revolution one wins or dies (if it is a real one).

Today everything has a less dramatic tone, because we are more mature. But the event repeats itself. I feel that I have fulfilled the part of my duty that tied me to the Cuban revolution in its territory, and I say farewell to you, to the comrades, to your people, who are now mine.

I formally resign my positions in the leadership of the party, my post as minister, the rank of commander, and my Cuban citizenship. Nothing legal binds me to Cuba...

Recalling my past life, I believe I have worked with sufficient integrity and dedication to consolidate the revolutionary triumph. My only serious failing was not having more confidence in you from the first moments in the Sierra Maestre, and not having understood quickly enough your qualities as a leader and a revolutionary.

I have lived magnificent days, and at your side I felt pride of belonging to our people in the brilliant yet sad days of the Caribbean [Missile] Crisis. Seldom has a statesman been more brilliant as you were in those days...

I am also proud of having identified with your way of thinking and of seeing and appraising dangers and principles.

I want it known that I do so with mixed feelings of joy and sorrow. I leave here the purest of my hopes as a builder and the dearest of my loved ones. And I leave a people who received me as a son. That wounds a part of my spirit. I carry to new battlefronts the faith that you taught me, the revolutionary spirit of my people, the feeling of fulfilling the most sacred of duties: to fight against imperialism wherever it may be. This comforts and more than heals the deepest wounds.

I state once more that I free Cuba from any responsibility except which stems from its example. If my final hour finds me under other skies, my last thought will be of the people and especially of you... I am not sorry that I leave nothing material to my wife and children. I am happy it is that way. I ask nothing of them, as the state will provide them with enough to live on and to have an education...

I embrace you with all my revolutionary fervour.
Che.'

Che arrived in DRC[27] in good spirits but his mood soon changed as he realised just how hard it was going to be to turn the Congolese into a professional guerrilla army. Not only were the Congolese rebels lacking in any modern military experience, their knowledge of political or economic theory was virtually non-existent and many didn't know why the Cubans wanted to help them. If this wasn't enough to contend with, many of the Congolese fighters believed that their witch doctor could protect them from bullets, which he couldn't, obviously. And then the whole mission nearly went up in smoke when their camp was burnt down after a rebel dropped his lighter. Yet this was still not the end of Che's ordeal. Not only was the humid climate causing him to suffer numerous asthma attacks, he also had to deal with a serious bout of dysentery and the news that his mother had died.

*

Back in Cuba, the U.S. trade blockade had caused the economy to contract by as much as 30%, yet the people still overwhelmingly supported Fidel and the Revolution. Frustrated, in 1964 Washington tightened the screws further and managed to bully every country in the Americas (except Mexico, Guyana and Canada) into halting all trade (except food and medicine) and all sea transportation to Cuba. In the following three years the number of ships from non-Soviet countries entering Cuban ports almost halved.

The effect was devastating and with even more shortages and more rationing, it was not long before the Cuban people became restless. So when the U.S. accused Fidel of keeping the Cuban people prisoner by preventing them from leaving he took the opportunity to release some of the steam by announcing that anyone who wanted to leave the island was free to do so – as long as the U.S. agreed to take them.

Standing in front of the Statue of Liberty, President Johnson declared any Cuban would be welcomed with open arms. In the first few months

---

27 Whilst Che was in Zaire, 250 other Cuban fighters were deployed to the Republic of the Congo. But they were not sent to help fight a guerrilla war – the Cubans were there to protect the government from a military coup, and help provide medical support for the general populace. Previously the country had just nine doctors for a population of nearly a million, so the Cubans awarded 250 medical scholarships and started a nationwide polio vaccination programme. To help with the costs, the Cubans apparently pressurised the Soviets to send free vaccines. In three days alone 61,000 children had been vaccinated.

alone several thousand Cubans left the country, including two of Fidel's sisters. Due to safety concerns, flights were opened up between Havana and Miami which allowed 4,000 people to leave each month. The flights stopped after seven years, by which time over 260,000 Cubans had left.

Fidel then walked into another PR disaster a month later when the government was re-branded the Cuban Communist Party and given a reshuffle. Che's name was notably absent from the list and rumours engulfed the island as people discussed possible explanations; had Che been assassinated? Had he been sent to work in a Gulag? Or had he accepted an offer to appear on the next series of TV reality show, Big Brother? To end the gossip Fidel decided to read out Che's resignation letter. It did stop the gossip, but the gossip was merely replaced with a stream of love-torn emotion from the Cuban populace who immediately felt the loss of their iconic hero.

Che was distraught upon hearing that his letter had been read out. The U.S. offensive meant defeat was staring him in the face, but how could he return to Cuba now that he had publicly revoked his citizenship and his position? It would be an admission of failure, and would cost him his dignity. In a letter sent shortly afterwards, he shared his anger with Fidel with unreserved frankness.

Realising his error Fidel pleaded with Che to return anyway, but Che was not interested and asked instead to be found a new mission, preferably in Latin America. Eventually the two compromised on a mission in Bolivia, and Che agreed to return to Cuba, albeit clandestinely.

Che went under the knife to alter his appearance from rugged revolutionary to mild-mannered businessman. Even when he said goodbye to his five year-old daughter Aleida he did not reveal his true identity. During his visit she hit her head and he instinctively comforted her and gave her a message 'from her father'. Returning to her mother Aleida whispered, "Mummy, I think that man is in love with me." It would be the last time she ever saw him.

*

Although 1966 was supposed to be the Year of Solidarity, by the end of it solidarity was nowhere to be seen. In Bolivia the Communist Party were becoming resentful towards Che's attempts to provoke an armed uprising and the Chinese had shown themselves to be about as reliable as the Cuban trains by reneging on trade deals and distributing anti-Soviet propaganda around the island. Meanwhile the USSR were delaying shipments of important commodities[28] so as to provoke more rationing in Cuba and pile more pressure on Fidel to follow Soviet orthodoxy.

The U.S. had also carried on with their economic attacks by applying more pressure on countries to halt their trade with Cuba. For example, annoyed at the French and Italians for buying Cuban nickel, they banned *all* French and Italian products containing nickel. And of course both countries buckled immediately and stopped buying Cuban nickel.

In April 1967 – in what was dubbed the 'Great Revolutionary Offensive' – Fidel ordered the nationalisation of all the remaining independent businesses. The reason was not just economical or ideological however. Fidel claimed that small enterprises – even hot dog sellers – were hotbeds of corruption and insulting to the hard working men and women in the fields and factories. He demanded, "Are we going to construct socialism, or are we going to construct vending stands?" Which is a question nobody had thought to ask before. Or since. The policy saw over 57,000 businesses brought under government control with many of the staff redeployed to the agricultural sector.

It was always going to be extremely difficult for an enormous, centralised state trading system to be as creative, innovative or efficient as independent traders who could more easily adapt their wares, pitch, or prices to suit demand. And with workplaces now centred in some distant government department, the links between effort and outcome were removed, which caused worker morale to nosedive, absenteeism to rise, and bottlenecks in production to increase.

The Cuban people were having to make a lot of sacrifice and were eager for a something to show for it. As ever, Fidel had an ace up his sleeve. Having ended illiteracy, dramatically increased home-ownership, and established a comprehensive healthcare system, Fidel made plans to provide the Cuban citizenry with one of life's most important of commodities – ice cream. After all, how can you build a utopia without ice-cream? It just can't be done.

So in 1966 work was undertaken in Havana to build one of the biggest ice-cream parlours in the world Coppelia (named after Celia's favourite ballet), would eventually boast up to sixty different flavours ranging from the ubiquitous vanilla and chocolate, to the more rare and exotic tomato and avocado. The building remains one of the architectural splendours of

---

28 The Soviets had already started holding back their oil shipments, resulting in yet more rationing in Cuba and some sugar mills began burning the waste products from the sugar-cane harvest to create an alternate source of energy.

Havana and 35,000 Cubans still flock daily to socialise beneath the stained glass windows and luscious Banyan trees. In fact, the provision of ice-cream became so important that when the Soviet Union collapsed in the early 1990s and Cuba found itself unable to import enough milk products to satisfy demand, it was faced with a stark hard choice between using what milk they had to make butter or ice cream. And they chose ice cream. Basically, the Cubans eat ice-cream the way British people drink beer, epitomised by the fact that the state ice-cream vans sell ice-cream by the pint rather than the cone. Now *that* is revolutionary.

*

Meanwhile, in the Bolivian jungle Che and his men were fighting off malaria, were weak from non-stop marching, and the CIA had got wind of where he was and had sent vast amounts of money and support to the Bolivian army to track him down. It was not looking good. And it wouldn't get any better.

As the net tightened around him Che began to make rash decisions. Fatigued, famished and despondent he led his men into an ambush in a small village. In the ensuing skirmish he was captured, taken to La Higuera and imprisoned in the local schoolhouse[29].

The next day, October 9th 1967, the CIA gave the fateful order to murder him, but stipulated that it should be made to look like he died in battle. The soldier appointed to the task was visibly unnerved by the affair and spent many minutes aiming, deliberating, and seemed unable to pull the trigger. With characteristic frankness, Che said, "Calm yourself man, and aim well. You're only going to kill a man." And so ended the life of Ernesto 'Che' Guevara, a defiant romantic revolutionary to the bitter end.

Strapped to the skids of a helicopter, Che's body was taken to the nearby town of Vallegrande where his throat was slit and injected with formaldehyde to prevent decomposition before the press arrived. If this was not disrespectful enough, they then cut off his hands and sent them to the CIA headquarters in the USA where plaster casts were made and used as macabre paperweights.

Upon hearing the reports of Che's murder Fidel broke down in tears, beating the walls in grief. He was inconsolable. He had lost not just an important cog in his revolutionary machine, but one of his most faithful friends and comrades. Yet it was nothing compared to what the world had lost – a beacon of socialism, of humanism, and revolution.

---

29 When a curious teacher came to see if it really was the infamous revolutionary. Che pointed out a grammatical error on the blackboard. It was *definitely* Che.

The U.S. had ordered that Che's body be buried in an unmarked grave. His body remained undiscovered until 1997 whereupon he was returned to Cuba to receive a proper funeral and provide his loved ones with some much needed closure. Whilst giving his eulogy, Fidel made clear how Che should be remembered. "If we want the model of a person, the model of a human being who does not belong to our time but to the future, I say from the depths of my heart that such a model, without a single stain on his conduct, without a single stain on his action, without a single stain on his behaviour, is Che! If we wish to express what we want our children to be, we must say from our very hearts as ardent revolutionaries: we want them to be like Che!"

Not everyone shared this sentiment – the U.S. establishment were ecstatic at hearing of Che's demise. Walt Rostow, special advisor under both Kennedy and Johnson, informed his staff that "They finally got the son of a bitch. The last of the romantic guerrillas."

Fidel declared 1968 to be the Year of the Heroic *Guerrillo,* in honour of Che, but it was Soviet imperialism that dominated the news that year. The leader of Czechoslovakia, Alexander Dubeck, had started to liberalise the communist state, allowing more freedom of speech and more democracy. Moscow was furious. On August 20th Soviet troops from East Germany[30], Poland, Hungary and Bulgaria invaded Czechoslovakia, arrested Dubeck, and ensured the new government reversed the reforms.

Most expected Fidel to deplore the Soviet action, as it was exactly the kind of behaviour he had been accusing the U.S of engaging in for years, but astonishingly he didn't, and still doesn't. He admits that "The decision made concerning Czechoslovakia can only be explained from a political point of view, not from a legal point of view," but justifies the action because "The essential point to be accepted, or not accepted, is whether or not the socialist camp could allow a political situation to develop which would lead to the breaking away of a socialist country, to its falling into the arms of imperialism. And our point of view is that it is not permissible

---

30 In June 1972 Fidel renamed one of the 400 islands that sits off its shores to try and increase tourism from East Germany. The island was previously called Cayo Blanco de Sur, but was renamed Isla Ernesto Thälmann, in honour of the East German Communist Party leader who had ran unsuccessfully ran against Hitler in the 1932 elections. A year later, on Hitler's orders, Thälmann was jailed and placed in solitary confinement where he would spend eleven years before being executed in August 1944. A bust of Thälmann was also erected on the island, but was knocked down and destroyed by Hurricane Mitch in 1998. Sadly the island failed to take off as a tourist destination for the East Germans, although pop star Frank Schöbel did use it as a backdrop for his many music videos.

and that the socialist camp has a right to prevent this in one way or another." It was a weak argument.

But Fidel certainly had a good reason to toe the Soviet line. In January 1969, Fidel spoke to over a million people in Havana's Revolution Square and solemnly announced Cuba was ten million tonnes of sugar in debt to the USSR. The good news however, was that he had a plan to triple production and pay it all off in just one year.

The mission to produce ten million tonnes was planned like a military exercise, which was just as well as terrorist and sabotage attacks were ramped up by the CIA during this period in an attempt to ensure the target was never met. Along with their 'usual' attacks on sugar mills, plantations, transport, utilities and infrastructure, planes were sent to seed rain clouds in order to ruin crops and cause flooding. They also managed to convince a foreign supplier to ensure the ball-bearings destined for Cuba were produced just off centre so as to destroy the machinery, and another supplier to add corrosive chemicals to lubricating fluid.

To give them a fighting chance of attaining their target the harvest period was tripled – meaning Christmas would have be postponed to the end of the harvest period so as not to distract from the mammoth task before them.

The armed forces and thousands of urban workers were assigned to the fields and refineries and even the Soviet Embassy staff found themselves toiling in the fields, albeit only for a day. But having enough workers was never going to be enough – cane-cutting is skilled, strenuous work, and as a result most of those drafted were useless, almost to the point of being counter-productive.

After a gruelling harvest, in July 1970 Fidel announced to the public that their battle for ten million tonnes had been lost. They had managed an admirable 8,531,688 tonnes, more than double the previous year's effort, and trumped the previous record of six million tonnes which had been set in 1965. But it was still a defeat, and it came at a cost. The failure meant even more shortages. Underlining his full responsibility, Fidel admitted that he and his government had been guilty of over ambition and bad planning. Having laid bare the situation he then shocked everyone by offering to resign. The crowd were momentarily stunned before shouting back enthusiastically, "No! No! No!" followed by "Fidel! Fidel! Fidel!"

Whatever people think of him, it was exactly this type of behaviour, this humility in admitting his mistakes directly to the people, which created such long-standing acceptance of his rule. To the Cuban masses

Fidel appeared honest, he led by example and was materially frugal. He lived a relatively austere life, as did the majority of government ministers, and did not used his position – like so many presidents before him – to feather his own nest. When mistakes were made, he took responsibility, apologised and explained how he would rectify them.

And so the people kept their faith in Fidel, and the Revolution. Things were hard but for the vast majority, they were still much better than before. Housing costs were minimal, or, as the vast majority now owned their own homes, they were non-existent. Every child now went to school, dressed in a smart uniform and provided with text books. Doctors came to visit *them,* child day-care was provided, and everything from funerals, sports events, utilities, and transport were now free at the point of use.

And although at the time the failure of the ten million harvest had been a devastating blow, the Cuban people would soon be rewarded for their sacrifices as the country entered the Golden Seventies. With the USSR reassured that Fidel had been brought to heel, they rewarded him with more aid in the form of machinery, food, oil, and consumer goods. In the first five years of the 70s the Cuban economy grew a staggering 10% annually, reducing to a respectable 4.4% through to the mid 1980s. In 1958, before the Revolution, the poorest 40% received an average per capital income of $182, whilst the richest 5% enjoyed $5,947. By 1978 the disparity in incomes decreased dramatically, with each group receiving $865 and $3,068 respectively. Not that money had much bearing on one's quality of life; with almost all necessities free money was for the 'luxury' items. The only problem was that there were still very few luxury things to buy.

The economic outlook was not the only thing Fidel saw improving in the 1970s – his relations with his neighbours were also on the up. A poll in 1973 showed that just over half of the U.S. public wanted both countries to normalize relations (with 33% against), and two years later the OAS (including the U.S.) voted to lift the diplomatic and trade sanctions that had been in place since the early 1960s. Soon after the U.S. again allowed foreign subsidiaries of U.S. enterprises to trade with Cuba.

Fidel was naturally delighted with such progress, but arguably the event that really put a spring in his step was Salvador Allende, leader of the Democratic Socialist Party, winning the Chilean Presidential election in October 1971. For a Latin American country to democratically elect a Marxist president was a political thunderbolt throughout the continent.

The U.S. were particularly shocked – and afraid. Richard Nixon had won the race to become president of the U.S. in 1968 and was determined to rid communist influence from the hemisphere[31]. Nixon's national Security Advisor Henry Kissinger warned that "The example of a successful elected Marxist government in Chile would surely have an impact on – and even precedent value for – other parts of the world... the imitative spread of similar phenomena elsewhere would in turn significantly affect world balance and our own position in it."

As could be expected the CIA employed every dirty trick in their book to topple Allende, including a plan to make the economy 'scream' and force upon the Chileans the 'utmost deprivation and poverty' so as to force "Allende to adopt the harsh features of a police state." Showing his disdain for the Chileans, Secretary of State Henry Kissinger remarked bluntly "I don't see why we have to let a country go Marxist just because its people are irresponsible."

Efforts were made to cause shortages, encourage riots, and create a situation whereby Allende could be removed by military coup or U.S. intervention. A programme of industrial sabotage was instigated, essential imports and exports were blocked or delayed, pressure was put on the World Bank to refuse loans or reschedule debt payments, and support was given to fascist groups who devastated the capital with a campaign of bombing and arson. A U.S. senate report also refers to the CIA funding opposition groups, media organisations, and private sector organisations.

As could be expected, Fidel was very excited about the role Chile could play in influencing and inspiring other Latin American countries to

---

31 Nixon was determined to take a hard-line on Cuba, but he was forced to negotiate with the regime when a spate of hijackings started to get out of control. Between 1968 and 1972 there were around 173 hijackings of U.S. passenger planes from people wanting to be taken to Cuba. The reasons people gave for this were numerous. One 28 year-old American dressed as a cowboy said wanted to defect to Cuba because he wanted to experience communism, a retired Green Beret said he wanted to go to Cuba to assassinate Castro with his bare hands, and a Cuban exile said he wanted to return to Cuba because he missed his mum's cooking.

Eventually the State Department suggested solving the problem by offering people free one-way flights to Cuba. All people had to was promise never to return to the U.S.. This time however Fidel turned down the offer. After all, it was better that people continue to hijack planes to Cuba as not only did airlines have to pay $7,500 to get them back, it provided excellent anti-U.S. propaganda.

With the situation getting out of control the Federal Aviation Administration asked citizens for ideas and were subsequently besieged with a wide range of strange and wonderful schemes; have stewardesses carry tranquilliser darts, force passengers to wear boxing gloves during the flight so that they cant wield a gun or a knife, and, best of all, play the Cuban national anthem and arrest any of the passengers who start singing along.

move towards socialism, and he wanted to help in any way he could to help galvanize the people behind Allende. Visiting the country in November[32] he spent over three weeks touring mines, visiting factories and attending press conferences.

The new Chilean government was more than happy to have Fidel as a friend and ally, but they were nervous as to how the U.S. would react to his presence and feared he would announce something controversial. But as it turned out Fidel managed to remain unusually moderate in his rhetoric and actually called for restraint from those wanting to hasten the socialist policies of Allende's party. He did not suggest using the Cuban model of socialism, instead advising the Chileans to navigate their own path, suited to their own country and conditions. In one speech, when he spoke of the country's sad history of exploitation by colonialists and giant corporations, he called for peace and compassion, saying that although the mood might be for retaliation, the time was for reconciliation. And with that he took a big gulp from a Coca-Cola bottle.

Unfortunately his mere presence was more than enough to antagonise the extremely anti-Castro, conservative opposition. He could have swum in a lake of Starbucks Coffee with Ronald McDonald for all they cared. It was bad enough that he was in Cuba, never mind *other* countries. They wanted him – and Allende – out. And the sooner the better.

Publicly Fidel seemed enchanted with Chile, but within his inner circle he shared concerns about Allende's chances of survival. Allende hadn't neutralised or sought control over the armed forces, leaving himself susceptible to a possible coup. Also his electoral mandate was not significantly strong, and his coalition of left-wing parties was liable to infighting and factionalism. Added to this, privately Fidel still had his doubts about the viability of building socialism under a 'bourgeois' multi-party democracy framework.

It would be several years before Cubans had the chance to vote in the political sphere, but before then, in early 70s, they were given opportunities to make their voice heard as they were encouraged to take part in nationwide discussions about how to solve the many problems facing the country. Thousands of meetings were held around the country in

---

32 Predictably the CIA used the occasion to involve themselves in more assassination plots against Fidel. One plan was to install guns in television cameras and shoot Fidel at close-range, but although this time the actual plan was actually plausible, finding the men with the necessary nerves to carry it out proved impossible – the chosen assassins pulled out at the last minute.

which people were asked to discuss and suggest new laws and measures to deal with low productivity and increase the participation of the people in the running of their workplaces and communities.

Out of these discussions came a process of decentralisation. Municipal assemblies were given control of local enterprises, such as shops, schools, hospitals, cinemas and sports facilities, as well as the power to select the judges which oversaw the local courts. One-man management systems were replaced with elected management councils whilst trade unions were further democratised and given more power. Production levels improved significantly, as did absenteeism levels.

The USSR may have been helping Cuba economically, but their involvement tended to harm it culturally. As Soviet influence grew, the Cuban government became stricter in their censorship of 'controversial' novelists and poets who challenged government policy.

Possibly the most alarming of these measures was the motion pushed through in April 1971 which ruled that a person's political views be taken into account when applying for jobs in sectors such as universities, media and culture, arguing that, "Cultural channels may not serve the proliferation of false intellectuals who plan to convert snobbism (sic), extravagance, homosexuality, and other social aberrations into expressions of revolutionary art, alienated from the masses and from the spirit of our revolution." So began the 'Grey Period' in Cuban culture which would last until 1976.

The most famous case involved a Cuban poet named Padilla who was arrested after authorities deemed his poems to be counter-revolutionary. One poem, for example, included the lines "The poet! Kick him out!/ He has no business here./ He doesn't play the game./ He never gets excited/ Or speaks out clearly./ He never even sees the miracles ..." But still, its hard to imagine that it could have caused the downfall of the regime. After all, it didn't even rhyme!

Naturally, the world's media reacted with horror and indignation, and even cultural figures previously showing support for the Revolution, called for him to be released.

Whilst in jail Padilla fell ill and was taken to hospital where he received a personal visit from Fidel, who implored him to admit his guilt and change his ways, emphasizing the need for unity during the struggle with their powerful neighbours. Eventually Padilla agreed and was released. He had spent thirty-seven days in prison but his international reputation was hit badly – as was Fidel's.

In need of a holiday, Fidel set out on a two month world-tour, visiting ten countries including Algeria, Sierra Leone, Bulgaria, Romania and Czechoslovakia, before ending up in the USSR. His relaxed manner, good humour and spontaneous banter was especially well received by the masses in Eastern Europe and the Soviet Union, whose own leaders had the charisma of a toilet brush and the intelligence of its cheap plastic sheath, and it was not long before he felt like his old self again.

A reinvigorated Fidel returned to Cuba, but it was not long before he was off again, this time to attend the Fourth Summit Conference of the Non-Aligned Movement in Algeria. The Non-Aligned Movement was the collection of developing world nations not aligned to either of the two superpowers, so some naturally questioned legitimacy of Cuba's inclusion. Yet this hostility didn't last long as Fidel declared that Cuba would be breaking all diplomatic ties with Israel (whom previously Fidel had publicly praised) due to their oppressive and immoral actions against the Palestinians. The announcement was received with wild applause by the delegates, especially Colonel Gaddafi who rushed over to hug him, which was all the more remarkable because just the previous day he had denounced Fidel for being a Soviet stooge. But of course when you are a dictator the only continuity that is important is your own rule.

After the summit Fidel travelled to Algiers and then onto Baghdad, before moving on to India and Vietnam. Cuba had played a small part in helping the Viet Cong overcome the full-force of the U.S. military by providing rice, blood donations, doctors, teachers and skilled workers to support the country in its self-defence. In gratitude the Vietnamese government secretly sent captured U.S. guns/ammunition to left-wing Latin American guerrilla groups.

As he enjoyed hospitality from the country which had forced the U.S. military into a humiliating defeat, Fidel heard the news that his friend and ally Salvador Allende had been deposed in a coup led by the head of the Chilean Army, General Pinochet. Despite accusations from all corners of the globe, on this occasion the U.S. had not organised it and in fact had only heard that it was being planned the day before it happened. That said, in private Kissinger admitted a few days later that Washington had 'created the conditions.'

Fidel had implored Allende to make proper contingency plans in case of a coup attempt but Allende remained steadfast in his belief in the democratic sovereignty of Chile, and that the army would protect it at all costs He believed that if he was to be deposed, it would be at the ballot box, not the barrel of a gun. His optimism, although highly admirable, was to be his undoing.

In the Presidential Palace, Allende and thirty-six of his supporters had tried in vain to scurry to safety as twenty-four rockets pounded into the building. Not wanting to surrender, Allende shot himself using a gun given to him by Fidel.

The Chilean socialist mission was over. And to make sure it was over, Pinochet immediately arrested 13,500 Allende supporters, massacred between 1,000 and 3,000 of them, and then went on to torture 30,000 Chileans including women and children as young as thirteen. Needless to say, relations with Cuba were severed.

Despite the U.S stopping its economic attacks and instead giving hundreds of millions of dollars and substantial food shipments to the country, ditching socialism did not bring Chile the economic miracle that was promised. Even the business leaders who had supported and helped organise the coup remarked later that it was "One of the greatest failures of our economic history." Under Pinochet[33] the country languished in recession and the following year achieved the dubious accolade of having the world's highest inflation rate of 375%. By 1987 bread took up an average of 74% of the average family income. Unemployment was rife, hunger was prevalent and essential public services such as education and healthcare had been all but eradicated.

The whole affair left Fidel sick with anger and ravaged with guilt. There was a strong argument that it was his presence in Chile that had sealed Allende's fate, with CIA Director Colby later saying in an interview, "The problem in Chile was not Allende. It was Castro."

It may have been Fidel that they were angry with, but it certainly wasn't because he was harming the Cuban people. U.S. Representative Stephen Solarz visited the island in 1972 and reported that, "the Cuban people are better fed, better housed, better clothed, better educated, and are healthier than before the revolution... There is no unemployment, very little crime, and no drug problem."

---

33 Despite the massive human rights abuses and blatant disregard for democracy British Prime Minister Margaret Thatcher remained steadfast in her defence his rule. She praised him for 'restoring' democracy to Chile, ignoring the inconvenient truth that Chile had been a democracy since 1891 until Pinochet installed himself as dictator.

VIII
Fidelista Democracy, South African Apartheid, worldwide terrorism

"Long live the Cuban Revolution. Long live comrade Fidel Castro... Cuban internationalists have done so much for African independence, freedom, and justice. We admire the sacrifices of the Cuban people in maintaining their independence and sovereignty in the face of a vicious imperialist campaign designed to destroy the advances of the Cuban revolution."
Nelson Mandela

From the very beginning, the foreign policy of the Cuban Revolution was based on humanitarian values mixed with an internationalist, anti-imperialist solidarity. Those who needed military assistance would receive it, and those who didn't would instead be sent doctors, teachers and engineers. All civilian aid was politically impartial, never making demands or asking for 'favours', unlike much of the aid offered by the developed nations. The Cubans' offers always came without any strings attached, though in part this was because the string was in short supply.

To the surprise of many Cuban aid would prove highly influential in the success of anti-colonialist movements in Africa. Che may have failed in the Congo, but Cuban military assistance proved relatively effective elsewhere. They had helped Algeria gain independence from the French in the early 1960s and were instrumental in Guinea-Bissau claiming independence from the Portuguese in the early 70s – an event that indirectly contribute to the overthrow of the Portuguese military dictatorship and the subsequent liberation of many other Portuguese colonies including Mozambique, Sao Tome and Principe, and Angola.

Of all the countries that were to free themselves from the shackles of colonialism it was Angola which arguably proved most important for the future of Africa. In the mid-1970s Portugal had agreed to grant Angola its independence, but it was clear from the outset that just handing over the keys was not going to be an option. For some reason best known to themselves, the Portuguese government decided that it would be in everyone's best interests that power should go to whichever political faction was in control of the country's capital, Luanda, on 11th November 1975. Ultimately it was a brutal, real-life game of capture the flag that turned what was an independence struggle into a bloody civil war.

There were three major Angolan political factions fighting for supremacy: The People's Movement for the Liberation of Angola (MPLA), the National Union of the Total Liberation of Angola (UNITA) and the National Front for the Liberation of Angola (FNLA).

But the geopolitics of the age turned the Angolan fight for independence into the Third World War for the third world.

The MPLA, led by a poet and doctor called Neto, were mainly supported financially and militarily by the Soviets and Eastern Bloc countries, as well as Cuba who had been helping to train their soldiers since 1965. Yet Neto, like Fidel, was not interested in adopting the Soviet model and wanted the country to tread its own path to socialism.

Ideologically, UNITA and the FNLA were a lot more complicated. UNITA were officially Maoist but were quite malleable depending on who they were trying to get backing from, whereas the FNLA were officially a centre-right Christian party... However both groups received arms, money and political backing from many of the same countries.

UNITA's principal supporter was the U.S., but they also received varying amounts of support from (amongst others); South Africa, Egypt, France, Israel, Morocco, DRC, Saudi Arabia, China and North Korea. Meanwhile the FNLA mainly gained their support from the U.S., South Africa, West Germany, Israel, France, and China.

The FNLA also included foreign mercenaries recruited via a private military firm in the UK. Most of the mercenaries were British or Portuguese, but there were also some Americans and Irish too.

It turned out the mercenaries were more trouble than they were worth. For one thing they proved to be completely inept. According to one of the mercenaries, David Tomkins, they spent most of their time just trying to find food and military supplies. And they weren't that effected on the battlefield either. On one occasion, fourteen mercenaries managed to accidentally open fire on their own comrades.

The mercenaries were led by a former corporal in the British Army (and former post-office robber) called Georgiou Costas. He ruled with an iron fist, known for abusing and torturing his own soldiers and captives alike. On one occasion, fourteen mercenaries managed to accidentally open fire on their own comrades. Fearing Costas would execute them for incompetence, they fled. Unfortunately they were caught soon after, and instead of being shot for incompetence, they were shot with desertion.

One of the biggest players in the war was the racist South African government. They were not only keen to spread their influence further across the African continent, they were also nervous about the MPLA offering support to the SWAPO guerillas who were busy fighting for their independence from South Africa. The South African government had already been aiding UNITA and the FNLA but with the MPLA looking certain to win the battle for Luanda in late October, the South African government took direct action and marched their troops into Angola via Namibia[34], advancing on Luanda at 40 miles a day.

With the FNLA attacking from the north, UNITA from the east, and South Africa from the south, the MPLA saw their chances of holding onto the capital dissipate with every passing day. In desperation they made an impassioned plea to the USSR for more support before it was too late. The MPLA only needed to hold on for another week to be recognized as the legitimate government, but the Soviets refused. The Cubans on the other hand, decided to throw their hat right into the centre of the ring. On November 7th Operation Carlotta began in haste as over a thousand Cuban volunteers (including 652 of the elite Special Forces) made their journey across the Atlantic along with large shipments of supplies. Tens of thousands more Cubans would soon follow.

Later interviewed for a BBC documentary, General Onambwe De Caralho of the Angolan Central Committee said that when they had asked Cuba for assistance Fidel was more than co-operative. "We'd asked, let's say, for a packet of sweets, and he said, 'No, not a packet of sweets. What you need is 80 sacks of sugar, however many litres of water, and a mixer... And you don't have any cooks, so I'll send you some of those too!'" Indeed, when Neto saw all the Cuban ships unloading in the Angolan port he apparently turned to his aide and remarked "It's not fair. At this rate the Cuba will ruin itself."

All of the Cubans who fought in Angola were of African descent, a stipulation of the Angolan government who were wary of the cultural and political impact of having white soldiers seemingly riding to their rescue. Of course this arrangement was also beneficial to the Cubans as it made it harder for the U.S. to estimate how many had been sent over, although the U.S. quickly devised a way to make an accurate guess. Cuban army rules state that there had to be a certain number of baseball pitches per unit of troops in the camp, so the U.S. just counted the numbers of baseball

---

34 South Africa had been occupying Namibia since 1920. They had legal means to do so under a UN mandate, but the UN had a change of heart in 1966 and revoked it. When South Africa refused to leave the UN deemed it an illegal occupation and a decade later recognized SWAPO, a group of Namibian freedom fighters, as the rightful representatives of the Namibian people. South Africa took little heed, and the UN did little to punish them.

diamonds they could see from their satellite pictures. Conversely a similar mathematical trick can be used to estimate the number of U.S. army troops in a given area by counting up the number of burger joints.

As the Cubans arrived the South African forces were just 25km from Luanda, and the FNLA and mercenary forces were just 20km away. But they would advance no further, as the Cubans made an immediate impact. According to an account by renowned author Gabriel Garcia Márquez[35], the leader of one of the mercenary columns sat next to a blonde film actress whilst conducting operations from a Honda sports car, and his, "Column moved forward with a holiday air, neglecting to send out advance patrols." Inevitably, he, "Could not even have realized where the rocket came from that blew the car to pieces. [All] that was found in the woman's bag was an evening dress, a bikini and an invitation card to the victory celebrations…" It was all getting a little bit too Hollywood.

It was not only the FNLA who were celebrating prematurely. The CIA had been so confident of being victorious that they were already partying in their headquarters at Langley when the news came in that they had, in fact, lost. With the help of the Cuban forces, the MPLA maintained control of Luanda and as the sun rose on November 11th Angola became independent and Neto was recognized as its first President.

Although the MPLA had won the right to rule Angola the civil war would rage on as UNITA refused to accept the result. Nevertheless the MPLA triumph over the South African white-imperialists sent a shock-wave throughout the entire continent. The South African newspaper, the *Rand Daily Mail* commented that, "Whether the bulk of the offensive was by Cubans or Angolans is immaterial in the colour-conscience context of this war's battlefield, for the reality is that they won, are winning, and are not white; and that psychological edge, that advantage the White man has enjoyed and exploited over 300 years of colonialism and empire, is slipping away. White elitism has suffered and irreversible blow in Angola, and Whites who have been there know it."

Fidel was beaming from ear to ear. Not only did Cuba win international recognition and admiration; the event added more fuel to the Revolutionary fire of the Cuban people whilst opening up an opportunity

---

35 He and Fidel would become good friends over the years. According to biographer Panichelli-Batalla "After reading his book The Story of a Shipwrecked Sailor, Fidel had told Gabo there was a mistake in the calculation of the speed of the boat. This led Gabo to ask him to read his manuscripts … Another example of a correction he made later on was in Chronicle of a Death Foretold, where Fidel pointed out an error in the specifications of a hunting rifle."

to fan the flames all across the African continent. During a public speech in Havana, Fidel said, "Why are they [the U.S.] so annoyed? Because they'd planned to seize control of Angola before 11th November... Some imperialists ask why we're helping the Angolans, what our interest is. They assume that countries only act out of a desire for petrol, copper, diamonds or some other resource. No. We have no material interest. Of course the imperialists don't understand this. They would only do it for jingoistic, selfish reasons. We are fulfilling an elementary, internationalist duty in helping the people of Angola."

With the Angolan government now responsible for trying to rebuild the war-stricken country, Cuba did all it could to help. It was not in a position to offer multi-million dollar aid packages but it could offer to share its other resources. Cuban construction workers helped to repair roads, buildings and telephone lines, and built over two thousand houses. There were 1,400 Cuban doctors working there by the end of 1976, making up two-thirds of total number in the entire country. Helping to build a basic national health care system, they established clinics in even the most remote areas, just like they had done in Cuba. Three years later the U.S. ambassador admitted to CBS News that, "There's a sense in which the Cubans bring a certain stability and order to Angola."

And Angola was not the only country to benefit. Throughout the 1970s around 20,000 Cuban 'internationalists' operated around the world, in forty countries on three continents. Made up of construction workers, physicians, technicians, engineers, agronomists and teachers, the groups were volunteers, the vanguard of the Cuban humanist and internationalist spirit.

Today Cuba does even more. Over 50,000 Cuban medical personnel work around the world helping those affected by humanitarian disasters, which is more Medecins Sans Frontieres (MSF), the Red Cross and UNICEF combined. This incredible, humanitarian achievement cannot be understated – it's like Swansea having more astronauts than NASA. It just doesn't seem feasible.

One of Cuba's most notable internationalist healthcare missions has been Operation Miracle. Launched in 2003, it has resulted in nearly three and a half million cataract sufferers from thirty-five developing nations regaining their sight. One of those to receive the treatment was Mario Teran, the Bolivian sergeant who killed Che. Because the Cubans believe that everyone deserves free healthcare, even the most hated of enemies.

In 2010 the Cubans were at the forefront of organising the medical response to the Haiti earthquake, though this went relatively unnoticed by the Western free press. One of the few exceptions to this was in December 2010, when the British newspaper *The Independent* ran an article by Nina Lakhani. She writes of how 1,200 Cuban, "Doctors and nurses have put US efforts to shame," whilst acknowledging that such deeds have earned the country "many friends, but little international recognition." She also describes how the Cubans are "The largest foreign contingent, treating around 40 per cent of all cholera patients."

One of the reasons the Cubans were able to react so quickly and efficiently was because they were already operating on the island. Between 1999 and 2007 Cubans made up 75% of Haiti's medical personnel, helping infant mortality to fall from 80 to 33 and life expectancy to rise from 54 to 61.

And Cuba does not just provide doctors – it helps to train them. A major problem for low-income nations is the Brain Drain whereby they lose well-trained personnel to developed countries, an issue Cuba is all too familiar with. So in 1999 Cuba established the Latin American School of Medicine (ELAM) – the biggest medical school in the world – where they offer scholarships to thousands of poor people from around the world on the provision that they practice for five years in their home countries after they have graduated. Students receive not only tuition, but also housing, three meals a day, textbooks, uniforms, toiletries, bedding and a small monthly grant of 100 pesos. By 2013 it had 19,500 students enrolled from 110 countries – including one-hundred from the poorest communities in the USA.

*

A few years before all this, back in 1974 President Nixon had resigned the Presidency after the Watergate scandal broke, and the Vice-president Gerald Ford had taken his place. At the start of his presidency U.S.-Cuban relations improved dramatically. The U.S. voted with the other countries in the Organisation of American States to lift the diplomatic and trade sanctions that had been in place since the early 1960s, and soon after the U.S. again allowed foreign subsidiaries of U.S. enterprises to trade with Cuba.

The reasoning for these concessions was two-fold, as Assistant Secretary Rogers explained to Congress; first of all it was a, "Measure to remove a recurrent source of friction between the U.S. and friendly countries," who were indignant at being told who they could and could not trade with, and secondly it was to show Cuba that the U.S. had "Put a policy of permanent hostility behind us. We are ready to begin dialogue." It was also in response to domestic pressure.

Unfortunately once Cuba's Angolan adventure began, talks broke down and Kissinger made plans to mine Cuban harbours, suggested airstrikes against Cuban military targets, and increase economic and political support to Cuban-exile groups. U.S.-Cuban relations were back in the freezer.

So far Fidel's government had been preoccupied with getting the economy on track and preventing a U.S. invasion, but as the Soviet subsidies and military protection brought much-needed stability, they could focus on finally addressing the country's democratic deficit. In 1975 the whole nation took part in a national discussion where they were encouraged to debate, suggest and choose the content of the new constitution. Hundreds of thousands of meetings took place in workplaces and educational institutions across the country and a year later, after dozens of changes, alterations and additions, the constitution was ratified by referendum (gaining 97.7% of the vote) and signed into law.

It was not going to be a democracy where the richest man wins. This was going to be different. This was going to be a *Fidelista* democracy. Nor was it going to be a democracy where people are forced to vote for the person most amiable to U.S. interests.

The new electoral system (still in place today, albeit with some minor tweaks) resembled that which Havana University used when Fidel was a student. The process started by citizens nominating candidates from their constituency to stand for election to the Municipal Assembly. The list of nominees were then reduced to two candidates per seat by the Municipal electoral commission. The people then elected their favoured candidate to become a Municipal delegate, after which all the municipal delegates nominated and elected people from their own numbers to represent them at the Provincial Assembly.

At national level, half of the parliament comprised of delegates nominated by the Municipal Assembly from their own numbers, and half were nominated by the major six mass-organisations; The Federation of Women, Workers Central Union of Cuba, National Association of Small Farmers, Federation of University Students, Federation of pre-University Students, and the Committees for the Defence of the Revolution (CDRs). The reason for this split was to try and ensure that politicians broadly reflect the nation as a whole, so that instead of career politicians, they had politicians with careers, such as doctors, teachers, athletes, economists, scientists, students, and cultural figures.

The new system saw all nominated candidates for parliament (the National Assembly of Peoples Power) scrutinized by the candidacies commission, which held mass consultations with citizens before whittling the list down until there was one candidate per seat (unlike the Municipal elections where there are two choices per seat). The list was then ratified by the Municipal Assembly.

After all the delegates were elected to the National Assembly, they nominated fellow delegates to serve as its prominent President, Vice-President, Council of Ministers, and secretary of Council of State. The candidacy commission then sifted through the nominations and delegates voted to accept or reject their selection.

The candidacies commissions, comprised of people elected from the major six mass-organisations listed above operate separately at each level. Critics point to their involvement in selecting candidates from those nominated as an easy way of barring 'undesirables' who do not share the socialist vision of the government from taking part. At first, critics certainly had a reasonable argument, as although you didn't have to be a member of the Cuban Communist Party (PCC) the PCC were allowed to interfere with the selection process. So being a member certainly helped! But since 1992 the candidacies commission have been fiercely independent and the PCC are forbidden from involvement in elections in any way.

The new electoral system, although it had faults (like all democracies), it did have some interesting features. Delegates are not supposed to represent what they think is best for their constituents, but instead represent what their constituents think is best for themselves. Delegates who do not abide by their constituents demands can easily find themselves recalled and replaced by someone who will.

If this wasn't unorthodox enough, the meetings of the Provincial and National Assemblies were to be conducted by consensus. This of course had its advantages and disadvantages. Making decisions by consensus can mean that minorities may be better protected by stifling majority rule, whilst decisions are implemented more efficiently due to everybody agreeing with them. On the other hand, it can make the decision-making process can be frustratingly slow, as experienced by anyone who has tried to organise the office Christmas party.

Another interesting aspect of the new system was the election campaign itself. To do away with a system where the biggest wallet wins, the new rules insisted that each candidate could offer no more than an A4 piece of paper explaining who they are, what they have done, what their views are, and what they would hope to accomplish after taking office. So although elections weren't as dazzling as they are in the U.S. or Britain, candidates were at least encouraged to muster real support from those who lived in the area. Although voting is secret and not compulsory the country boasts a high voter turnout, currently averaging at around 97%. This is achieved without the need for compulsory voting laws, fines, or midnight visits from he authorities.

The new democratic model also coincided with the end of the cultural 'Grey Period', and from herein artists found themselves with more and more freedom to express themselves and challenge many social taboos.

Needless to say, neither the democratic system nor the reduced level of state censorship did much to placate the U.S. or the counter-revolutionaries, and so the terrorist attacks continued. In early 1976 Cuban exiles attacked Soviet freighters and Cuban fishing boats. In April they murdered two Cuban diplomats by bombing the Cuban embassy in Lisbon – and when a Cuban radio host in Miami had to temerity to criticise them they detonated a bomb under his car. Luckily he survived, but he lost both his legs. In July terrorists armed with machine guns fired upon the Cuban Embassy in Columbia and a Cuban official was killed in Mexico. The following month two Cuban consulate security agents were kidnapped and a bomb was set off at the Cubana airlines office in Panama City. Not content with just attacking Cubans officials, Cuban exiles also teamed up with Chilean secret service to murder former Chilean ambassador Orlando Letelier and his colleague Ronni Moffitt by planting a car bomb under his car in Washington D.C..

Yet arguably the most deplorable attack happened in October of that year. A Cubana passenger plane was the victim of a terrorist attack, killing all seventy-three people on board. The CIA, on this occasion, were not *directly* responsible but declassified records show that they knew about the planned attack but decided not to inform the Cubans about it[36]. The culprits were two Cuban exiles based in Miami, Luis Posada and Orlando Bosch.

Luis Posada had been recruited by the CIA for the Bay of Pigs invasion and was later given explosives training and made one of their 'principal agents'. However by 1968 his relationship with the CIA had

---

36 In response to this Fidel ripped up the hijacking accord signed between the two countries during Nixon's presidency.

become distant. Not only was he suspected of being involved in smuggling cocaine, which presumably annoyed the CIA by treading on their turf, Posada also threatened to assassinate Kissinger because he felt he was not taking a hard enough stance on the Cuban issue.

Posada ended up in Venezuela, where he temporarily became head of their secret intelligence agency before turning 'freelance'.

Orlando Bosch, another Cuban-exile, had an equally colourful background. Bosch fled Cuba in 1960 and eight years later found himself arrested in Florida and sentenced to ten years in a U.S. prison after firing a bazooka at a Havana-bound Polish freighter. He had previously been caught trying to smuggle 18 bombs out of the country and for towing a torpedo through the Miami streets in rush-hour (like you do). He had also threatened the President of Mexico, General Franco of Spain, and British Prime Minister Harold Wilson.

Bosch was released on parole four years later and was quickly involved in more controversy when he was alleged to have been involved in the assassination of a rival exile leader. When the authorities closed in he went to Venezuela, but he was forced to flee when he was found in a room full of weapons. He turned up in Chile, and, undeterred from his task, he sent letter bombs to four Cuban embassies around the world, tried to assassinate a Cuban diplomat in Argentina, and bombed the Mexican Embassy in Guatemala.

In early 1976 he was arrested in Costa Rica on suspicion of trying to assassinate Henry Kissinger – who was about visit the country. When quizzed by the U.S. secret service, Bosch assured them that he had no intention of killing Kissinger. They had obviously jumped to conclusions. Just because he was a well-known terrorist and had turned up a few days before a meeting of leading world figures, it didn't mean he was there to assassinate Kissinger. They couldn't be more wrong. He was there to assassinate the nephew of ex-Chilean President, Salvador Allende.

He was expelled to the Dominican Republic where he set up a new counter-revolutionary organisation with Cuban exiles on the island before making his way back to Venezuela.

When Posada and Bosch met in Venezuela they got on like an Embassy on fire. By their own admission, between them they had masterminded around fifty bombings in Miami, Mexico, Panama, Venezuela, Argentina, and New York. Just before the Cubana bombing the pair orchestrated attacks on Cuban airline facilities in Jamaica, Barbados (twice) and Panama.

They considered those aboard the Cubana flight as legitimate targets in the ongoing war with Fidel and his Revolution, yet the most notable passengers were the twenty-four members of the Cuban National Fencing Team. Yet at no point had the regime terrorised the populace by having people dress up in tight-fitting bee-keeper costumes armed with long, thin sticks.

Following the Cuban airlines attack, Cuba descended into mourning, Fidel declared, "We can say that the pain is not divided among us. It is multiplied among us."

It did not take long for the Venezuelan authorities to learn that Bosch and Posada were behind the plot and the following month the pair were arrested and put on trial and subsequently imprisoned. Nine years later Posada escaped after bribing a warden, whereupon he fled to Honduras before popping up in El Salvador where he began working once again with the CIA in their struggle against the left wing guerrilla movement, the Farabundo Marti National Liberation front (FMLA).

In 1990 in Guatamala Posada was shot twelve times whilst working as a private security consultant. Miraculously, he survived the assassination attempt and was soon organising more terrorist attacks against Cuban economic targets. Having been involved in numerous plots to kill Fidel, in November 2000 he decided to have another go, this time in Panama. He was caught along with four co-conspirators but after serving less than four years in prison he was given a pardon by Panamanian President Mireya Moscoso. It would be the last known assassination attempt on Fidel's life. In 2005 Posada turned up in the U.S. but just two years later he was found guilty by a judge in Texas of using false identity papers to enter the U.S., and also of fraud, and making false statements. To his relief a different judge overturned this decision, but then the U.S. appellate court overruled *that* decision and ordered a retrial. He was eventually found not guilty on all charges in 2011 and lives happily in Miami.

Bosch's life meanwhile has had its own ups and downs. Having been arrested in Venezuela for his part in the Cubana bombing he would be forced to undergo two court cases and endure eleven years in prison before being acquitted. Wanting to put the past behind him, Bosch then went back to the U.S.. The problem was, he *couldn't* put the past behind him. The reason he had left the U.S. in the first place was that had been under suspicion for the murder of a rival Cuban-exile leader, and by leaving he had violated the parole he was under following his conviction for firing the bazooka at the Polish freighter. And the U.S. weren't too happy about that and so he found himself spending another three years in jail.

But his luck finally changed. In 1990 President Bush Snr. over-ruled his justice department, ordered Bosch's release and granted him residency. So basically this meant a U.S president had officially pardoned a convicted terrorist, which must have made Osama Bin Laden feel pretty hard done by.

*

In 1977 Jimmy Carter was sworn into office, having narrowly beaten the Republican candidate Ronald Reagan in the recent Presidential elections. Having witnessed the ineffectual attempts of his predecessor at unseating Fidel, he decided instead to try a more mature approach. In the hope he could 'out-statesman' him he raised important issues in a calm and reasonable manner, and made some conciliatory gestures such as putting an end to the reconnaissance flights over Cuba, and again permitting U.S. citizens to again travel to the island.

Fidel was clearly impressed by the humble, soft-speaking President and the two agreed to begin secret back-door negotiations to try and end the long running dispute between the two countries. And as could be expected, the negotiations suffered a few hiccups along the way.

One problem was that the Cubans seemed to have a habit of taking more liberties than Donald Trump at a Miss world contest. For example during one meeting in a New York Hotel the negotiating teams stopped for lunch and according to a U.S. official 'I was told by the department that I could cover the cost of coffee and sandwiches. I made a fatal error and asked for room service… The Cuban eyes lit up. They ordered a five course meal with steak and everything else, and I had to explain it to the State Department accountant.' And that was not all. On another occasion the hotel management approached the U.S. officials after the Cuban delegation had left and said "Who's going to pay for the towels and linen? Your friends on the other side have just left and they've taken all the towels and linen with them." Luckily the U.S. saw the funny side, with one of them remarking, "see, the embargo is working!"

At first the relationship between the two countries improved during Carter's rule, but there were red lines in the sand for both countries that in the end that meant all efforts were destined to fail. For example Fidel had previously stated quite adamantly that reconciliation talks between the two countries could not take place whilst the trade blockade remained in place. However it was clear he saw some hope in Carter so softened his approach and suggested that talks could start if the U.S. merely relaxed the trade blockade to allow food and medicine.

Carter's first reaction was to accept this, but after pondering on the proposal, eventually changed his mind. The sticking point wasn't Cuba buying food and medicine from the U.S., it was Cuba *selling* food and medicine. After all, Cuba's principal export was sugar, and sugar was food and as Secretary of State Cyrus Vance pointed out in a memo "To give him [Fidel] access to the U.S. sugar market at the beginning of the process would be to give away most of our bargaining position."

Needless to say Fidel was less than impressed at Carter's decision. In an interview Fidel commented that Cuba was no interested in one-way trade. "We would not buy anything at all in the U.S., not even an aspirin for headaches, and we have a lot of headaches."

Yet whereas the Fidel may have been concerned about trade, as far as Washington was concerned the biggest barrier to the two countries mending their ties was foreign policy. Or to be more specific, Cuba's foreign policy. The issue had again become a hot topic as Carter had barely walked through the doors of the White House when Fidel again managed to embarrass the U.S. on the battlefield as Cuban troops proved decisive in helping Ethiopia repel a U.S.-backed Somalian invasion. And like almost every war in Africa in the 1970s, it was rather complicated.

Initially it was all the other way around. Cuba had supported the Marxist Somalian government and helped to train their troops for their fight against the invading U.S.-backed Ethiopian army. The U.S.-backed Ethiopian emperor was then overthrown and replaced by a Marxist emperor, Haile Miram in the mid-70s. Unsurprisingly, Fidel quickly established a good rapport with him.

With two bitter enemies now both converted to Marxism, Fidel may have innocently hoped that they would put the past behind them and unite against the common enemy of Western imperialism. But if so he was to be gravely disappointed.

As it turned out, the Marxist Somalian government gave diddly squat about what Ethiopia's ideological convictions, but cared rather more about creating a Greater Somalia by making a smaller Ethiopia. This would be achieved by taking a large amount of territory in the Ogaden Desert, and in July 1977 Somalia sent in tens of thousands of troops to claim it.

Embarrassed to see two supposedly Marxist countries butchering each other, and incredulous to find that they were ultimately arming both sides, both the Soviets and Cubans stopped supporting the Somali aggressors, upped their support for the Ethiopian defenders (which included sending 1,500 Soviet military advisors and 15,000 Cuban soldiers). They had hoped that this would bring an end to the bloodshed but instead the Somalians gave up their Marxist cause and turned to the U.S., who were more than happy to wrestle another country away from the USSR's sphere of influence – even though as National Security Council member Paul Henze admitted "The Soviets and Cubans have legality and African sentiment on their side."

At first the Somalians had the Ethiopians on the ropes, but they could not press their advantage due to – amongst other things – the rainy season making all the roads unusable. It was a costly reminder that before starting any war it is important to check the weather forecast first.

The Ethiopians, emboldened by the sudden influx of Cuban soldiers and Soviet advisors, launched a counter offensive in February 1978 and soon fought the now U.S.-backed Somalians into retreat.

Having given him a bloody nose on the battlefield, Fidel took Carter on in a war of words on the political stage. Taking umbrage at Carter's suggestion that he was not respecting the human rights of his people, Fidel retorted, "With what moral authority can they speak of human rights — the rulers of a nation in which the millionaire and beggar coexist; the Indian is exterminated; the black man is discriminated against; the woman is prostituted; and the great masses of Chicanos, Puerto Ricans, and Latin Americans are scorned, exploited, and humiliated? How can they do this — the bosses of an empire where the Mafia, gambling, and child prostitution are imposed; where the CIA organizes plans of global subversion and espionage, and the Pentagon creates neutron bombs capable of preserving material assets and wiping out human beings; an empire that supports reaction and counter-revolution all over the world; that protects and promotes the exploitation by monopolies of the wealth and the human resources of whole continents, unequal exchange, a protectionist policy, an incredible waste of natural resources, and a system of hunger for the world?"

Needless to say, negotiations between the two countries broke down within a couple of years. Yet there was one diplomatic project – spearheaded by a Cuban-born Jewish banker called Bernardo Benes – that proved surprisingly fruitful. Benes lived in Miami having fled Cuba after Fidel came to power during the 1960s. At first he had actually funded Cuban exile terrorists, but by the mid-70s he had started to work constructively towards peace. Encouraged by Carter's accession to the Presidency, Benes helped establish a diplomatic mission with the aim of encouraging the Cuban government and Cuban exiles to resolve their differences. The Dialogue, as it became known, proved extremely successful and by 1978 Fidel had agreed to release 3,600 political prisoners.

Yet even though 'The Dialogue' resulted in a better outcome than any of the acts carried out by the Cuban exile extremists, the people who had participated in the two conferences (held in Havana) were not welcomed back to Miami as heroes. Instead they were vilified. Incredibly, even some of the prisoners who were granted their freedom because of 'The Dialogue' condemned it. Things got so bad two people who took part in the conference were assassinated, one in front of his thirteen year-old son. Benes' meanwhile saw his bank bombed and he was forced to wear a bullet proof vest everywhere he went. He even stopped seeing his family because he felt it would put them in danger. Commenting on the situation in Miami, Benes said, "You see, no one is interested in free speech in Dade County. Only in Havana."

Despite Benes achieving some measure of success in dealing with Fidel through respect and reason, by the end of 1978 talks between Havana and Washington had broken down and Carter started to take a more hard-line approach. This involved, amongst other things, pressurising European countries to stop providing Cuba with much needed credit and preventing Cuba becoming a member of the UN Security Council, a position that was almost inevitable as Fidel was made Chair of the Non-Aligned Movement.

Officially established in 1961 the Non-Aligned Movement was a group of countries[37] in the developing world (representing approximately 55% of the world's population) who were not allied with either Superpower. Its main aims were to push for peaceful coexistence between *all* countries, give solidarity with independence movements, reject racism, promote equality, and encourage cooperation between members. Cuba had long been involved – indeed it was the only founding member from Latin America – and Fidel had long cherished the opportunity to lead it.

His opportunity came in 1979. Having impressed the developing world with his solidarity with African independence movements – especially in Angola – he was voted as Chairman in 1979[38], the tenure of which lasted

---

37 It began with around 25 countries, rose to 96 in 1979, and today it encompasses over 120 countries

38 One of his first duties was to give a speech at the UN General Assembly in New York. Whilst being interviewed en route, he was asked if he was wearing a bullet-proof vest, causing a moment of amusement from the bearded revolutionary. Smiling from ear to ear, he

for 3 years.

However having just attained his much-coveted position Fidel was galled to see the USSR attack Non-Aligned Movement member Afghanistan the following December[39].

Inevitably this would prove to be a true test of Fidel's loyalties. Condemning the USSR would bring an end to the generous trade contracts, but not condemning them would seriously damage the legitimacy of his rule as the President of the Non-Aligned Movement. Fidel was forced to take the pragmatic option and wait a year to assess the situation before eventually supporting the Soviet action – even sending thousands of Cuban troops to help.

As this meant Cuba was going against the cornerstone of the Non-Alignment charter – respecting the sovereignty of nations – Carter was able to successfully lobby Latin American and Non-Aligned countries to vote against Cuba being included in the UN security council – a position that traditionally went to any country who was Chair of the Non-Aligned Movement.

---

unbuttoned the top few buttons of his fatigues to show a bare chest, "I shall land in New York like this. I have a moral vest, which is strong. That one has protected me always." And with that he placed his obligatory cigar back between his big grin and re-buttoned his fatigues.

39 The Soviet invasion was a reaction to the rapid increase of Islamic fundamentalist militants (supported heavily by the U.S.) who were threatening the rule of the country's pro-Soviet President and spread its war across the border.

IX
The 1980s... What did they ever do for us?

"If you're losing your soul and you know it, then you've still got a soul left to lose."
Charles Bukowski

Having more or less sauntered through the Golden Seventies, Fidel was to find the 1980s a much more unpleasant and difficult slog. The decade started in sorrow as the country mourned the passing of Celia Sanchez who died of cancer on January 11th 1980. The following day millions of Cubans made their way to Havana's Revolution Square to pay their respects at her casket.

Her death hit Fidel hard. Celia had been his most loyal confidante, and his best friend. He was lost without her. One of those present at the private burial that was held later remarked, "When you see any man cry, it is very impressive, but to see Fidel Castro cry... I was on the other side of the coffin and Fidel was facing me. He was very red, like a pomegranate. And tears flowed down both sides of his face."

The 1980s also saw the country face many economic challenges. Sugar was still the lynchpin of the economy but its price fell by a third in the first two years alone. And worse was to come as disease wiped out a third of the 1980 sugar crop and *all* of the tobacco cop. To compound the problem the USSR had started demanding Cuba actually repay all the loans they had given them over the years. Fidel had not been expecting this. He seemed to think the USSR would never *actually* request repayment on all their billions of dollars of aid. He thought it was like borrowing a fiver off your parents and that if they did insist that he pay it back he could do some washing up or mow the lawn instead. It turned out they preferred cash.

With the good times looking like they were coming to an end, disillusionment increased considerably which led to an increase in people fleeing the island. Most Cubans wanted to go to the U.S., but found it hard to obtain a visa due to the U.S.' strict immigration policy. They could, however, gain automatic residency by illegally setting foot on U.S. territory. So that is what they inevitably did.

Some decided to gate-crash foreign embassies in the hope of claiming asylum. In one incident twelve Cubans were handed over to the authorities by the Peruvian embassy after they ran their station wagon through the embassy gates only for the Peruvian government to condemn the actions of the Peruvian diplomats and demanded the twelve Cubans be returned and granted asylum.

Needless to say, the incident served as a dangerous precedent and soon the situation spiralled out of control. Just a few months later, in April 1980, another group of Cubans hoping to claim asylum also ram-raided the gates of the Peruvian Embassy, however this time a policeman was killed in the process.

This complicated things; although the Peruvians were happy to ignore the manner of which the group of Cuban asylum seekers gained entry, Fidel was not. Gaining illegal entry into an embassy was one thing, but the murder of a Cuban guard was quite another – he wanted the men turned over to the Cuban authorities so they could be tried for murder. One of Fidel's aides reported that "When we told the *Commandante* of the policeman's death, his face turned deep red... I have never seen him so angry." When the Peruvians refused to hand them over, Fidel retaliated by removing all the Cuban guards from the embassy. But this backfired, massively.

To his horror approximately 10,000 Cubans took the opportunity to descend on the embassy and claim asylum. It was a major embarrassment – and it was far from over.

Forced onto the defensive, Fidel tried to downplay the number of people trying to flee the country by calling them 'lumpen' (a Marxist term for an 'undesirable') traitors to their country, and 'victims' of U.S propaganda. Then he announced that anyone else who wanted to leave was free to do so. He may have thought that all those who wanted to leave were already in the Peruvian Embassy and that not many other Cubans would take up the offer, but he would be seriously wrong.

The numbers of Cubans wanting to leave just kept growing until there were 125,000 Cubans congregated at the port in Mariel. This was proportionally equivalent of everyone in London packing their bags today and moving to France, although in such an event it's unlikely anyone would have been that bothered, except maybe the French.

Believing that the U.S had been the main instigators of the affair, Fidel was determined to have the last laugh and laid out a little present for the U.S. border officials. Because what he hadn't initially made clear was that nearly 1,700 of those gathered at the docks were criminals who had been offered early release on the proviso that they travel to the U.S. with the other migrants.

Overnight, Miami suffered a massive increase in crime and U.S.

border control slumped into a state of catatonic consternation. The Mayor of Miami quipped, "Fidel has just flushed his toilet on us." Carter appeared completely clueless as to what to do and the whole affair quickly turned into a public relations disaster as many of the new immigrants arriving on the shores were praising the Revolution's healthcare, education, and welfare provisions, adding that their emigration was for economic, and not political reasons.

Indeed, those that were emigrating comprised mainly those from the less well-off segments of society who although having their basic needs met, dreamed of a more materially rich life. They wanted the same preferential treatment as the other Cubans who had previously emigrated and to make a better life for themselves. They were in for a rude awakening. A U.S. official in charge of the resettlement agency claimed that they were only willing to sponsor Cuban refugees if they were white and came as a 'family package', as if they were buying crockery and weren't willing to spend any money on the teapot and sugar bowl unless they came with the matching milk jug.

This was not the only incident of racism. Around this time 14,000 Haitians had also made their way on the prevailing tide in the hope of starting a new life in the U.S., but they were all scooped up by the coastguard and taken to Guantánamo Bay (ironically) where they were held in conditions so bad they started rioting. Why, asked reporters, were the Cubans being given entry to the U.S. so readily, but not the Haitians?

To be fair to Carter, on his part at least, it was not to do with racism. It was politics. They wanted the Cubans because it would harm the Cuban economy and image of Fidel and his Revolution. They didn't want the Haitians because their psychotic murderous dictator was happy to appease Washington's interests. And no doubt Disney wanted all their cheap labour back. But the harm had already been done and Carter's standing in the polls continued to nosedive. Hoping to put an end to the affair, Carter soon ordered that all Cubans would be picked up at sea and sent to refugee camps instead.

The first to be released were the Cuban immigrants who had family members living in the U.S. who were willing to support them, but the rest were sent to one of four minimum security prisons so they could be 'processed'.

They may have been treated better than the Haitian but the Cubans were still far from happy. During one incident in Arkansas, 300 of around 1,800 of the Cubans being held there broke through a security gate and made for freedom. The U.S. guards shot five of those fleeing before the rest realised the game was up and returned to prison 'voluntarily'. They had learned a very valuable lesson about U.S. freedom: If they wanted to live in the free world, then they had to do exactly what the government said.

The Mariel Crisis, as it became known, was damaging to Fidel's image but it did nothing to improve Carter's either and it was little surprise when Republican Ronald Reagan romped home to victory in the late 1980 U.S. Presidential election.

Reagan, a rabid anti-communist, was to take a much tougher line on international issues and was not interested in détente with the Soviet Union or any other communist nation. And that included Cuba.

The first thing Secretary of State Al Haig did when taking office was to ask for a Cuban invasion plan. "You just give me the word," he said to Reagan, "and I'll turn that fucking island into a parking lot." Reagan resisted the urge but did beef up the trade blockade by increasing pressure on third countries to desist from trading with the island, banned all products that contained Cuban nickel, reinstated the travel ban that Carter had rescinded, and placed Cuba on the list of terrorist states.

There was little dialogue between the two countries, and what dialogue there was centred around migration. The U.S. was still unwilling to keep to its promise to take the 2,500 ex-prisoners that Fidel had released in the late 70s, but were eager for Cuba to repatriate over 2,500 'excludables' (those who had acquired criminal records before – or after – leaving Cuba) who had arrived during the Mariel Crisis. The negotiations were tense, but there were some light-hearted moments. Apparently during one meeting, a U.S. official was reading out names of the 'excludables', when suddenly the Cuban counterparts burst out in hysterics. It turns out that one of the Cuban 'excludables' who arrived in Miami had been asked what his name was and had replied in Spanish 'No me Jodes' which translated as 'Don't Fuck with Me'. But as the immigration officer didn't speak Spanish he simply recorded it as his name! In 1984, a deal was finally reached. Cuba agreed to take the 'excludables' and the U.S. agreed to take the ex-prisoners and issue 20,000 visas to Cubans annually.

Other than the migration agreement, the relationship between the two countries was incredibly frosty. Determined to given Fidel a hard time, Reagan gave Cuban exiles in Miami more and more support. Mas Canosa was one of the most powerful of the Cuban exiles, and in 1981 he established an organisation called the Cuban-American National Foundation (CANF) whose leadership comprised of many veterans from

128

the Bay of Pigs.

CANF operated as a tax-exempt business whose predominant purpose was the overthrow of the Cuban regime, directly or indirectly. They quickly secured strong links with congressmen and senators, and Mas Canosa found himself directing U.S policy on Cuba across three different presidencies, even making adjustments to presidential speeches. In 1983 he pushed the U.S. government to launch Radio Martí, and later TV Martí in 1987 which broadcast counter-revolutionary material into Cuba from its station in Miami. Although the shows reached absolutely nobody in Cuba because the signal was easily jammed by the government, it didn't stop the U.S. taxpayer picking up the tab. And it was no small tab. Between 1990 and 2007 alone it cost $500m. One wonders if the money might have been better spent elsewhere, such as on public housing, healthcare or a chocolate teapot the size of Manhattan.

CANF also helped finance terrorists and assassins, and attacks on Cuba[40] would peak during this period. The attacks were becoming much more sophisticated too. In 1981 type II dengue fever was introduced to Cuba for the first time in its history. A Cuban exile later admitted responsibility, whilst also accusing the CIA of telling him the virus would only affect Russians. And although the U.S. hasn't admitted their complicity many international bodies have questioned how such a virus could have spread to the island naturally. Of the 350,000 people affected, 158 died, one-hundred of whom were children.

Just days after Reagan's inauguration, Cuba fell victim to three sabotage raids by the Cuban-exile terrorist group Alpha 66, who released a statement threatening to, "Create as much havoc as we can," and dared the U.S. authorities to arrest them. Not long after, five more exiles were arrested by Cuban authorities whilst on a mission to assassinate Fidel, who was predictably frustrated. "How is it that in the U.S. news conferences are held in public offices announcing the landing of mercenary commando groups to carry out attacks... and yet the U.S. government does not say a word?"

Cuba was not the only socialist country on which Reagan set his sights. In March 1979, in nearby Grenada, a communist called Maurice Bishop overthrew the country's dictator in a bloodless coup. Bishop was a lawyer who became a radical politician like Fidel, and like Fidel would

---

40 And it wasn't just Cuba in the firing line. Between 1983-1985 several businesses operating in Miami's Little Havana were bombed after being found trading with the regime, even those businesses supplying only medical goods.

later ensure that there would never be a fraudulent election again by refusing to hold any elections at all until he had time to come up with a new democratic system that would work wildly in his favour.

At the time, despite being a dictator, Bishop was wildly popular amongst the masses and had been declared Prime Minister without one person killed, shot, or injured. Labour rights were introduced, as were women's rights, including equal pay and maternity pay. Bishop declared that, "No country has the right to tell us what to do, or how to run our country, or who to be friendly with... We are not in anybody's backyard, and we are definitely not for sale."

He did have one big problem though, Grenada was a small country with few natural resources and a population of a little over 100,000, (about the size of Crawley). So, making the best of what they had – a tropical paradise – the government decided to develop the tourism sector. But they needed help. Delighted to have a friendly neighbour, and a socialist one at that, Fidel sent hundreds of technicians and engineers, doctors and teachers to assist in any way they could.

However it was not long before a spanner was thrown into the works. Bishop's reign came to an abrupt end in 1983 after a group of communist extremists launched a power grab and killed him. Their motive is still unknown today, and although Fidel publicly rebuked those involved he agreed to allow Cubans to carry on working on the island.

The U.S. meanwhile were watching events closely. Since Reagan had come to power, a more hard-line stance was taken to those countries who did not embrace capitalism. And Reagan saw Grenada an easy target. He just needed an excuse to invade. The obvious choice would be to declare the new government illegitimate due to taking power through violent, undemocratic means. Yet for some reason Reagan chose to suggest that the Grenadians were a threat to world peace because they had a plan to lay down some tarmac. To be more precise Reagan argued that the airstrip that the Grenadians were building as part of their efforts to expand the tourist industry would be used by the USSR to bomb the U.S..

Reagan's allies over the pond were far from happy when they hard of his intentions. In the UK the Queen was running around her palace with smoke coming out of her ears, declaring it to be an attack on the Commonwealth. Prince Philip was just a tranquilliser dart away from grabbing his elephant gun and taking on the whole U.S army himself, and Parliament was in uproar. Meanwhile the British Prime Minister Margaret Thatcher phoned Reagan and pleaded with him not to invade, reminding him that it was a British matter and the U.S. had no right to interfere. She was adamant. They were *not* to invade. She was the Iron Lady and she would not be defied. Which put Reagan in a predicament – because the invasion had already begun.

So ironically, the Grenadian airstrip that the Cubans had helped to build would be used by neither tourists nor (as Reagan outlandishly claimed) the Soviet Union but by tens of thousands of U.S. Marines who caused one hell of a mess and left without paying. They didn't even give the place a good review on TripAdvisor.com.

Official Cuban records indicate that Fidel had ordered his men to refrain from joining the fighting, but many joined the defence force anyway. The Grenadian-Cuban defence force fought well, but inevitably were no match for the U.S. military machine. Of the 784 Cubans on the island, 24 died in battle and 57 were wounded.

As usual, the U.S. did make some military mistakes, such as sending in its air-force to fire upon their own ground troops. Although due to the gigantic gulf in strength between the two sides this was possibly their way of trying to level the playing field... along with the schools, hospitals, and everything else in sight.

It was an easy victory for Reagan, but the wider world was not impressed. After much deliberation, the UN ruled[41] that having an airstrip does not constitute a threat to world peace. Because it doesn't. It also declared that the U.S. invasion was illegal and contrary to international law. Which it was. Normally if you are found guilty of violating international law there is a good chance you may face fines, sanctions or penalties but the U.S. simply brushed the issue aside and vetoed the decision.

Another group on Reagan's radar was the Sandinistas in Nicaragua. In 1979 the Sandinistas had ousted the U.S.-backed President of Nicaragua, Anastozio Somoza[42] and announced that, "For us, the efficiency of a political model depends on its capacity to resolve the problems of democracy and justice. Effective democracy, like we intend to practice in Nicaragua, consists of ample popular participation – a permanent dynamic of the people's participation in a variety of political and social tasks... For us democracy is not merely a formal model but a continual process capable

---

41 108 to 9, with 27 abstaining

42 Somoza went the country where all Latin American dictators go for their retirement, the U.S.. It seems few dictators can resist the lure of Disneyland's Space Mountain.

of giving the people that elect and participate in it the real possibility of transforming their living conditions, a democracy which establishes justice and ends exploitation." The U.S. were livid.

Fidel was delighted. He had helped to bring the left-wing groups together to topple Somoza, and Cuba now provided much needed civil support in the form of doctors, teacher and technicians. He visited the country to make a speech, but warned them about moving too quickly and called for a slow, peaceful transition to socialism.

But with Reagan in the White House, the transition was never going to be peaceful. In his first year alone Reagan sent $14 million to Nicaraguan opposition parties, and $19 million to the main counter-revolutionary group, the Contras. Anti-Sandinista propaganda was increased, attacks were made on schools, hospitals and other important infrastructure targets, whilst members of the Sandinista government were threatened of assassination.

In an attempt to quell outside interference and criticism the Sandinistas held free and fair elections in 1984, with delegations from the Carter Centre, Canada, the U.S State Department, Europe, and the Organisation of American States (OAS) overseeing them. When it became obvious that the Sandinistas would triumph the U.S. pressurised the opposing parties to pull out of the election and claim fraud. The Sandinistas won with 91% of the people voting. True to form the U.S. accused the government of rigging the elections whilst all the other organisations accepted the result unquestionably.

The result reinforced Washington's belief that the Latin Americans had no idea what democracy was all about, and so they carried on funding the civil war that was sapping the strength of the government and its welfare policies. They also carried on with more direct terrorist attacks of their own, and were soon found guilty by the International Court of Justice of planting mines in the harbours of Nicaragua.[43] True to form, the U.S. refused to recognize the court's jurisdiction and suffered no penalty.

Unable to see a way out of the hostilities, in 1989 the Sandinistas made the U.S. an ultimatum. They would hold another set of elections. If they won then the U.S. must put an end to the war, and if they lost they would bow out gracefully. It was a very risky gamble. The war, terrorism and sabotage by the U.S. backed counter-revolutionaries had cost the Nicaraguan economy an estimated $12 billion, and 30,000 of the populace had lost their lives. The people were exhausted and the Sandinistas also

---

43 The mines hit ships from the Netherlands, Japan and the Soviet Union.

started showing signs of corruption, and thus lost much of their trust and respect.

Being one of the world's biggest sceptics of multi-party democracy, Fidel was horrified, especially as the Sandinistas did nothing to stop the U.S. directly funding the opposition. And it was a lot of funding. Having already spent over $1 billion in ten years trying to oust the regime, the U.S had decided to throw a few more chips onto the table in the hope of securing the jackpot. They provided another $30 million, equal to $20 per voter. To put this in perspective, when George W. Bush won the American presidency in 2000 he spent an average of $4 per voter. Fidel's fears proved true and the Sandinistas were beaten in the elections, with the coalition of opposition groups gaining 55% of the vote.

*

Back in 1982 Yuri Andropov had replaced Brezhnev as leader of the Soviet Union and upon reviewing the dire economic situation he had inherited, he duly informed Cuba that they could no longer count on military protection or generous trade agreements. This was extremely bad news and it was not long before Cuba was unable to pay its debts to international creditors.

Paintings from the Cuban National Art Gallery were sold off, and in an effort to circumvent the crippling U.S trade blockade, a Convertible Currency Department was created within the Ministry of Interior that would clandestinely run businesses in countries such as Panama so they could access U.S. products, including much-needed computers.

The efforts were in vain and by the middle of the decade Fidel announced that the country would be suspending its repayments of all commercial debt, lamenting to the Communist Party leadership that, "We have never experienced... such a small supply of convertible currency."

Cuba's fortunes then went from bad to worse when in 1986 Mikhail Gorbachev took the helm in the USSR. He had a plan to create a more hospitable environment for free speech whilst transforming the county's economy to a more market-socialist model, partly inspired by the Scandinavian social democracies. The emphasis was on creating cooperatives rather than U.S.-style corporations and was popular amongst the majority of Russians, but it didn't take long for Fidel to start criticising the reforms,[44] claiming that Gorbachev was in danger of allowing

---

44 There are many jokes about the Soviet leaders that were popular amongst the masses, but this is definitely my favourite; A man goes to buy some vodka but finds that due to Gorbachev's reforms there are long queues of other people waiting to buy vodka. He takes his place in the line but soon becomes increasingly agitated and yells "I can't stand this any

capitalism to take hold by decentralising the economy and allowing rival, autonomous enterprises.

In response to Gorbachev's perceived lurch to the right, Fidel wanted to ensure Cuba was firmly on traditional socialist ground and so introduced a programme of change that became known as the Rectification of Errors and Negative Tendencies.

The main thrust of Fidel's reform was, for all intents and purposes, a return to Che's economic model from the 1960s. Foreign trade was recentralised and again there was an effort to diversify to create more exports and reduce imports. An emphasis was once again placed on moral rather than material incentives. Yet although material incentives were taking on less importance, agricultural workers were no doubt delighted to hear that their wages were increasing by as much as 40%. But this came at a price – the elimination of small-scale enterprises. Again.

As ever, Fidel had his reasons. Since the 1960s private farmers could only sell their produce directly to the government, but in 1980 a law was been passed to allow more flexibility. The new law permitted farmers who had fulfilled their government quota to sell any excess stock direct to the consumer on the open market. This *did* lead to an increase in production, but it came at a cost. The main problem was that farmers generally had little time after work to take his produce to market and so a legion of shrewd middlemen emerged. The middlemen did what all middlemen do and immediately moved to distort the market in their favour to increase profits. For example some would hold back supplies until the demand had caused the price to soar, whilst more brazen 'entrepreneurs' would simply pilfer from the state warehouses and sell that. As far as Fidel was concerned they had had their chance and had blown it, and now the private farmers were again forced to sell *all* their produce to the government.

The reforms also included the establishment of construction brigades to help build large infrastructure projects such as roads, dams, hospitals and airports. All workers in these brigades were volunteers and were able to decide amongst themselves as to the hours they should work and wages each worker should receive.

These brigades were also complemented by smaller, 'micro-brigades' made up of unpaid volunteers who were tasked with building

---

longer, I'm off to kill Gorbachev!" A little while later he returns and again takes his place in the line, leading to the others to ask how he had fared. "Well I got to the Kremlin," the man replied, "but the queue to kill Gorbachev was even longer."

houses, child care centres, clinics, schools and recreational facilities in their local neighbourhoods. The government would provide the materials, machinery, and technical assistance, and each neighbourhood would organise its own construction projects. This push into community-based building not only helped to ease the chronic housing shortage (though did not solve it), it also provided another benefit – residents would take care of their self-built houses and were equipped with the skills to maintain them.

*

In 1987 a defection of a high-level Cuban secret service officer to the U.S. alerted the CIA to various Cuban operations and left around twenty of Cuban agents severely compromised. The CIA were horrified and shocked to discover the breadth and sophistication of the Cuban spies operating and all the more galled to discover an incredible amount of money and technical equipment had been lost to double agents – one double-agent alone managed to glean a total of $250,000.

Always willing to try and make the best of a bad situation, Fidel reckoned the only thing to do with secret agents that are no longer secret, was to make them the most famous secret agents in the world. An eleven-part series called *The CIA's War Against Cuba* was broadcast which included incredible footage of 'secret' meetings between CIA agents and counter-revolutionaries. Just to ensure the point was hammered home, it was also dubbed into English and a copy sent to the FBI. It was yet another embarrassment for the CIA.

Having ridiculed the U.S. establishment in the field of espionage, Fidel then proceeded to embarrass them on the battlefield – again. And again the arena of battle was to be Angola. Since the MPLA victory in the mid-70s South Africa had been repeatedly invading southern Angola despite the UN decreeing these actions illegal. Now they again teamed up with rebel group UNITA – who themselves were again receiving large quantities of aid from the U.S. – to eradicate the MPLA once and for all.

The USSR had been in overall control of the Angolan armed forces, but they proved to be more hindrance than help as their tactical incompetence led to scores of embarrassments on the battlefield. By November 1987 the MPLA in Angola were on the ropes and were again forced to send an urgent plea for help to the Cubans.

Fidel responded immediately but insisted he oversee the operations; the Cubans were willing to die in solidarity but that did not mean they wanted to be killed, and the best way to avoid that was to ensure the Soviet generals stayed well away.

A massive military airlift was organised, including 22,000 troops (adding to the 30,000 Cuban troops already in Angola), fighter jets and artillery. Not content with that Fidel ordered some of the anti-aircraft batteries in Cuba be dismantled and sent as well. Raúl explained to the chief of the soviet mission in Havana, General Zaitsev, that the Cubans were so determined to defeat the South Africans "we will send everything to Angola, including our underpants." Cuba would ensure that Angolan commandos would not go commando.

Fidel became obsessed with the struggle, spending almost every waking hour at headquarters in Havana planning and organising all aspects of the mission, down to the amount of rations each man received and how much sleep each man should be allowed.

According to the acclaimed novelist Gabriel Garcia Márquez, "Castro kept himself informed of the minutest details of the war. He personally saw off every ship bound for Angola, having previously addressed the fighting units in the La Cabana theatre; he himself sought out the commanders of the special forces battalion who went on the first flight and drove them in his own Soviet Jeep right to the aircraft stairs ... By then, there was not a single dot on the map of Angola that he was unable to identify, nor any feature of the land that he did not know by heart. His absorption in the war was so intense and meticulous that he could quote any statistic relating to Angola as if it were Cuba itself, and he spoke of its towns, customs and peoples as if he had lived there all his life. In the early stages of the war, when the situation was urgent, Fidel Castro would spend up to fourteen hours at a stretch in the command room of the general staff, at times without eating or sleeping, as if he were on the battlefield himself."

In a strange twist, around 2,000 Cubans with Soviet weapons were sent to defend the U.S.-owned Gulf Oil Company platforms from being destroyed by U.S.-backed UNITA forces. Now, warfare can be strange thing. Sometimes you can lose, sometimes you can win, and sometimes you can make a dignified exit with all limbs still attached, but very rarely does a side defend the opponent's assets from being attacked by those very same opponents. The Iraqi's insurgents did not form militias to protect McDonald outlets, nor did the Vietnamese dig a complex series of tunnels to keep U.S. sweatshops intact. But then very rare moments are remarkably common when the Cubans are involved.

As the invading forces advanced to Luanda, the stage was set for the final of the World War Cup, and the playing field would be Cuito

136

Cuanavale, a strategic area south-west of Luanda.

Fidel again showed himself to be the master tactician and the Angolan forces, supported by the Cuban army, proved too much for the opposition. Outfought, outwitted, and forced into a hasty retreat, South Africa fled south into Namibia whilst UNITA moved across into the Democratic Republic of Congo (DRC). The Angolan-Cuban alliance had triumphed once again.

As the Cubans and Angolans celebrated their triumph, their ecstasy turned to bemusement when they learned that the South Africans and UNITA were claiming that *they* had won the war. Showing more cheek than a *Victoria's Secret* fashion show, South Africa and UNITA argued that they were the victors because they hadn't been completely annihilated; but being the magnanimous people they were, they offered to negotiate a compromise in the name of peace.

Fidel was happy to carry on fighting but the USSR and Angolans were weary of the conflict and so negotiations began. And again it was the Cubans who had the upper hand. The U.S. Assistant Secretary of State for African Affairs, Chester Crocker, sent a cable to Secretary of State George Shultz 'They [the Cubans] are prepared for war as much as they are for peace... We are witnesses to a great tactical virtuosity and a true creativity at the negotiation table.'

Finally in December 1988 a peace accord was signed with Cuba agreeing to leave Angola in return for South Africa agreeing to respect Angolan independence, withdraw from Namibia and release various political prisoners. The last Cuban left Angola one month ahead of schedule. In the end, between 1975 and 1991 approximately 375,000 members of Cuban armed forces had served in Angola, along with 50,000 volunteers to carry out various civilian responsibilities.

Revelling in his latest triumph, Fidel made a speech in Havana in which he announced, "The history of Africa is at a turning point. They will write about 'before Cuito Cuanavale' and 'after Cuito Cuanavale'. The power of South Africa, the whites, the 'superior race', has come unstuck in a little parcel of land defended by blacks and mulattoes. We do not seek a great military victory, but a reasonable and just solution. They might not only lose Namibia, but apartheid too. We want a solution now. I believe we are witnessing the beginning of the end of Apartheid."

Two years later in 1990 Nelson Mandela was released from prison, and his first foreign visit was to Cuba where he thanked Fidel and the

Cuban people[45] for the monumental support they had given to Africa. Four years later, during his inauguration as President of South Africa, Mandela turned to Castro and – not realising the microphones were still on – whispered "You made this all possible."

Four years later he would go on to say, "If today all South Africans enjoy the rights of democracy; if they are able at last to address the grinding poverty of a system that denied them even the most basic amenities of life, it is also because of Cuba's selfless support for the struggle to free all of South Africa's people and the countries of our region from the inhumane and destructive system of apartheid. For that, we thank the Cuban people from the bottom of our heart."

Chas Freeman, from the U.S. Department of African Affairs said in an interview for a BBC documentary, "He [Fidel] could think of himself as having been the father of Namibian independence and in the end, the man who ended colonialism in Africa. Cuba in fact, demonstrated a level of responsibility in its behaviour and maturity in its judgement that arguably should have been recognized by the U.S. as an important gesture deserving some response. But the politics of this in the U.S., that is the politics of relations with Cuba, are poisonous in the extreme. So in the end, Cuba which acted responsibly and should have been acknowledged for doing so, got no such acknowledgement."

---

45 When Mandela later flew to the U.S. to be presented with the key to Miami, he took part in an interview on Nightline in which he praised the Cuban support for the freedom of Africa and their support in bringing apartheid to an end. This did not sit well with the Cuban-exile groups who duly ensured that the key was withdrawn and the locks changed.

X
Back to the Future

"A failure is not always a mistake, it may simply be the best one can do under the circumstances..   The real mistake is to stop trying."
B. F. Skinner

As the Cuban troops returned home from Angola they brought with them a new revolutionary triumph and a significant morale boost. But they also brought with them a new disease that was starting to spread itself across the world – HIV/Aids. When the virus came to international attention in the 1980s Cuba was quick to act.

The first known case in Cuba was in 1985. At first, when there was more fear than knowledge about the disease, the government decided to quarantine all those infected in specially built sanatoriums. The word 'sanatorium' conjures up images of dark, sinister hospitals worthy of any Stephen King horror-story, but the World Health Organisation described the Cuban sanatoriums as "suburban communities on several acres of land with modern one- and two-story apartment duplexes ... surrounded by lush vegetation and a small garden."

Patients were well looked after at the sanatoriums, but controversially, they could not leave. Fortunately, this arrangement did not last too long. By the end of the 1980s, with more understanding of the disease, quarantine was relaxed and although patients still had to live at the sanatoriums, they were given the freedom to come and go as they pleased. By 1993 patients were asked to attend the sanatoriums daily so that they could receive specialized treatment and learn more about the disease, but were permitted to return home at the end of each day. The only patients forced to stay at the sanatoriums were those who refuse to practice safe sex.

To help prevent HIV/Aids patients being discriminated against, laws were created to ensure people with the disease were not unfairly treated at work and allowed patients to continue to receive their full salaries whilst undergoing treatment. A national project to demystify and de-stigmatise the disease was also carried out.

At first Cuba was having to treat patients with drugs bought on the world marketplace, but by the turn of the millennium Cuba was starting to produce its own. Today all Cuban citizens living with HIV/Aids have access to the antiretroviral drugs they need, compared with just 37% of their U.S. counterparts.

Cuba's approach to controlling the disease has been extremely successful. The percentage of its population battling the disease is just 0.2%, which is far less than the Caribbean average of 1%. In 2006 the UN would note that Cuba's program was 'among the most effective in the world' and a decade later, in 2016, Cuba became the first country in the world to officially eradicate mother-to-child transmission of the virus.

*

Along with HIV/Aids there was another disease that was quickly becoming a major concern for the government – corruption. In 1988 evidence was found that implicated some senior Cuban officials in various underhand schemes, although at first only one person was under investigation - General Ochoa. He was considered one of the finest minds in the Cuban military and had been one of the major players in Angola, but it had become apparent that his success had rather gone to his head. Privately he mocked Fidel and had found ways to enrich himself by taking part in the illegal trade of drugs and ivory.

As the investigation progressed it caused a worse stench than a Portaloo at a music festival, and similarly its contents soon spilled over into other areas.

To Fidel's horror it was shown that there had been a serious amount of corruption taking place at the Convertible Currency Department, an arm of the Ministry of Interior whose purpose was to secretly establish businesses in foreign countries with the aim of circumventing the U.S. imposed trade blockade. In the end fourteen people (including Ochoa) were arrested and charged with corruption offences.

One of those arrested was the head of the Convertible Currency Department, Tony de la Guardia. He had been an important figure in the regime and had an extremely colourful life-history. He had fought alongside Che in the Congo, trained guerrilla fighters in various Latin American countries, acted as a spy, and helped launder money for the Palestinians. His twin brother, General Patricio de la Guardia – also well-respected after having fought in Angola – was also heavily implicated.

The investigation found that not only had they been trafficking cocaine to the U.S. since 1987, they had involved themselves in the illegal ivory and diamond trade too.

The seriousness of the offences could not have been higher. They had laid themselves open to blackmail, brought the country into disrepute and taken part in activities that could give the U.S. enough pretext to invade[46].

The trials of those accused were broadcast on television. All fourteen defendants contritely pleaded guilty, but if the ringleaders were expecting clemency it was not forthcoming. Whilst eleven of the defendants were given jail terms ranging from ten to thirty years, Ochoa and the La Guardia twins were sentenced to death by firing squad. It was a dark day for the Revolution.

*

To Fidel's immense frustration, over the past decade Marxism had been in decline around the world. In the late 1980s the Soviet Bloc had started to collapse as one by one the satellite countries had gained independence and rid themselves of the chains of Soviet Communism. Fidel was mortified, saying in December 1989: "Why must the so-called reforms go towards capitalism? If those ideas are truly revolutionary, as some claim, why do they receive the imperialist leaders' unanimous, enthusiastic support?" He went on to say, "In history there has never been a truly revolutionary idea that has received the enthusiastic support of the leader of the most powerful, aggressive, and voracious empire known to mankind."

With the days of the USSR clearly numbered, it was not that surprising when Gorbachev flew to Cuba in 1989 to inform them that their trade subsidy from the USSR was coming to an end. There would no longer be any special treatment – they would have to face the U.S. alone.

Yet if Fidel had reservations over Gorbachev's policies, he would be absolutely mortified at those enacted by his successor, Boris Yeltsin. Whereas Gorbachev wanted to improve communism, Yeltsin was eager to destroy it. Having first dissolved the Soviet Union he then – under advice from U.S. economists – instigated an explosive change to a free market economy, selling off all the state assets for a fraction of their price, and unleashing a raft of spending cuts to public services.

It was not long before the Russian people found themselves mired in economic, political and social despair. Due to Yeltsin's reforms the middle-classes lost all their savings, workers were left unpaid for months, and there was 40% less consumption. A third of Russians fell below the poverty line and unemployment soared to previously unseen levels. The figures are truly startling; within just a few years those living on less than a dollar a day increased from 2 million to 74 million, of whom 37 million were described by the World Bank as living in 'desperate' poverty. Drink

---

46   This was a serious threat – the U.S. had invaded nearby Panama in late 1989 under the pretext that the government had been colluding with drug cartels

and drug abuse soared, as did homelessness and violent crime. By 1996 the suicide rate was double what it had been in 1986, all of which contributed to the country's population decreasing by 6.6 million between 1992 and 2006. By the year 2000 male life expectancy had fallen from 63 years to 58 and it would take two decades to recover.

With the Soviet empire finally eradicated, the Western world began a massive celebration. The party was a wild free-for-all extravaganza in which riches seemed to be as inexhaustible as the champagne. One of the most fervent of the party-goers was renowned U.S. political scientist Francis Fukuyama, who became so inebriated he claimed that the world was experiencing 'The End Of History'. Normally people would laugh at such a ludicrous remark, but everyone else in the room was just as drunk as he was and so instead they decided to venerate him as one of the most perceptive intellectuals on the planet. It was as if they hadn't noticed that when he made this claim he was gyrating to Spandau Ballet with his pants on his head.

The partying continued for nearly two decades as the Western powers assured the world that as long as they kept on drinking, the party would never end. But in 2008 they found out the champagne had been paid for on credit, and the people entrusted to buy more from the off-licence had gambled the last of their money on scratch-cards. The party was over.

The collapse of the Soviet Union was clearly not the end of history, but it was the end of an era, especially in Cuba. Almost overnight the country became even more isolated; an island of socialism in an ocean of capitalism. It was arguably the biggest challenge Fidel and the Revolution would face – and nobody outside of Cuba thought The Revolution could survive. Hawks in Washington and Cuban-exiles in Miami were licking their lips in anticipation. But not for the fist time, their hopes were dashed.

With no trade with the old Soviet states the economy shrank 40% whilst the amount of hard currency, the kind that other countries would accept in exchange for imports, dwindled down to just 17% of the 1989 total. A UN Economic Commission report in 1997 described the effects as "More severe than that brought about by the Great Depression." Shipments of rice, soap, steel, metals, refrigerators, fertiliser, chemicals and machine parts all came to a complete stop.

Oil and petrol supplies dropped a staggering 90%, causing frequent blackouts. Around 60% of factories were forced to cease production due to lack of fuel. The country was thrust back decades in technological terms and old pre-industrial skills suddenly acquired a new importance. Under such conditions the CIA may have been hopeful for a coup – and they got one – but not the type they were expecting: due to communication lines being hampered by electrical blackouts, carrier pigeons were reintroduced.

Around 300,000 oxen had to replace 30,000 tractors which Cuba could no longer afford to run, milk production halved, powdered milk production dropped by 90%, beef production fell 75%, poultry production fell 80%, the number of pigs fell by 70% and the sugar harvest dropped from 8.1 million tonnes in 1991 to 3.3 million tonnes in 1995.

If that wasn't enough, prices on the international markets for two of the country's major exports, sugar and nickel, fell 20% and 30% respectively, whilst the price of much needed imports such as wheat, chicken, milk and petroleum rose steeply.

So began the 'Special Period in Time of Peace'. Hunger was prevalent and queuing became a social norm. Average calorie and protein consumption halved as people found their monthly rations lasted just two weeks. By 1994 the average Cuban had lost 20lbs in weight. This led to 50,000 malnourished Cubans being struck by a medical condition called Optic Neuropathy which caused poor vision and sometimes blindness as parents starved themselves in order to give their pitiful portions to their children. Whereas previously Cubans had eaten relatively well compared to their Latin American and Caribbean counterparts, most now ate just one meal a day. In 1993 UNICEF estimated that around half of Cuban children aged between six and twelve months were malnourished and a third of women in the first trimester of pregnancy were anaemic.

With no oil the entire transport system came to a grinding halt. The Cubans had shown fantastic ingenuity in maintaining their old Yankee auto-mobiles left over from the Batista era but they could not make them run on thin air, public transport was running at just 10-20% of its previous capacity. As a result people turned to old forms of transport like horses and mules, but it was the bicycle which soon became the new favourite. 700,000 were imported from China in 1991 alone, along with 60,000 tricycles.

Other than bicycles, there were shortages of just about everything. The trade in goods on the black market increased dramatically, and accounted for 50-70% of a typical household's yearly expenditure. There was also an increase in 'socialismo', the term jokingly corrupted by Cubans to mean 'sharing one's pilfered goods with one's friends'. One Cuban man put it like this: "If my brother is well connected politically, he can get a good job in a tourist hotel. Not only does he get to earn some American dollars, he also gets access to the hotel's storeroom (which represents a supply of desirable consumer goods that are unavailable to most Cubans). One day he may walk away with some towels for his neighbour, who has none. Say his neighbour works in a factory bottling beer. To repay his *socio* he'll smuggle a case of beer out of the factory and give it to the hotel employee. The hotel employee will then trade the beer to the maid for a supply of soap, which he'll either give to his *socios* or sell on the black market. Everyone does it. It's the only way to survive."

The period also saw a rise in prostitution, especially when the tourist industry started to increase. A crack-down ensued whereupon prostitutes were rounded up and taken back to their surprised parents, who were told to keep a better eye on their children. Homeless people became more numerous on the city streets, and crime increased dramatically, including cattle rustling, vehicle theft, muggings and armed robberies.

The inevitable increase in emigration saw the country again suffer a severe brain drain. Not only were doctors, teachers and technicians leaving, so were prominent cultural and sports figures. In one event alone, at the Central American and Caribbean Games in Puerto Rico in 1993 around 40 Cuban athletes stayed behind including two of the most famous and talented baseball players. Yet despite the material incentives to head for the USA, there were other strong incentives to remain, as one former athlete – and member of the national parliament – Quirot Moret explained; "Well, we Cuban athletes are also multimillionaires from the following point of view – there are many millions of people living in Cuba... and so, since we, the athletes, are loved and admired by millions, we are also multimillionaires in a sense. Even today, when I am no longer active in racing, when I go into the streets, people show their love and affection."

With the U.S. still not allocating all of the 20,000 visas they promised, many emigrating Cubans decided to make home-made vessels and set sail across the perilous sea towards Florida. Such people were nicknamed the 'rafters' and many lost their lives trying to make the voyage. The number of rafters increased from 2,000 a year in 1990 to 3,500 a year in 1993, and as the numbers increased so did the international criticism of the Cuban regime. Fidel, as always, argued that the problems were the result of the economic war conducted by the U.S., and made the point that "Mexico [which sees higher levels of emigration] has plenty of oil, faces no U.S. embargo, and is not going through a 'Special Period in Time of Peace'. In comparison we have all these problems and only a few people leave illegally." Going further, he also pointed out that "If a Mexican goes to the U.S. illegally, he's expelled," he says. "If a Cuban enters illegally, he's given a house."

It would take something special to turn Cuba's fortunes around, and as ever Fidel immersed himself in the struggle. He had determined that the Revolution would not collapse no matter how bad their situation might be. Advisers had been sent from the Soviet Union and Europe to help Cuba through the economic quagmire, and they pressed Fidel to adopt a more market-based model. But Fidel had never been an advocate of capitalism and was not about to be converted. Everyone else may have given up on socialism, but Cuba had not. They would find their own way.

Fidel spent much of his time making public appearances and writing articles, trying to boost morale, production, and the economy. During his many television appearances and public speeches he would explain the crisis and the measures being taken in exhaustive detail, all the while trying to boost morale by telling jokes and trying to keep a positive outlook. He pointed out that not only were bicycles cheaper and healthier, they were also a lot more reliable than the poorly designed, gas-guzzling vehicles from the Eastern Bloc. And he mockingly made reference to the time when they ordered a fleet of tractors from the Soviets, only to be sent snowploughs. Which obviously weren't much use on a tropical Caribbean island.

Despite the times being extremely tough, Fidel still retained the support of the vast majority of the populace, and as the years went on it looked less and less likely that there would be any major opposition to his rule. This left the U.S. extremely frustrated. They just could not understand why the people continued to put up with it. They could not see that most Cubans were grateful and proud of the successes of the revolution. They also failed to r4ealise that most Cubans had a deep rooted fear that the U.S. and the Cuban exiles would return to take control. After all, what would happen to the people of Cuba if that happened? Would they end up like nearby U.S.-dominated countries like Haiti and the Dominican Republic? Would they lose their land? Their houses? If the U.S. reclaimed the companies nationalised by the revolution, would the profits be spread throughout the country or spirited offshore? Would they keep their jobs? Would the state provide for them if they were unemployed? Would they have to pay for health insurance and tuition fees? The Cubans had too much invested in the Revolution to let it fail.

These sentiments are well-documented by the many journalists who visited the island, including Ole Hansen of *The Independent* newspaper who wrote about his visit to the island in 1994; 'Even those who complain are aware of the advantages that the revolution has brought in terms of health, education and welfare. They also know that while the regime has its repressive aspects, it compares favourably with some other Latin American countries. No one to whom I spoke expressed any support for the Miami exiles or any desire that they, or any other US- backed group, should take over the government.'

In 1996 the UN Human Rights Commission Special Rapporteur for Cuba, Carl-Johan Groth wrote that Fidel and his government still commanded "[in] broad sectors of the population, a credibility and a margin of confidence far greater than observers have believed." And that "The philosophical good humour with which most rural people seemed to confront their difficulties was impressive."

That is not to say there was no dissatisfaction with the political and economic situation – the tension on the streets was palpable. However, whereas many international critics may have expected the Cuban government to revert to a siege mentally and usher in tougher civil restrictions, instead they actually made efforts to decentralise power even more.

A few months before the Soviet collapse, a Cuban Party Congress was held in during which a raft of measures were put forward, discussed and finally voted for by the people in a referendum held in 1993. The resulting reforms meant that the National Assembly would finally be voted in directly by the people, and Workers' Parliaments would be established to give employees more power in their places of work. *Consejo Populares* (People's Councils) were also brought into existence which decentralised economic and political power to individual neighbourhoods. People elected a councillor for their area who would be responsible for dealing with social problems and local economic issues, helping to promote self-government within the community and bringing local issues to the attention of the municipal delegate. Also, from now on there could be multiple people on the ballot for the representatives for both provincial and national positions.

Small businesses were again allowed to operate so as to lessen the burden on the state bureaucracy, and there was a move to allow openly religious people to take on positions of power. In the early years of the regime the relationship between the government and the religious community had been fractious, not helped by the Catholic Church being complicit in the kidnapping of thousands of Cuban children during

Operation Peter Pan in the early 1960s. Now, nearly forty years later, relations between the two groups had thawed and a law was passed in 1992 that allowed people of religious faith to be elected to government.

Naturally, the dissident groups and anti-Castro exiles in Miami did not believe the reforms went far enough. Hoping to profit from the economic disarray they turned the 1993 referendum into a vote of no-confidence in Fidel's government and the socialist system itself by asking citizens to spoil their ballot, or simply abstain.

In the resulting free and fair election almost all the population – 99.6% – turned out. The spoilt ballots and non-voters gained just over 7% and the referendum was passed with a 95% share of the remaining votes. Fidel had won convincingly. The result was gallantly accepted by the leading Cuban dissident, Elizardo Sanchez.

During the first few months of 1994 another round of debates were arranged with three million citizens taking part in 80,000 meetings. People decided on the implementation of various new measures, such as placing a tax on cigarettes and rum (to help keep prices of rationed goods down) and introducing ticket prices for sporting events which had previously been free.

In the 1998 elections the spoilt ballots and non-vote share fell to just over 5% with little improvement in the 2003 elections. Today, with the economy in better shape, spoiled ballots account for roughly 4% of those cast.

*

After 1959 Cuba had zealously followed the developed nations' mass-industrial farming and the use of fertilisers was especially high, with Cuba using twice as much per acre as the U.S., and three times more than the Latin American average. Now, unable to import much food or fertiliser, nor the fossil fuel to manufacture it, the island needed a drastic overhaul of its entire food production system. The belief that science and 'progress', in the form of oil-based fertilisers and heavy machinery would solve all of their problems had been one of Fidel's greatest dogmas, but now that all seemed to be at an end.

Acknowledging that the transition from oil-based agriculture to a low-fuel organic system was not going to be easy, vast amounts of research was undertaken. The investment quickly bore fruit and today over 80% of the agricultural land is farmed organically and Cuba exports organic fertilizers and pesticides to Central and Latin America.

To no-one's surprise the Cuban army was asked to pitch in. The

British socialist MP Tony Benn once said, "If we can find the money to kill people, we can find the money to help people," though Raúl Castro put it more bluntly: "Beans are worth more than cannons." Which must have caused a moment of consternation on wall-street. But as it turned, out the army proved very efficient in its new task and was soon responsible for producing and distributing around a quarter of the nation's food.

Another radical policy change was to divide two-thirds of state farmland into smaller plots and leased it for free to newly emerging farm cooperatives. The deal was that these autonomous cooperatives supply the state with a certain amount of produce at a set price, and were allowed to sell their excess on the open market.

To accompany these changes *autoconsumos* were established, through which volunteers cultivated fallow land to supply food to the community, including to schools, factories, retirement homes and hospitals. Workers volunteered to tend to plots near their workplaces, with the produce donated to the staff canteens and any surplus sold to their fellow workers. Urban gardening was also heavily promoted in the attempt to maximise agricultural use from even the smallest of areas. It was a staggering success, with around 8,000 city farms sprouting up in 1994 alone. By 1995 80% of the gardeners in Havana were donating some of their harvests to local community institutions and by 2005 this accounted for half the fruit and vegetables eaten in Havana.

Expertise in sustainable food production almost became the new rock and roll in Cuba. One community project saw two scientists thrust to national fame for their flashy new methods of organic cultivation, food preservation and their farm education programmes which provided classes and instructional materials to all those interested. Soon schools and other local community institutions became involved and the state provided television and radio time to help promote their programme.

Cuba's surprising success at organic farming has brought international acclaim. One 2004 report by Oxfam America reported that, "Under the circumstances facing Cuba – the U.S. trade blockade, loss of trading partners, little international aid and economic collapse – the agricultural recovery is nothing short of extraordinary."

The new forms of collaborative food production brought other benefits too, in terms of building communities and helping people stay connected to one another. In the documentary *How Cuban Survived Peak Oil*, Roberto Perez of The Foundation for Nature and Humanity, a Cuban NGO explains that "They do it for free. And they don't do it because it's compulsory, they do it because they want it, they want to do their little part to the society. But in other places people do not know their neighbours... Here no. The neighbour knocks on the door and says, 'I need some salt,' or, 'I need some sugar', whatever. 'I brought you an avocado.'"

With no more investment coming from the USSR, there was a need to encourage investment from elsewhere so the government decided to form collaborative projects with western companies, mainly in the tourism and biotechnology sectors. China also became interested in investing in Cuban electrical generation and nickel mining and from having just two partnership agreements with foreign corporations in 1990, by 1993 this number had risen to 112.

The Special Period saw the much-loved national health service come under much strain. Patients were asked to bring their own bedding, food and toiletries, and some hospitals fell to ruin.

With the U.S.-imposed trade blockade, Cuba found it very difficult to acquire certain medical products because 80% of patents in the medical sector were held by U.S.-based companies. One upsetting example was that they couldn't acquire the products needed to treat retinal cancer in children, meaning that the doctors were left with the only other option of removing the whole eye. But the trade restrictions prompted large investments in biological research, genetics, neuroscience, and pharmaceuticals, and eventually Cubans were able to develop many of their own medical products. Not only did this help improve the country's healthcare system, it also proved to be a good source of revenue for the government.

In the mid-1980's Cuba became the first country in the world to create a Meningitis B vaccine[47], all but eradicating the disease from the island within five years. Meningitis affects hundreds of thousands of people every year, and can be fatal, but as the BBC reported in 1999, "The vaccine has since been sold in Brazil, Argentina and Colombia," but "US domination of the big international pharmaceutical companies has made it very difficult to commercialise elsewhere."

Historically Fidel hated international tourism. Before The

---

47 Peter Bourne, Chairman of Medical Education Cooperation with Cuba (MEDICC), a Californian-based non-profit organization that promotes US-Cuban healthcare collaboration, noted in 2003 that, "Significant investment in sophisticated medical research has resulted in Cuba leading the world in some areas. Its development of a vaccine against meningitis B caused an embarrassing situation for the U.S. Americans, because of the embargo, could not get access to the vaccine even though several hundred die from the disease every year."

Revolution Cuba had been the tropical playground for wealthy U.S. citizens, and the tourist sector was regarded as a breeding ground for gambling, prostitution and corruption. But it was also a massive cash cow, and with the country in desperate need of money huge investments were made to develop it.

Cuba proved to be a popular destination for western tourists, providing unspoilt beaches, a dazzling range of wildlife, a glimpse into a rose-tinted, pre-consumerist past, and a rich and vibrant culture. In 1990 Cuba was receiving 350,000 tourists a year, and within five years that number had more than doubled. By 2006 it had reached 2.1 million, and in 2014 the number past 3 million.

Without doubt the tourist industry helped the country out of a massive financial black hole. Between 1993 and 1995 earnings from tourism doubled, reaping an extra $1 billion for the treasury each year. By 2006 the total had risen to $2.4 billion and constituted around half of Cuban foreign exchange earnings.

The figures were impressive, and they did not even tell the full story. In other developing countries for every $100 of tourist dollars spent in the country, usually only around $5 is retained and re-spent there. But Cuba had ensured that foreign companies could never own more than 49.9% of any enterprise which meant a larger chunk of the tourist income was kept in the country.

In 1992, just when Fidel had managed to get Cuba's head above water, he submerged himself in controversy. Afraid that Cubans would become disillusioned if they were in contact with these well-off western tourists, Fidel tried to devise ways of keeping tourists out of sight. Many of Cuba's surrounding islands and its sandy peninsula, Varedero, were made into tourist enclaves complete with hotels, sun loungers, bars and beaches – but no Cubans, with the exception of hotel workers and taxi drivers.

Cubans were banned from the hotel complexes, the beaches, and even from talking to tourists when they came into contact on the streets. These policies were horribly reminiscent of the Batista days when Cubans had been treated as unwelcome onlookers. Yet for some reason Fidel decided it was a good idea. It wasn't. And incredibly it would take over two decades for this ridiculous policy to be overturned.

The economic changes were helping to spur the country's recovery, but they were breaking it ideologically. The egalitarian dream based on a 'moral economy' seemed to be put on hold.

In 1993 it had again become legal for shops in Cuba to trade in U.S.

dollars, mainly to cater to tourists and their desire for familiar, imported 'luxury' goods. Many of the stores were government-run, so this provided another way that the treasury to get its hands on foreign currency. But it came with problems. Cubans who worked in the tourist trade or had relatives living in the U.S. had access to dollars and could therefore manage to shop in these luxury stores, whilst many ordinary Cubans – including otherwise fairly well-off workers like teachers and doctors could not. Around 40% of the population had no access to dollars at all, so while their neighbours bought shampoo and mobile phones and designer clothes, they were stuck with Cuba's adequate, but old-fashioned factory fare. Those with dollars became Cuba's nouveau riche. In the 1990s the ratio of income between the highest and lowest deciles of earners soon grew from 4:1 to 25:1.

The Cuban government tried its best to capture and redistribute the valuable tourist dollars but they couldn't fight the tide. The lure of dollars also caused an internal brain drain as highly skilled workers in sectors such as healthcare, engineering, or education began finding alternative employment in dollar-accessible industries such as tourism. The logic was unquestionable. A bell-hop could earn ten times more than that of a brain surgeon, a taxi driver could earn twenty times that of a state engineer, and a hotel waiter earned more in two weeks than a physician made in a year.

Yet in a strange twist this new inequality actually helped bolster the popularity of the government. As state employees politicians were also deprived from access to dollars, so they too did not enjoy luxurious expenses or comforts. There were no millionaires in the National Assembly, and the country's Vice-President Carlos Lage would often be seen riding his bike to work (and without a Rolls Royce behind to carry his briefcase). People could see that they were, at least, really all in it together.

Within a few years Cuba had almost starved, and had then found new unique ways to turn things around. Entirely by accident they had invented a sustainable way of feeding the people, and by sheer necessity, had become a leader in medical research. All in all, the Special Period had been special in every sense of the word.

XI
When Pianos Were more Dangerous Than Nuclear Weapons

"If you only have a hammer, you tend to see every problem as a nail."
Abraham Maslow

With the Cold War a fading memory the legitimacy of the trade blockade against Cuba became all the more questionable, especially when the U.S. had normalised trade relationships with most other communist regimes such as China and Vietnam. It wasn't as if Cuba presented a direct threat to the U.S., but then, that wasn't the point and it never had been. They could not forgive Fidel for having outfoxed them for so many decades or for showing that there could be another way to organize society. They were also concerned that if they ended the blockade now it would lessen dissent in Cuba, the economy would improve, and it would allow Fidel to declare another victory against the Yankee imperialists. The trade blockade, despite its obvious logical and moral failings, was there to stay.

Not only was the trade blockade remaining in place, it was going to get even more punitive. In 1990 President Bush Snr. passed the Mack Amendment which decreed that any foreign vessel that had docked in Cuba would not be allowed to dock in the U.S. for the next six months. This was a massive impediment to Cuba's ability to import goods and it resulted in millions of dollars being sucked out of the economy due to foreign firms insisting that Cuba cover the cost of these tedious separate shipments.

Fidel may have hoped that Democratic Party leader Bill Clinton – favourite to win the 1992 Presidential election – would take a more liberal approach, but he was to be sorely disappointed. Although Clinton did assert that the U.S. would not attack Cuba militarily and made some effort to crack down on Cuban-exile terrorist groups operating on U.S. soil, during his electoral campaign Clinton threw his support behind the 1992 Torricelli Act (also known as the Cuban Democracy Act). The act again prohibited American subsidiaries abroad from trading with Cuba (the ban had been lifted in 1975 and was worth around $700m in trade annually). He also restricted Cuba's use of U.S. dollars for international transactions, and stopped U.S. citizens from sending money to family members in Cuba. The idea, in Torricelli's words, was, "… to wreak havoc on that island."

Which it did. But its aim to force Fidel's regime to crumble "in a matter of weeks" was much less successful. And yet again it was the Cuban people who were caught in the firing line.

With an ever tighter blockade, many in Cuba deemed the situation untenable and were even more desperate to escape. In July some hijackers managed to commandeer a tugboat. They were immediately confronted by the Cuban coastguard who tried to impede the vessel using a high-powered water cannon but tragically they only succeeded in sinking it. All forty-one one of those on board drowned. Not wanting such a tragedy to repeat itself the government decreed that in future no vessel would be stopped, but this only gave encouragement to would-be hijackers.

The following month tensions broke. Rumours spread through Havana that somebody was going to hijack a ferry, resulting in over two-hundred people flocking to the harbour hoping to take advantage whilst trying to look inconspicuous and nonchalant. This, it can be assumed, was quite difficult. "Oh no, we're... we're all part of the Seagull Appreciation Society. Look there's one. What Luck! I call that one George because he looks my Grandpa."

When the police arrived the crowd became more agitated. Loud shouting turned into stone-throwing before groups of men split away from the crowd and ran through the capital's streets shouting anti-Castro slogans and breaking into government warehouses. Yet it was not the massive uprising that his enemies had been anticipating. One Canadian tourist who witnessed the event remarked that, "It was chicken feed compared to a routine hockey riot in Canada." But then apart from a full-scale nuclear war, what isn't?

It was no doubt a nerve-racking experience for the Cuban police as they had never had to deal with such an event. How would the government react? Would it apply the methods of the Chinese and send in the tanks? Would they take inspiration from the U.S. and use tear gas and rubber bullets? Or would they copy the British police and stand still and wring their hands as the whole area was set alight and the violence spread to other cities?

As ever, the Cubans had decided to deal with the rioters in their own way, and the police remained surprisingly restrained. For instance when a man was arrested for tipping over a police-van, he was allowed to bring his bicycle along in case it got stolen – and the police even helped him load it into the van.

Not all responses to the riots were quite so genteel however.

Sensing that having the police politely ask the rioters to 'stop all this nonsense and get a haircut' wasn't going to work Fidel called into action his 'rapid action brigades', which were comprised mainly of construction workers (i.e. big beefy blokes). As they weren't allowed guns they just picked up whatever was near to hand, which being builders tended to be big sticks and iron bars. Then – accompanied by Fidel and many other members of the government – they marched up and confronted the rioters who quickly dispersed.

Whether out of genuine loyalty or simple curiosity most people on the streets joined in and the event turned into a huge pro-government counter-demonstration. In classic Fidel fashion, the government had managed to flip the situation on its head.

Fidel's tactics had been morally dubious but he remained defiant in the face of criticism from the world media. He had stopped raids on the warehouses and restored order on the streets, and he had done it without killing anyone – not even an innocent newspaper seller. "Our enemies want to provoke violence and make us lose our head. I am proud of the way our people behaved... We have to exercise great self-control. In that sort of situation it is better that our own side should be the ones suffering casualties. We cannot abuse our power when we are fighting unarmed individuals... Weapons should be reserved for invaders and mercenaries..."

Soon after this the Cuban government relaxed their border controls and it was announced that anyone who had a boat could leave if they wanted to – as long as they had a vessel to do so. It was another dramatic, albeit not unexpected, embarrassment for the regime as 35,000 Cubans quickly took advantage of the offer. On the plus however, those thinking about hijacking planes or boats or gate-crashing embassies were now suitably distracted, spending their time with other wannabe migrants building their own boats on the seafront, overlooked by the inquisitive gaze of tourists and diplomats.

Over in Washington President Clinton followed developments closely. Wary of wading into another Mariel Crisis he made plans to have Cubans picked up at sea (so they couldn't take advantage of the Cuban Adjustment Act and claim immediate-residency) and had them interned at makeshift camps at the U.S. base at Guantánamo Bay. Then he sat down with the Cuban government to find a way of ending the crisis. The talks resulted in Clinton promising to actually process the 20,000 visas a year as agreed in previous migration agreements, and to return rafters to the Cuban authorities. Soon after Clinton also approved more cultural, academic, and religious exchanges. Most famously, however, Clinton started the wetfoot/dryfoot policy. Previously, under the 1966 Cuban Adjustment Act, *any* Cuban could gain permanent residence in the U.S., but under the new policy only those who set foot on American soil were allowed to stay - any Cuban picked up at sea would be returned to Cuba.

Yet despite these openings, Cuba's relationship with the U.S. was still strained. And it did not take long for the tension to break.

Still working hard to destabilise the regime, the Cuban-exile groups had formed another organisation in 1991 called 'Brothers to the Rescue'. The organization was founded and led by Bay of Pigs veteran José Basulto, who by his own admission "was trained as a terrorist by the U.S., in the use of violence to attain goals." Officially the organisation's 'mission' was to fly over the Florida Straits to search for Cuban rafters, but it also had a side-line in venturing into Cuban territory to drop anti-government propaganda.

Becoming frustrated with the repeated violations of their airspace, the Cuban authorities gave repeated warnings that the planes risked being intercepted by the Cuban air-force and shot down. During secret talks between the Washington and Havana, Fidel agreed to release three prisoners on the understanding that the U.S. authorities would ensure that the Brother's to the Rescue flights would no longer make incursions into Cuban airspace. Fidel released the prisoners, Clinton broke his word. The flight continued and the Cuban warnings that military action could be taken were not heeded. In late February 1996 – just six months since the last warning – three planes from the Brothers to the Rescue made another sortie over the island. Finally losing patience, the order was made for the air-force to intercept them. One of the planes managed to escape and make its way back home to the U.S. but the other two were shot down, killing four Cuban-Americans.

A UN investigation found that both Cuba and U.S. were to blame for the incident, but the U.S. were furious that (although the planes *had* ventured into Cuban airspace) the planes were actually shot down in international airspace. Things then got really heated when an audio recording was released of the Cuban pilots celebrating their success over the radio, saying, "We blew his balls off!" They shouted, "Homeland of Death you bastards!" Evidently they were better fighter pilots than they were diplomats.

In response to the incident Clinton not only tightened the trade blockade, he also enshrined it into law in what became known as The

Helms-Burton Act. It completely prohibited any import of any goods that *may* contain Cuban materials, and placed restrictions on entry visas for people who worked for companies who merely traded with Cuban enterprises. Meanwhile any Cuban-Americans who had had property expropriated by the regime could file for restitution in U.S courts. Even more controversially, it included a clause which prohibited *foreign* companies from trading with Cuba, if they also wanted to also trade in the U.S..[48] This was economic warfare on an epic scale and like many U.S. wars, many innocent people would be hit in the crossfire[49].

After a few months the lumbering bureaucracy of the European Community managed to find time to pass a resolution condemning the U.S. bill, but withdrew the threat of sanctions at the last minute. The UN General Assembly passed a resolution expressing concern at the extraterritorial nature of the law, but they were powerless to do anything. The UN only takes action against small countries – the major countries hold a veto.

Here are a handful of examples of the blockade in action in recent years:

- **2003 - Scottish Whiskey producer Glenfiddich finds their Havana Reserve whiskey banned in the U.S.. The problem was that the whiskey had been aged in Cuban rum barrels.**
- **2004 - U.S. fines Chiron Corporation $168,500 for exporting vaccines for children to Cuba despite the company having been given a licence to do so by UNICEF.**
- **2006 - The UN Environment Programme ran a children's painting competition. One of the winners was a 13 year old Cuban boy, but he was told that he could not be given his prize, a brand new Nikon camera because it contained parts made in the U.S..**
- **2007 - When a Cuban trade delegation arrived at the Hilton**

---

48 Interestingly, the Helms-Burton Act also contains twenty-eight separate grievances against Fidel's regime and according to Lars Schoultz in his book *That Infernal Little Cuban Republic*, 'No similar list appears anywhere else in the history of the U.S. legislation. The closest historical parallel is the Declaration of Independence list of grievances against King George III, and his indictment was limited to only eighteen transgressions.'

49 According to Noam Chomsky, "a detailed study by the American Association for World Health concluded that the embargo had severe health effects, and only Cuba's remarkable health care system had prevented a 'humanitarian catastrophe'"

Hotel in Oslo, Norway, they were refused entry. Vice-president for communications Linda Bain later explained to journalists that, "We are a U.S. company. The dilemma we face is that [if we took a booking from a Cuban delegation] we would be subject to fines or prison and if anyone [from the company] tried to enter the U.S., they would be arrested."

- 2008 - Chinese firm Minxia Non-Ferrous Metals, Inc. paid a $1,198,000 fine for investing in the Cuban nickel sector.
- 2008 - A British businessman living in Spain had his travel website disabled by the U.S. authorities because he was offering trips to Cuba and the company who sold his domain was registered in the U.S.
- 2010 - Dutch Bank ABN is fined $500 million for allowing transactions to be made between Cuban nationals. Over the years various other banks have also been fined heavily, including Lloyds TSB, HSBC, and Barclays Bank.
- 2010 – The U.S. fines Swedish firm Innospec $2.2m for selling a gasoline additive to Cuba.
- 2011 - $4.2 million designated by UNICEF for the Global Fund to Fight AIDS, Tuberculosis and Malaria is confiscated because they were giving to projects in Cuba.
- 2011 - French firm is fined $374,400 for providing shipping services to Cuba.
- 2013 - PayPal froze the accounts of UK online store York Coffee Emporium because the store sold Cuban coffee. Although the York Coffee Emporium did not trade in the U.S., PayPal did, and they were scared of being fined in the U.S. for dealing in the transaction.

And it wasn't just businesses that were getting caught in the crossfire of the U.S. government's economic war machine. In April 1996 two U.S. citizens, a man and his elderly father sailed to Cuba. So as to avoid breaking U.S. law by spending money there, they took with them enough food to last three months, but on their return voyage their boat was damaged in a storm and had to be dragged back to the port in Havana by the Cuban coastguard.

This left the men in a quandary. They needed materials to fix their ship, but they if they bought anything they would be in breach of U.S. law. The U.S. authorities helpfully suggested abandoning their boat and their dog, then make the return journey by plane. It could also be assumed that they would be expected to walk to the airport as getting a taxi would also be breaking U.S. law. Thankfully some nearby foreign sailors heard about their plight and fixed up the boat for them, but this was not the end of the saga. After finally reaching home soil they were stopped, questioned, and then fined tens of thousands of dollars after they let slip that they had given some medical gauze and tape to a Cuban chef who had cut his hand.

If this wasn't petty enough, when U.S. citizen Benjamin Treuhaft travelled to Cuba to personally tune dozens of antique pianos suffering from old-age (he also ran a charity which shipped unwanted pianos to the island), he was given a $10,000 fine. When he not only refused to pay up but also defiantly returned to Cuba to tune more pianos, the U.S. authorities increased the fine to $1.3million and threatened him with a ten year prison sentence. When he continued to ignore them the U.S. authorities reduced the fine to $3,500, but he still refused to pay. He wanted his day in court, but the U.S. authorities refused to escalate the situation that far for fear of becoming a laughing stock when they tried to argue piano's were a threat to national security.

And this was not the only piano fiasco. In 2016 British charity Cubanos en UK organised a fundraiser so they could buy a second-hand grand piano and send it to Cuba. Unfortunately they chose to use U.S.-based online crowdsourcing company Eventbrite, who claimed this breached the embargo and seized their funds.

It is incredible to think that the U.S. had twice as nuclear weapons than they do colleges and universities, yet appeared to be scared of plasters and pianos.

*

Clinton's hard-line stance on Cuban paid off as he won the 1996 Presidential elections. As the constitution prevented him from running for a third term, he felt more free to push for policies that he thought were 'right' morally and logically rather than what he thought was right electorally. And inevitably, that meant taking a much more liberal and mature approach to the Cuban issue.

Not only did he allow nearly a dozen U.S. news agencies to set up bureaus in Havana and agreed to sell machinery to Cuban private farmers, he also eased restrictions on the remittances that could be sent to people in Cuba, allowed more U.S. to travel to Cuba, and permitted more cultural and educational exchanges.

One group who weren't happy with Clinton's new direction were the Cuban-exile extremists in Miami. They were keen to keep the pressure on the Cuban government, and so decided to take matters into their own hands by unleashing a new wave of terrorism on the island. They mainly targeted the tourist sector, detonating nine bombs in hotels between April and October 1997 alone, killing foreign nationals and Cubans alike.

Terrorist veteran Luis Posada claimed responsibility, and in the hope of gaining his extradition the Cuban authorities shared intelligence documents with the FBI that proved it conclusively. However the U.S. ignored Cuba's request and instead hunted through the documents for clues about the activities of Cuban spy networks operating in the U.S.. When it became apparent that the U.S. authorities were on to them, twenty Cuban spies managed to escape back to their homeland, but a handful of agents – later dubbed the Miami 5 – were caught and arrested in September 1998.

The Miami 5 were imprisoned for seventeen months before being tried and sentenced to life. During the trial the defence team were not allowed to see any of the evidence being used against the men. Eight Nobel Prize winners wrote a letter to the U.S Attorney General, pleading for clemency, a sentiment similarly conveyed by politicians around the world, including over a hundred British Members of Parliament. It had little effect. One of the men was paroled in 2011 and a while later allowed to return home to his family. The rest were finally released in late 2014 as part of an effort to heal the historic feud between the two countries.

The arrest and jailing of the Cuban spies may have caused a diplomatic thunderstorm but it was the plight of a young Cuban boy who would preoccupy the hearts and minds of the world media, becoming a pawn in an ideological tug-of-war between Fidel and the Miami-exiles.

In December 1999 – just over a year after the Miami 5 were arrested – twelve people from two families sailed away from Cuba in a small aluminium boat. The Cuban authorities saw the vessel but chose not to intercept it after they noticed that there were children on board. Instead they deemed it safer to follow it to the edge of Cuban water and inform the U.S coastguard of the boat's position and bearing. The U.S coastguard took no notice of the information and all but three of the people on board the boat drowned after the boat capsized in the turbulent sea.

One of the survivors was a five year-old boy called Elian González. Elian's mother and her boyfriend had been amongst those who had drowned during the crossing. His father Juan Miguel who was still alive and well in Cuba expected his son to be returned to him but Elian's other relatives, notably his Great Uncle Lázaro González who lived in Miami, moved swiftly to gain custody with the aid of the anti-Castro exile groups.

As part of the propaganda offensive, Lázaro's team draped young boy in the American flag, lavished him with gifts and took him to Disneyland. They thrust him in front of the media, made him pose for numerous photo-shoots and forced him to answer questions from journalists. But few were fooled. Lázaro had four drink driving offences resulting in him having to attend an alcohol treatment programme, whereas even President Bill Clinton admitted that Juan Miguel genuinely loved Elian and they had a strong relationship. When a poll was taken, 70% of the U.S. public sided with Juan Miguel.

Facing an uphill battle, the Cuban exiles in Miami responded by intensifying their campaign, part of which included giving Elian a scholarship to the Lincoln Martí School in Little Havana where history textbooks were filled with passages such as, "Richard Nixon got a raw deal when he was forced to resign as President," and, "Americans now regret this and honour him." The school's curriculum summary, meanwhile, asserted that the school was to teach students to oppose abortion and homosexuality and, "In no way support Cuba or people in Cuba who believe in that system."

On January 5th the U.S. Immigration and Naturalisation Service ruled that Elian be returned to Cuba, but less than a week later the Cuban exiles had a massive breakthrough after they took the custody case to the family court and the judge, Rosa Rodriguez, gave emergency custody to Lázaro after ruling that sending the boy back to Cuba would be considered child abuse.

Feeling the need to up their game, Juan-Miguel's team sent Elian's grandmothers to Miami to meet with Elian. Unfortunately, rather than give the world a beautiful heart-warming moment that would ensure the U.S. public demand his return to Cuba, they unwittingly made themselves out to be perverted old women.

The controversy occurred during an interview when the grandmothers were asked how Elian was doing, and they replied that they had bitten his tongue and peeked down his pants to check 'if it had grown', and saw everything was fine! As you could imagine this did not sit well with the American public. Yet it was an honest mistake. In Cuba it is an innocent (if not somewhat bizarre) custom on the island and in no way denotes child abuse.

And they weren't the only family members causing making PR gaffs. Elian's father Juan Miguel appeared on U.S. TV talk show *Nightline* and when asked what he would do if he met his relatives in Miami who

160

were fighting for custody, he said he'd shoot them. Which wasn't the best thing to say when you're entire legal defence hinges on you being regarded as a level-headed, responsible adult. That said, he recovered well and gave a staunch defence of his homeland, pointing out that he, unlike many millions of Americans, he did not need to fret over his family's health and education. He loved his country, he loved his child, and he wanted to be reunited with both. And he had the support of his country. Vicki Huddleston, U.S. director of Cuban affairs noted that, "Every Cuban – the human rights activists, the man on the street, it didn't matter – they wanted Elian back. He was their child..." She also noted that the stance of the Cuban-exiles was "terrible propaganda against us, more effective that 40 plus years of Fidel's propaganda."

The case was taken before the U.S. Supreme Court who ruled Elian should be returned to his father. The Cuban people took to the streets in celebration. The whole ordeal was finally over. Almost.

It started when the Mayor of Miami Alexander Penalas ordered people to block the federal police from taking the boy, stating that any violence would be the fault of the President and Attorney General. As could be expected, the scene at the house had all the trappings of a great episode of Police, Camera, Action as a SWAT team, six Border Control agents and an INS agent stormed the house to remove Elian. Meanwhile the crowds outside – included several members of anti-Castro terrorist group Alpha 66 – were pepper-sprayed. For his part in the sorry débâcle, Penalas was made a laughing stock. Subjected to accusations that he was turning the city into a 'banana republic', protesters started throwing bananas at the City Hall. His reputation would never recover and his political career was left shattered.

In April 2000, Elian was once again reunited with his father, and photos of the beaming pair were broadcast around the world. Not everyone was happy of course. Violence involving Cuban exiles groups broke out in Miami who proceeded to smash store windows and set fire to rubbish bins, leading to over a thousand police officers in full riot gear and armed with tear gas being sent in to combat them.

When Fidel Castro died in late 2016 Elian would say of him, "Fidel was everyone's friend ... Fidel was that friend who was with my family, with my father at the most difficult moment, and who made it possible that I came back to my father and back to Cuba. And so that what I will always be thankful for... Fidel prepared us for exactly this moment, because that's precisely what he did: He taught us to fly, he taught us to dream and it's now up to us".

*

The struggle to have Elian returned to Cuban shores caused a groundswell of national unity and anti-U.S. sentiment which Fidel was eager to turn to his advantage. Despite the clear economic improvement, Fidel was aware that the market measures the government had enacted after the fall of the Soviet Union had not only diluted socialist framework, it had also diluted the socialist consciousness. And that was not all. Inequality had widened considerably as those who did not have access to the 'dollar market' were left behind, theft and corruption had increased sharply, and many of the Cuban youth who had grown up knowing nothing but the hardship of the Special Period had become disillusioned and politically apathetic. Knowing something needed to be done before the whole socialist project fell in on itself, Fidel launched the 'Battle of Ideas'.

The Battle of Ideas would ostensibly be Fidel's last-ditch attempt to prove to the Cuban masses that human and social development was more important than economic progress, that a socialist culture was richer than a capitalist culture.

It would encompass hundreds of projects in dozens of areas over several years. Colleges and universities were expanded, more investment was ploughed into the healthcare sector, hundreds of computer clubs were formed, educational TV channels were launched, book fairs were held, and rural schools were provided with solar panels. Showing just how serious he was, Fidel spent 7,000 hours planning the campaign and had a new Cabinet office created to help manage the initiative, bypassing the old bureaucracies.

Naturally Fidel was the figurehead of the campaign, but the 'vanguard' was the Young Communist League who worked with the government to organise mass public demonstrations and help reinvigorate the country's socialist soul. But to truly win the battle Fidel realised he needed an army and so unemployed youths (mainly from the poorest segments of society who had missed out on university education) were paid to train as 'social workers' and sent to serve in their local communities.

These social workers were extremely well received by the populace. Not only did they uncover tens of thousands of pensioners in need of personal care (and made sure the government did something about it), a leaked memo from the U.S. Special Interests Section mentioned that when they were deployed at petrol stations and oil refineries to reduce corruption

"Locals and foreigners… commented that revenues at the pumps doubled immediately.'"[50]

These social changes were one thing, but Fidel and his socialist hard-line supporters in government were determined to also bring the economic sphere back under more orthodox lines. Therefore in 2003 all state enterprises were again forbidden from financial independence (including the joint-ventures with foreign corporations) and their profits were diverted to social and welfare projects via the National Bank. Many critics claimed that this would lead to economic suicide, but growth actually increased from just under 2% in 2002, to over 12% in 2006.

The economy was helped along by some other factors too, not least the support of oil-rich Venezuela and rising commodity prices, but another major factor was the 2004 decision to again ban the use of the American dollar and have the people (and tourists) convert them to a 'convertible currency' pegged to the dollar (known as the CUCs). This considerably bolstered the state's supply of much needed international currency which was used to buy essential imports.

During the Special Period with its relaxation of religious freedoms there had been a substantial rise in people openly practising religion, and possibly keen to boost his share of the new market, Pope John Paul II made a visit to the island in 1999 where he was invited to give a speech to 10,000 Cubans in the Plaza de la Revolución.

He was given complete freedom to choose his own itinerary and was not restricted as to what he could say. Yet if the world was hoping he was going to castigate Fidel and the Cuban Revolution they were to be tremendously disappointed as he instead called for the U.S. to end the trade blockade and spoke about the dangers of consumerism. It was a fantastic propaganda coup for Fidel and the Revolution – it seemed God was on the side of the Atheists.

Indeed, as Cuba stepped into the twenty-first century it did seem that most of its prayers had been answered. Foreign investment had climbed to $5bn, food and drink production was up and cigar exports had also started to show improvement. Investments in nickel and cobalt were also starting to show returns, and Cuba was becoming much more self-

---

50 And it wasn't just the 'social workers' who were helping to fight against corruption. The same memo also goes on to say that when the Cuban Army took over management of the port in Havana the port inspector who had been displaced later complained that it 'had deprived him of his usual means of support (thieving) for the past five months, imposing serious financial hardship. According to the American, the port inspector was looking forward to a possible transfer to a port in Venezuela, where oversight might be more lax.'

sufficient in medical goods. Unemployment had fallen back to a much more respectable 4,1%, compared with averages in both Latin American and Europe of 9.3% and 8.6% respectively. The U.S. unemployment rate stood at 6%.

As the health of the economy improved, so did that of the average Cuban citizen. They had few material possessions but enjoyed a life expectancy to rival any developed nation and infant mortality rates were amongst the lowest in the world. In 1992 400 more physician home-offices were established, and by the end of 1999 there was one doctor for every 170 citizens.

The achievements were not missed by even the most developed nations. Western analysts remarked how 'It was most intriguing to observe a population that was not only determined to find solutions to all obstacles but did so with a great passion for communal welfare.'

Even World Bank President James Wolfson was forced to admit, "I think Cuba has done – and everybody would acknowledge – a great job on education and health," and "They should be congratulated on what they have done."

One area that did not seem to be improving was the sugar trade. The harvests had begun to improve in the mid-1990s but it had long been in decline. The sugar price fell year on year, and only ten of the 156 Cuban sugar mills were able to produce sugar more cheaply than the world market price. By 1997 the harvest had risen to a respectable level of 4.5 million tonnes, but it slipped back to 3.2 million tonnes in 1998 and 2.2 million tonnes by 2002.

Sugar had been a major focus for the country for hundreds of years. At first physically enslaved to it, they were then economically dependent on it. Yet with sugar prices dropping it was clear its future was doomed. In 2002 the government closed seventy-one of its 156 sugar mills. It was a monumental moment in Cuban history, akin to the British closure of the coal mines in the 1980's. The only difference was that the 100,000 Cuban workers who had lost their jobs as a result of the closures were not left to stagnate in the dole queue. Instead the were given ample remuneration and the opportunity to retrain in other areas, with many choosing to take up work in a similar profession, such as farming or ranching.

XII
New Beginnings of the Same Old Problems

"Getting older is no problem. You just have to live long enough."
Groucho Marx

Over the in the U.S. the new millennium saw the inauguration of a new President, George Bush Jnr, who would soon become infamous for such intellectual repartee, such as; "You know, when I campaigned here in 2000, I said, I want to be a war president. No president wants to be a war president, but I am one," and, "Our enemies are innovative and resourceful, and so are we. They never stop thinking about new ways to harm our country and our people, and neither do we."

It could be assumed that Fidel would be happy to take on such an intellectual lightweight, but an intellectual lightweight in charge of the biggest nuclear arsenal in the world was arguably much more dangerous.

Then on 11th September 2001, the U.S was struck by a terrorist attack which demolished the World Trade Centre's Twin Towers and left a gaping hole in the Pentagon. Almost immediately President George Bush Jnr. showed off his geography skills when he declared that because the hijackers were from Saudi Arabia, the U.S. was going to invade Afghanistan This resulted in a long drawn-out war that did nothing but make a poor, desolate country, much poorer and more desolate – very much like Aberystwyth in winter.

Bush's War on Terror (which would prove to be as successful as the War on Drugs) also saw the U.S. taking a more aggressive stance to all those who did not accept U.S. global hegemony. Naturally, that included Fidel.

But Fidel – and Cuba – had more pressing concerns. As the dust began to settle in New York, Mother Nature had struck the island with the strongest hurricane in fifty years. Hurricane Michelle, caused immense devastation to homes, farms, factories and infrastructure; basically destroying anything that was upright. The scenes were so horrific even the U.S. felt obliged to allow $30m of food and medicine to be traded, albeit on the condition that all purchases were paid for up front. And in cash. Considering his past behaviour it's startling that Fidel didn't respond by making the payments in five cent coins.

Nearly every year strong hurricanes hit Cuba, flattening tens of thousands of houses, destroying crops and crippling infrastructure. And as devastating as Hurricane Michelle was, the costliest weather was still to come – in 2008 Hurricane Ike caused damage estimated at $7bn (around 10% of Cuba's GDP) and came just days after Hurricane Gustav which caused damage of over $2bn.

Nevertheless, Fidel had always tried to ensure that the human cost of these disasters was kept to an absolute minimum. The United Nations' International Secretariat for Disaster Reduction said in 2005 that, "Cuba is a good example for other countries in terms of preparedness and prevention," whilst one Oxfam report notes Cuba's "Political commitment at all levels of government to allocate all resources at hand for the preservation of life in emergencies. This allows the Cubans to make use of any and all available resources, such as using local schools as evacuation shelters, securing boats and buses for evacuation purposes... [and a national] communications network." It later suggests that the U.S. could learn from the Cuban model, stating that thousands of lives could have been saved during Hurricane Katrina in 2005 had they done so.

But it is not just the hurricanes themselves which can cause the most heartache and hardship – it is the aftermath. But with tens of thousands of homes to rebuild, infrastructure to repair and food to distribute Cuba finds itself again outperforming its neighbours. With everything coordinated with military precision resources are more easily (and readily) allocated to the areas of most need. Nobody has to wait years for insurance companies to pay out only to be told it was an 'Act of God'.

*

After more than forty years at the helm, it was clear that time was starting to show on the old revolutionary, and not just in the greyness of his beard. In June 2001 Fidel passed out whilst making a televised[51] speech to sixty-thousand Cubans in El Cororro, although, being an incredibly hot day, so did hundreds of other people in the crowd. Though quickly recovering and continuing his speech later that day, it wasn't the first time he had lost control. It is claimed that during a diplomatic lunch he passed out and his head slammed against the table, then just seconds later he fully recovered and acted like nothing had happened.[52] But in late 2004 Fidel would give a public display of his increased frailty when he fell and broke his knee in

---

51 Most Cubans now had televisions and some of those unable to procure a satellite dish on the black market or state shops instead constructed their own from bin lids and broom handles. Which worked, apparently. The Cubans really are a very, *very* innovative people.

eight different places at a televised press conference.

The anti-Castro Cubans living in Miami were delighted at his sudden decline, though they themselves were also a dying breed. The head of the Cuban American Foundation (CANF), Mas Canosa, had died in 1997 and the organisation fell into disarray. The majority of Cuban-Americans in Miami were now much less hostile to the regime and were actually starting to protest *against* the trade blockade, leading to CANF falling into a period of ideological infighting. Without Canosa pulling the strings, CANF started to follow a more tolerant, open-minded policy towards Fidel's regime, leading to some of the organisation's extremists leaving in 2001 and setting up a new organisation – the Cuban Liberty Council – which like CANF before, helped shape U.S. policy towards Cuba, and sent delegations to the UN to have them condemn Fidel's regime on its Human Rights record.

With Fidel appearing to be on his last legs, the dissidents gained confidence. Part of the Cuban constitution allows citizens to propose legislation to be debated and voted upon in the National Assembly, if they can find ten thousand people to sign it. So a group called the Christian Liberation Movement led by Oswaldo Paya collected eleven thousand signatories on a petition calling for more free speech, the release of political prisoners, multi-party elections, and more freedom for private businesses. Fidel was not best pleased. First the signatures were scrutinized and accusations made that there were numerous duplications and forgeries.

The furore caused by the petition had not entirely gone away when former U.S. President Jimmy Carter visited the island a few months later. And of course he wasn't going to let the issue go away without a mention.

Fidel had invited Carter to address the Cuban people as part of a political campaign to normalise relations between their respective countries. Carter was under no conditions or limitations, with no subject off-limits and no questions prohibited. He spoke to students at Havana University, with television cameras from CNN broadcasting events to television sets all over the island. Most Cubans now had televisions and, in another example of the incredible powers of the black market, some 20,000 satellite dishes had been smuggled into the country. Many began constructing their own using dustbin lids and broom handles. Which apparently actually worked! The Cubans really are a very, *very* innovative people.

---

52 This is not the worst that has happened to a leading world statesman however, as President Bush Snr. Passed out and threw up on the Japanese Prime Minister in 1992.

In his speech Carter called for the abolishment of the trade embargo, before speaking at length about what he perceived to be the Cuban government's totalitarian nature, its human rights record, and its handling of Oswaldo Paya's petition. Fidel was in good spirits from the outset (upon greeting Carter at the airport he said "The band is going to play your national anthem... Excuse them if they are a little rusty") and despite Carter's harsh criticisms he listened politely throughout. Later, in a moment of mutual respect and friendship, Fidel took Carter to a baseball game and asked him to throw the first pitch in front of the 60,000 Cuban audience.

Fidel was less happy with the sitting U.S. President, George Bush Jnr. also waded into the Paya petition a few days later. Bush Jnr. was clearly delighted with the dissident's petition and decided to compliment it by publishing his own 'Initiative for a New Cuba'. The policy made regime change the prerequisite for normalising relations, set further travel restrictions on Americans wanting to travel to the island and promised more support for dissidents.

The U.S. suspended licences for mutual educational and cultural programmes and further restricted visas. Amongst other things this meant a 70 year-old Cuban singer and their four collaborators were unable to pick up their Grammy Award in person because the U.S. deemed it 'detrimental to the U.S.' interests'. The new measures also decreed that Cubans living in the U.S. would only be permitted to travel home once every three years, and only allowed to take with them a maximum of $300 spending money, a tenth of the previous limit.

U.S. Deputy Assistant Secretary of State Daniel Fisk was as honest as he was stark, "An individual can decide when they want to travel once every three years and the decision is up to them. So if they have a dying relative they have to figure out when they want to travel." Which if nothing else, does seem to put an unfair amount of pressure on those on their deathbed; that they be lucid enough to say their last goodbyes when their relatives arrive but also be dead in time so that they can also attend the funeral.

The punitive sanctions on Cuba coincided with a 2002 report by the U.S. Commission for the Assistance to Free Cuba which read less like a report and more like a manifesto for regime change. Not only did it declare that the U.S. would only normalize relations when Fidel had been deposed and the Cuban Revolution dissolved, but it also called for all property that had been nationalised since January 1st 1959 to be returned to their original owners or families, the privatization of public services such as healthcare and education, the dissolution of cooperatives, and pension payments ended. Around $80m was allocated to bring this plan about, including $31m to disseminate directly to Cuban dissidents.

In a rebuke to Bush's new policy (that clearly impeded Cuba's sovereignty) and, more directly, Paya's petition, Fidel decided to announce his own initiative and start his own petition which called for socialism to be enshrined into the constitution, removable only by referendum. Quickly mobilizing the people he soon collected more than eight million signatories. As per the constitution, both Paya's and Fidel's petitions were discussed in the National Assembly, and somewhat unsurprisingly it was Fidel's petition which was accepted.

*

Whilst securing socialism in Cuba Fidel was delighted to see many other countries in Latin America finally start to follow suit as the people on the continent fought back against U.S. domination.

Starting in 1998 Latin America was slowly submerged under a 'pink tide' as country after country started electing leftist governments, including Venezuela, Brazil, Chile, Costa Rica, Ecuador, Guatemala, Honduras, Paraguay, Peru, Argentina, Bolivia, Uruguay and El Salvador. Many of those elected heads of states or their cabinet ministers had at some point studied in Havana or travelled there for conferences. Some even had links with Fidel personally.

For Cuba the most important of all the countries to turn to the political left was the first. In 1998 the socialist candidate Hugo Chávez was elected to the Presidency in oil-rich Venezuela[53] and proved himself to be one of the most democratic leaders of the continent. In the first six years of his presidency Chávez organised eight national referendums which were deemed free and fair by accredited international organisations. When he won the 2004 election and the opposition claimed the result was fraudulent, Chávez agreed to have another one, which he won again, taking 60% of the vote. Two years later he won another election, this time with 63%.

For some reason the fact that he won a dozen elections, overseen by reputable international bodies did not stop the western world – especially the U.S. and UK media – brazenly describe Chávez as a dictator, cleverly altering the definition of the word dictator from 'someone who rules

---

53 Seemingly unperturbed by all their previous failures to assassinate Fidel, they tried again as he attended Chávez's inauguration. Needless to say, they failed. Again.

without the consent of the people', to 'someone who the rules without the consent of the U.S..' And the U.S. did *not consent* to Chávez being in power.

Upon being elected he immediately established cordial relations with the Cuban government and trade between the two countries increased dramatically, reaching $7 billion annually by 2009. Cuba supplied Venezuela with much needed doctors, specialist medical services and helped to create a national health infrastructure whilst the Venezuelans in return provided them with much-needed oil.

The Cuban medics provided health services to areas where people had rarely, if ever, seen a doctor. Many were so well respected that when some thieves discovered one of the bicycles they had stolen was owned by a Cuban medic they returned it immediately.

While many Cuban medics signed up for the programme through genuine altruism, the scheme provided a rare opportunity to earn a bit more cash. They were paid $100 to $200 dollars per month, compared to around $30 a month for doctors that stayed at home in Cuba.[54]

The U.S. were not happy. Not only had Chávez offered Cuba an invaluable supply of oil, he went on to nationalise U.S companies in order to fund his welfare reforms. He was a danger to their 'economic interests'. He had to be stopped.

Colluding with private media companies, the Venezuelan military and opposition groups, the U.S. began organising a coup to oust him. The scale and tactics used were shockingly brutal; the plan was to have snipers shoot anti-Chávez campaigners; blame Chávez and his supporters for it; force a coup and take power.

In April 2002 the plan was set in action. An anti-government demonstration was directed away from the official route and sent towards the pro-government demonstration that was happening in another part of the capital. Snipers then took position on the roofs lining the route and fired down upon them with wanton abandon.

The private television networks who were in on the plan then manipulated their footage to make it seem like Chávez supporters were the ones doing the shooting. Only after extensive independent analysis was it proved that the footage had been fabricated by stitching different scenes together. The chaos this unleashed gave perfect cover for the coup plotters

---

54 For those with their eyes on bigger prizes it also provided a handy means of escape to other countries – mainly the U.S. – where skilled salaries were higher and no one talked about tedious ideas like 'sharing the wealth'.

to send the army in and remove Chávez from power.

As the army surrounded the Presidential Palace, Chávez phoned Fidel to ask for advice. Scared he would suffer the same fate as Allende, Fidel implored Chávez not to do anything rash, not to resign, and reminded him that he was worth more to the country alive than he was dead.

Fidel then spent the next several hours trying to contact the leaders of the coup, offering two planes to pick up Chávez and his government and take them to Cuba. The offer was refused. Instead they took Chávez to an undisclosed location and a fake letter of resignation was circulated to the media.

Realising what was happening Chávez managed to send a message to his daughter Maria Gabriela, informing her that he had not resigned and to spread the word. He also told her to contact Fidel.

More than happy to take an active role, Fidel arranged for Maria and many of the other leading Venezuelan figures to give recorded phone interviews for foreign news stations to try and get the message out that Chávez had not resigned but had in fact been removed by a coup d'etat. "[I] became a kind of news reporter," Fidel says, "receiving and broadcasting news and public statements."

Having ousted Chávez, a new government led by Pedro Carmona – then President of the Venezuelan Federation of Chambers of Commerce – was sworn in. He immediately tore up the constitution which had been voted for in a referendum and scrapped the progressive welfare reforms already underway. He then received a message of congratulations from the U.S government who offered millions in aid to help the new regime. Cuba's trade contracts were ripped up and discarded. It looked like Cuba was yet again going to be forced into isolation in the hemisphere. U.S. democracy was being restored in Venezuela whether the people wanted it or not.

However this time things were different. Latin America was different. Venezuela was different. They would not roll over quietly. As news started to circulate of what was really going on, the people were quick to respond. Chávez had given them hope, offered them dignity and had already done so much to ease the poverty and ill-health that plagued the country. He had not abandoned them when he came to power, and they would not abandon him now. Those living the barrios of Caracas streamed down to the Presidential Palace in their tens of thousands forming an ocean of defiance that lapped up against the walls of the Presidential Palace. Like King Canute, there was nothing Carmona could do to fight back the tide.

Left with few options that would result in him keeping his head (to which he was in may ways firmly attached) he resigned, leading Fidel to assign him the disparaging moniker 'Carmona the Brief'.

Fidel then spoke to Carmona's replacement Diosdado Cabello and advised him to release Chávez before the people took justice into their own hands. Chávez was duly released and restored to power. The people had spoken and Venezuela was once more a *real* democracy – much to Washington's chagrin.

*

As much as the U.S. wanted to get rid of Chávez, they still hadn't forgotten about Fidel. After more than forty years, you would have thought the U.S. would have admitted defeat, but they were still hard at it.

In the latter part of 2002 the U.S. sent James Carson to head the Special Interests Office in Havana (The U.S. embassy in all but name). Soon after arriving Carson started supplying significant quantities of money to counter-revolutionary groups on the island, as well as radios so they could listen to the U.S. propaganda machine, Radio Martí. His meetings with such groups raised eyebrows among the Cuban security services, especially when on one occasion he stated his intent to travel all over the island to stir up anti-government sentiment. As well as being a bit cheeky, his actions were a clear violation of the 1961 Vienna Convention on Diplomatic Relations. Unsurprisingly Fidel soon informed Carson that he could no longer journey round the country with impunity and that if he wanted to travel anywhere on the island he had to ask permission seventy-two hours beforehand.

Tensions increased on the eve of the 2003 Iraq War when Fidel set about arresting the seventy-five main protagonists that had received money and supplies from Carson. In fact in the year leading up to these arrests the U.S. had doled out just shy of $9 million to counter-revolutionary groups and individuals in Cuba in the quest for regime-change.

When the U.S. appeared content ignoring international law by invading Iraq, and also included Cuba on the proclaimed 'Axis of Evil' list, Fidel understandably feared that he would be next in the firing line. In fact U.S. Undersecretary of State John Bolton made the wild assertion Cuba "Has at least a limited offensive biological warfare research-and-development program," as did Otto Reich and Condoleeza Rice.

Upon hearing the news of the arrests, the European Parliament condemned Fidel and the Cuban government and imposed strict trade sanctions. Yet at the same time they only half-heartedly wagged a finger at the U.S. and UK for not only launching an illegal war against Iraq, but also kidnapping *hundreds* of people, torturing them and keeping them in solitary confinement, under no jurisdiction and without charge in Guantánamo Bay.

*

As well as trying to deal with U.S.-financed counter-revolutionaries, Fidel was faced with another spate of hijackings by Cubans wanting to emigrate. There were many reasons Cubans wanted to leave their homeland. Most of the time it was for economic reasons, sometimes it was for political reasons, sometimes for cultural reasons, and sometimes it was to flee justice. One problem they all faced however was that there weren't many places better to live in Latin America, and even if the Cuban government sanctioned their travel the Bush administration had again made it much more difficult to obtain a visa to the U.S..

However the U.S. still had its 'Wet foot/Dry Foot' policy, whereby any Cuban who managed to stand on U.S. soil could automatically claim asylum (but anyone who was picked up at sea would be returned). It was therefore easy to understand why some Cubans came to the conclusion that if their only chance of gaining entry to a country was arriving there illegally (i.e. without a visa), they might as well go the full hog and travel there illegally too. After all, if you hijack a plane you'll probably be able to bump yourself up into first class.

As expected, the number of hijackings increased. The most notable one was on March 19th 2003 when six knife-wielding Cuban men hijacked a small passenger plane flying between the mainland and the Isle of Youth (formerly the Isle of Pines). They forced the pilot to fly to the Key West Military Base in Florida and although they were arrested upon arrival, less than a week later a U.S. judge ordered their release and they were awarded green cards. The plane of course, was impounded.

No doubt spurred on by their success, another passenger plane was hijacked two weeks later, this time carrying forty-five passengers. What the hijacker had not foreseen however, was that the plane didn't have enough fuel to go anywhere except Havana, leading to a tense stand-off at Havana airport as the hijacker reiterated his threats to blow the plane up with a grenade unless it was refuelled and flown to the U.S..

After being informed of the situation Fidel rushed to the airport to negotiate with the hijacker directly. When the hijacker refused to believe that the U.S. had no interest in offering him sanctuary, Fidel had someone wake up Carson at the Special Interests Section so that he could come and

173

tell the hijacker in person. But the hijacker still refused to give himself up.

Frustrated, Fidel had the pilot patch him in to the cabin whereupon he brought the passengers up to speed on events so far, asked them to act quickly should events escalate out of control and described the hijacker as 'totally irresponsible.' This was bad news for the passengers as up to this point they had been under the impression that he was one of those responsible hijackers who paid the fare for his journey, reimbursed the other passengers for the inconvenience, and kept the children entertained with magic tricks during the flight... The situation was tense.

Eventually the hijacker told Fidel he would release all the male hostages, but the male hostages were not willing to leave the women and children and so they were back to square one. Meanwhile the authorities finally worked out the hijacker's identity and promptly escorted his brother to the airport in the hopes that he could convince him to give it up. But he couldn't do it either.

In the end the hijacker was given permission to fly to Miami where he was arrested upon arrival, and although the U.S. had given the Cuban authorities assurances that their plane would not be impounded, they impounded it anyway. Fidel just didn't understand American humour.

Then another serious hijacking occurred just ten days later when a boat containing fifty people – both Cubans and foreign tourists – was seized by a group of seven men and three women armed with guns and knives. But it was not long before the hijackers realised that they had commandeered a flat bottomed boat which was incapable of making the arduous journey to Miami. Hoping to improve their situation by making it worse, they subsequently threatened the lives of all those on board unless a more suitable boat was found.

Fast becoming a veteran hostage negotiator, Fidel made his way to the harbour and met with a 'representative' of the hijackers. Then events quickly sped out of control. It started with one of the hostages bravely jumping off the boat, followed by another. Then another hostage grabbed one of the hijackers in a bear-hug whereupon they both fell into the water, and in the subsequent commotion all the other hostages jumped into the water too.

In the end all the hijackers were caught and put on trial. The three women involved received sentences ranging from one to five years, and of the remaining seven men, four received life sentences and three were given the death penalty.

The spat with Carson, remained alive and kicking. In December

2004 for example, Carson decided to erect a large Neon sign commemorating the 75 dissidents that had been arrested. In retaliation, the Cuban government erected various billboards showing the brutal treatment of prisoners metered out by the U.S. government at Guantánamo Bay, and a picture of Carson dressed as Santa riding a sleigh full of bombs.

Carson was eventually replaced in 2005 by Michael Parmly, who seemed intent on ratcheting up the tension even further. Within months of arriving he erected a massive electronic billboard on the U.S. Interests Section that showed counter-revolutionary messages. Naturally Fidel was less than pleased and so decided to obscure the billboard with 138 black flags to represent the 3,000-plus Cubans who had met their demise through U.S. terrorist attacks.

XIII
Conserve Energy – Give Up Work

"I retired from Parliament in order to devote more time to politics."
Tony Benn

Although it has been widely accepted that, unlike many other heads of state, Fidel had not used his position for personal enrichment, in 2006 *Forbes* magazine claimed he was more than twice as wealthy as the Queen of England with personal fortune of $900 million. Fidel defiantly refuted their claims; "If they can prove that I have a bank account abroad, with $900 million, with $1 million, $500,000, $100,000 or $1 in it, I will resign." No evidence was forthcoming. Not even the CIA, who would no doubt jump at the chance to have Fidel resign, could provide any evidence. Later Forbes quietly admitted that its calculations were 'more art than science' which in the language of public relations translates as 'we made it all up.'

Finally, in early 2005 Fidel announced the end of the Special Period in Time of Peace. He was not, however, ushering in a Special Period in Time of Plenty. There was still a long way to go. But things were looking up.

Following the anti-corruption drive, Fidel dubbed 2006 to be the Year of Energy Conservation as he unveiled a number of projects including upgrading the county's electrical infrastructure to make it more efficient, providing households with more energy efficient appliances such as slow-cookers, made the country the first in the world to phase out incandescent light-bulbs, and had social workers go from house to house to teach people about how they can reduce their energy consumption. By the end of the year the country had saved nearly one million barrels of oil, reduced CO_2 emissions by 5 million tons, whilst the economy grew by a whopping 12.5%.

So all this considered it was even more startling when, on July 31 2006, at the ripe old age of seventy-nine and just over a month before he was due to take over the reigns as leader of the non-aligned movement, Fidel announced that due to health reasons he was temporarily handing over his responsibilities to his brother Raúl. He would never again take up the post, and officially retired two years later stating that, "It would be a betrayal of my conscience to accept a responsibility requiring more mobility and dedication than I am physically able to offer."

This caught the U.S. establishment by complete surprise. They had only just released a report stating that any succession of power should be made to fail, and now it was happening they just stood by slack-jawed and impotent. Right up to the last moment Fidel had kept one step ahead of them.

Though Fidel may have retired from front-line politics, he would continued to play host to visiting foreign government officials and sporadically wrote articles in the state newspapers under the title 'Reflections of Comrade Fidel.' The articles usually focused on world affairs, carefully steering clear of anything that could be seen as interfering with government policy. He basically combined the roles played by Queen Elizabeth II and Prince Philip, in that he would not even think about talking about domestic issues but he would be occasionally take the time to insult foreigners, especially if they happened to be the U.S. President.

The Cuban people, on the whole, were more concerned with his health than his absence from the political stage. In her book *Cuba, What Everyone Needs To Know* U.S. scholar Julia Sweig describes how in 2010 she saw Fidel give a speech to some medical students, and when he made some rather macabre comment about how he would probably not 'return to these steps' many in the crowd starting crying. It seemed that although many Cubans wanted change they were respectful of what they had – and how they had got it.

*

With Raúl in charge things were going to be different. For one thing, Presidential speeches were going to be much, much shorter.

At the expense of his family Fidel had devoted his entire waking life to politics whereas Raúl was a devoted family man who generally undertook a 9-5 work schedule. And although Raúl's beliefs had been forged in the same fire as Fidel's, his own half-century of revolution had led him to develop a rather different conception of social justice. For decades, Fidel's focus on creating national wealth and sharing it equally had paid little heed to people's desire to live on their own terms. Raúl understood people's longing to be free – free from rules whose purpose they could not understand; free from the burden of having to pull everyone up with them if they wanted a better life for themselves. Raúl was still a staunch socialist but like his peers across Latin America, he was determined to find ways to create a decent, fair, equal society while cutting people free from the government's apron strings. Twenty-first century Cubans expected better – it was time for a new approach. And that also meant redefining the equality that the Revolution would offer; Speaking in 2008 Raúl explained that "Socialism means social justice and equality, but equality of rights, of opportunities, not of income… equality is not egalitarianism." Socialism wasn't being discarded, but the rules were being redrawn.

Giant government-run farms were divided up into more manageable chunks and leased for free (a practice known as *usufruct*) to groups for people who would farm them as co-operatives. Farmers could now also sell most of their produce directly to the public leading to markets springing up in towns and villages across the island, whilst the farmers, incentivised by the opportunity to turn a profit, worked hard to produce as much as possible from their land holdings.

Along with entrepreneurial independence, Raúl signed the UN's International Covenant on Civil and Political rights and the International Covenant on Economic, Social, and Cultural Rights and gave the UN Human Rights Council free access to investigate the island.

Raúl also oversaw a nationwide discussion that led to some new revolutionary measures being suggested, agreed, and implemented. One of the most popular reforms was to quash the ban on Cubans entering tourist hotels, a hangover from the tourism boom at the start of the Special Period when Fidel deemed the mingling of Cubans and wealthy western tourists as too 'dangerous'. It was one of the most stupid policies Fidel had ever enacted and for the decade or so it was in force, it made a mockery of all the Revolution was supposed to stand for.

Other measures saw the restrictions on ownership of certain electrical goods such as mobile phones removed, the death sentence abolished (except for crimes of terrorism) and in 2012 all musicians and artists who had defected or spoken out against the regime were taken off the blacklist and again allowed to play and sell their art. This was considered by many to be a positive move until someone pointed out that Gloria Estefan could again be played over the airwaves, but by then it was too late.

Less than a year after Fidel announced his retirement, Barack Obama took over the reigns at the White House. He had won the elections promising – amongst other things – the closure of the Guantánamo Bay, and a change in the relationship with Cuba.

To do this he faced huge political obstacles, namely, the Republican Party, right-wing media, and Cuban-exile extremists in Miami. They were going to make sure that he paid a high political price domestically if he tried to normalise relations.

Then again, he faced huge political embarrassment if he didn't. As part of the plan to isolate the Cuban Revolution, in the early 1960s the U.S. had pressurised other countries in the hemisphere to ban Cuba from the Organisation of American States (OAS). But since the 'Pink Tide' things had changed. The U.S. did not have the hold on Latin America they once had. It was no longer *their* backyard. And in 2009 those countries made the U.S. an ultimatum; allow Cuba to come back into the fold or there will be no future summits.

Obama proceeded the only way you can when navigating a political tightrope; slowly, cautiously and preferably not on a unicycle. Needless to say, not much changed during the first few years of his presidency. He did agree to revoke Cuba's expulsion from the OAS, and also lifted some restrictions on Cuban-Americans travelling to Cuba and sending remittances. But he also kept open the regressive policies of the Bush era, including the $20million budget for USAid's covert plans for 'democracy promotion' (but which ostensibly meant 'regime change' whilst Guantánamo Bay remained open and operational throughout his entire term of office.

Maybe, with Fidel pretty much out of the picture, Obama thought he might find dealing with 'the Cuban issue' an easier task than previous Presidents had. If he did, he was sorely mistaken. In 2014 he was forced to admit that his administration was behind the creation of the Cuban version of Twitter, ZunZuneo (ZunZuneo is Cuban slang for the sound of a hummingbird) in the hope of creating anti-government sentiment and fomenting a 'Cuban Spring', but all it achieved was to give the Cuban government tens of thousands of dollars in text messaging fees.

Launched in 2010, the website was financed through USAid, though they were eager to keep their links secret. One leaked memo from Mobile Accord, one of the contractors working on the project, states, "If it is discovered that the platform is, or ever was, backed by the U.S. government not only do we risk the channel being shut down by Cubacel [Cuban state phone company], but we risk the credibility of the platform as a source of reliable information, education, and empowerment in the eyes of the Cuban people."

Their deception was achieved by setting up a string of 'fake' companies. For example, the money for the project was channelled through a company was set up in the Cayman Islands, whilst a UK-based company was used to set up another company in Spain that would actually run the website.

An important element needed for success was to let users know that when using the site they could not be identified or monitored by Cuban authorities. However they were not so keen to let users know that they were being identified and monitored by the U.S. authorities who were busy collating a gigantic database that included users' gender, age, 'receptiveness' and political tendencies. It was hoped that they could use this information to help make future 'projects' more effective.

To help increase access, a scheme was created whereby people could 'tweet' by simply sending a text from their mobile phone. The service proved quite popular and by 2011 had attracted 40,000 subscribers (from two million mobile phone users) but to the frustration of the U.S., Cubans weren't using it to organise counter-revolutionary actions or even criticise the government – they were using it to keep up to date with the sports news and to keep in touch with friends and family – meanwhile the U.S. government was shelling out tens of thousands of dollars in text messaging fees to the Cuban state phone company. So rather than bringing down the Cuban government, they were actually helping to finance it! Eventually, in 2012, the U.S. pulled the plug on the project and took down the website. The only trace of its existence was a Facebook page with 300 'likes'.

In his second term Obama still appeared to be dragging his heels and it seemed the only thing that would hurry the process along would be divine intervention. And fortunately divine intervention is actually what happened as former nightclub bouncer turned progressive pontiff, Pope Francis .

Leogrande and Kornbluh note in their book 'Back Channel To Cuba' in which they give an extremely detailed account of the talks between the two countries over the decades following Fidel's triumph in 1959: 'One of the most striking things about the long history of antagonism between Cuba and the U.S. is how often the Cubans have tried to find a way to bridge the divide…. Every time a new president took office in Washington, Castro held out an olive branch…' And 'If anything, the historical record suggests that the Cubans have been too eager to negotiate and too gullible in believing U.S. promises, which, time and after time, were not kept.'

Now the pontiff leaned on the President of the U.S. to accept it for the betterment of both countries, and the world, before it was too late. He even offered to act as a mediator and host talks between both parties. And history was made.

Both governments sat down together and made real progress for the first time in over five decades. The first biggest breakthrough was announced in 2014. In return for a very important U.S. spy who had been languishing a Cuban jail for twenty years and Alan Goss (a USAid worker jailed for fifteen years in 2009 for working with 'enemy intelligence services'), Obama released the remaining members of the Cuban Five and took Cuba off the list of terrorist states.

Obama also agreed to increase the amount of remittances that could be sent to Cuba to $2,000 (previously set at just $500), relax the rules on food sales and agricultural supplies (including machinery), ease visa restrictions to make it easier for Americans to visit Cuba, allow U.S. telecommunication companies to enter deals to modernise Cuba's telecommunications infrastructure (including internet provision) and again permitted the importation of Cuban cigars – albeit limiting the amount to $100 per person per visit. In an historic moment, in early 2017 Cuban charcoal – sourced from hundreds of co-operatives on the island and channelled through state-run company CubaExport – became the first legal export to the U.S. in over 50 years.

In January 2017, just days before he was due to leave office, Obama announced he was rescinding the wetfoot/dryfoot policy (whereby the U.S. would return Cuban immigrants intercepted at sea, but automatically accept Cuban immigrants as soon as they set foot on U.S. soil. Now Cuban immigrants would be treated like any other[55].

One of the lesser mentioned deals however, was also the most surprising: In 2015 a hell-fire anti-tank missile that the U.S. were transporting from France ended up in Cuba after being accidentally put aboard the wrong aircraft.[56] The Cubans could have sold it to the Chinese or Russians, or even North Korea, but in a gesture of goodwill they returned it. Presumably after they'd stopped laughing.

To cement the new friendship in 2016 Obama actually travelled to Cuba to meet with Raúl, becoming the first U.S. President to set foot on Cuba soil since Calvin Coolidge in 1928. He didn't try and give anyone a poisoned wet-suit either – he was just there to chat and watch some baseball.

---

55 It was clear the Cuban people were expecting this announcement as there was a surge in those trying to get to the U.S. (from 24,278 in 2014, to 43,159 in 2015) to take advantage of the policy before it was revoked.

56 The U.S. were also red-faced when a missile fell off one of their helicopters during a training exercise and had to put out a statement asking citizens if they had seen it.

His visit was a truly monumental moment in Cuban-American relations, yet it was evident that Obama was not about to allow Cuba to seen as a friend, or equal. Nothing emphasized this more than when Raúl grabbed Obama's wrist and held it aloft in a show of camaraderie, only for Obama to make his reluctance clear by awkwardly allowing his wrist to go limp which made it look like the two world leaders were about to perform a rendition of 'I'm a little tea-pot' in front of the world's media. Raúl's embarrassment then turned to anger when one U.S. reporter in the room asked about political prisoners. "Give me the list of those political prisoners right now and they will be released." He said, "Tell me the names, and if those political prisoners exist they will be freed before nightfall." Tellingly, no names were forthcoming.[57]

So although in some ways Obama's administration still seemed enthusiastic in meddling in Cuban affairs, his determination to stop the U.S. continuing down the same path of bad ideas should be applauded. U.S. allies – especially those in Latin America – also seem to have been pleased with the progress he made as John Kerry noted in 2017 that, "Our new relationship with Cuba has also removed an irritant in our relationships throughout the Western Hemisphere".

Then came a big cloud of obnoxious gas called President Trump. During the Presidential election he complained that Obama had made too many concessions without getting anything in return, and promised to put Cuba back in the diplomatic freezer unless the Cuban government gave in to his demands.

The Cubans, of course, had heard all this hard-line rhetoric before. One street performer interviewed by CNN remarked, "We are watching him. If Trump is tougher, he is going to find a tougher people here," And, "The people will resist him here and he will be just one more that goes into history. He should loosen the screws, like Obama did."

Nevertheless Raúl deemed it would be best to play it safe and sent Trump a message in which he congratulated him on attaining the presidency. But he also scheduled a five-day military exercise to prepare the nation for any upcoming hostilities.

*

Then, on 25th November 2016, surrounded by his family, Fidel passed away. Despite his age, the news was still a major shock to many around the world. Nobody saw it coming – to the very end Fidel was full of surprises.

---

57 Mainly because Raúl had already released all those Amnesty International had decreed 'prisoners of conscience' back in 2010.

His last request was that he be allowed to remain humble in death and ensure no cult of personality be made of him; no monuments or roads were to be named after him, nor statues or busts made. His body was cremated and, after a nine-day pilgrimage[58] around the country so people could pay their respects, his ashes were placed in a large rock next to the resting place of his idol and Cuba's other independence hero, José Martí. The rock was supposed to represent a kernel of corn, in reference to one of Fidel's favourite José Marti lines 'All the glory of the world fits in a single kernel of corn'.

As the country descended into mourning even the country's most infamous (that is, the one most supported by the western powers) dissident group, the Women in White[59], called off their usual weekly protest against the government for the first time in thirteen years.

One 90 year-old Cuban woman interviewed for the BBC burst into tears when asked what he meant to her. She explained he had given her 'everything' and that "Fidel was like a father to me." And it wasn't just the older generation who remembered what life was life under Batista, and how much things had changed for the better under Fidel. One Cuban student noted that "If you walk around here, you'll see that the majority is young people. We're young people who are well-educated, we know what ideas we have and know what we want our country to look like. And we're not going to abandon those ideals."

An Al Jazeera article meanwhile quotes a ninety-five-year-old Cuba called José Perez who, even though he had his business nationalised by the revolution in the 1960s, says "I lost my business but I'm with him [Fidel Castro] 100 percent, because that man got us out of capitalism... He is the greatest thing nature has ever given."

The world-famous Cuban artist, Alejandro Lescay known for his incredible sculptures remarked that "As a man, he was extremely simple, and had a common appearance, but within seconds of talking to him, you realized that, no, although the way he communicated was ordinary, his thinking was monumental, extraordinary. I feel very sorry. But men like

---

58 Because life likes an irony, the vehicle transporting Fidel's remains broke down nearby the Moncada barracks and had to be pushed along by the soldiers who were escorting it.

59 The Women in White are widely reported in the western media's critical articles of the Cuban government, but Dr Denise Baden, Associate Professor in Business Ethics at the University of Southampton, noted in a BBC interview that "they're paid for by Americans – people don't realise that; an American agency pays for them. The Cubans don't take them seriously."

him do not die — death is not for those men. The legacy of Fidel will be eternal — he will be missed by the whole world, not just Cubans, but all humanity."

The UK newspaper *The Daily Telegraph* interviewed his personal chef, who, upon being asked if Fidel had any regrets replied "I don't think he had any, actually," he said. "He was human. He knew he made mistakes. But he didn't do any damage. He kicked out of the country those that had exploited the people. And then he gave the country back to the people." Upon being asked about the celebrations in Miami he replied, "It's really unpleasant. And inhumane. You have to respect his work – even if you don't like him as a character. I would love to go there and talk to them, [and] tell them what he was really like."

Of course, not everyone was going to miss him. Donald Trump – giving a worrying precedent of what Cubans might expect of him, tweeted 'The tyrant Castro is dead. New hope dawns. We will stand with the oppressed Cuban people for a free and democratic Cuba. Viva Cuba libre!'

There were also mass celebrations from the hard-line anti-Castro extremists in Miami and Cuban-born mayor of Miami Regaldo said to a Miami Herald reporter that "…what's happening right now [during the celebrations in Miami] is a sign of solidarity with the people of Cuba". Yet the people of Cuba he claimed to champion were far from impressed. A 42 year-old in Old Havana interviewed by the New York Post remarked "It really seems pretty sick to me… I can't understand one person celebrating the death of another," whilst a 33 year old called Diuber Perez said "Fidel was a human being with virtues and defects, that explains why they're crying here and raising glasses there… But it's really ugly to go after someone who's dead, regardless of who they are."

If this was not enough of a poke in the eye to the Cuban-exile extremists, the same New York Post article noted that 'the personal enmity toward Castro that is so widespread in Miami is largely missing even in private conversations on the island'.

*

The debate of who would replace the Castro brothers has been going on for many decades. At the time of writing the leadership of the Council of State is still in the hands of the elder generation, but with 95% of government posts staffed by people less than forty years of age it will not be a shock when the old guard depart.

A 2008 U.S. diplomatic cable from the U.S. Special Interests Section in Havana – released by whistle-blower website WikiLeaks – notes that, "We see very little evidence that the mainline dissident organizations have much resonance among ordinary Cubans."

This is echoed in the electoral results. At every election, dissidents plead for people to spoil their ballots to show their dissatisfaction with the regime, yet spoiled ballots rarely account for more than 4% of those cast., and with around a 97% participation rate, this result cannot be the result of people simply not voting through apathy. Neither could it be blamed on voter intimidation as ballots are secret. Elections are often overseen by schoolchildren, and the most intimidating behaviour they are likely to show is perpetually spitting out random questions like "Who invented the duvet?' or 'How many raccoons can you fit in on a spaceship?'

There is still a danger that the U.S. could return to dominate the island, or that an oligarchical system could spring up like that in post-Soviet Russia. But what is more likely is that Cuba will keep on experimenting, reinventing its unique jumble of compassionate, humanist market economics and surprising government schemes, and keep on being a glorious independent island in the sun.

But Fidel will be remembered, always.

Final Summary

Fidel Castro tried his best to create a better world, and maybe that is all we can ever ask of anyone. He did not use his position to feather his own nest, he did not instigate a cult of personality like Stalin or Mao. Instead he provided his people with first rate healthcare and education and built the world's only country to meet all the UN development goals whilst using a sustainable amount of energy. Most of all, he has always worked hard to provide for his people. And he has always stood side by side with other countries who, like him, wanted to be free to try a better way of living. He has made many mistakes, through ignorance, arrogance, stubbornness and naivety, but they were on the whole *honest* mistakes. As Kissinger admitted in his memoirs, Fidel 'was probably the most genuine revolutionary.'

It could be said that for all his failings and successes over the past fifty years, possibly the most incredible is how he had managed to outfox the greatest superpower the world has ever seen. As one U.S diplomat wryly noted, it appeared that the U.S. were "playing checkers whilst Castro is playing chess."

Former U.S Attorney General Ramsey Clark was much more forthcoming in his appraisal, and probably sums up Fidel's story better than anyone else; "The government of Fidel Castro has shown the world that is teeming with impoverished people, that it is possible for a very poor country emerging from the sickness and ignorance and corruption and poverty of the Batista regime, to within a few short years, educate all of its children, to create a system of education that is comprehensive, that reaches the entire society; that abolishes illiteracy, that is capable of export to other countries, to help them learn to read and write and grow and know."

Fidel meanwhile was much more humble in his reflections. "I was a thirty-two year-old inexperienced man who by mere chance survived many risks. I was simply lucky, and that is not something to take credit for." And "I feel no fear about myself personally. Glory and my place in history do not worry me. All the glory in the world can fit into a kernel of corn," he said, invoking the 19th-century Cuban patriot José Martí. "More people know about Napoleon because of the brandy than because of the battle at Austerlitz. We should be more concerned about the fate of ideas than the fate of men."

After all, ideas cannot be killed.

Bibliography

The CIA Targets Fidel: Secret 1967 CIA Inspector General's Report on Plots to Assassinate Fidel Castro. Ocean Press, 1996

The Cuban Missile Crisis 1962: Selected Foreign Policy Documents From the Administration of John F Kennedy. The Stationary Office, 2001

Cuban Revolution Reader: A Documentary History. Ocean Press, 2001

Acosta, Tomás Diez. *October 1962: The Missile Crisis as seen from Cuba.* Pathfinder, 2002

Agee, Philip. *CIA Diary: Inside the Company.* Penguin, 1975

Anderson, Jon Lee. *Che Guevara: A Revolutionary Life.* Bantam Books, 1997

Andrew, Christopher. *The KGB and the World: The Mitrokhin Archive II.* Penguin, 2006

August, Arnold. *Cuba and its neighbours: Democracy in Motion.* Fernwood Publishing, 2013

Bardach, Ann Louise. *Cuba Confidential. The extraordinary Tragedy of Cuba, its Revolution and its Exiles.* Penguin, 2002

Benjamin, Medea. *No Free Lunch: Food & Revolution in Cuba Today.* Institute for Food and Development Policy (USA), 1989

Blum, Denise. *Cuban Youth & Revolutionary Values: Educating the New Socialist Citizen.* University of Texas Press, 2011

Blum, William. *Rogue State: A Guide to the Worlds' Only Superpower.* Zed Books, 2003

Caistor, Nick. *Fidel Castro.* Reaktion Books Ltd, 2013

Castañeda, Jorge. *Compañero: The Life and Death of Che Guevara.* Bloomsbury Press, 1997

Castro, Fidel. *Cuba & Angola: Fighting for Africa's Freedom and Our Own.* Pathfinder, 2013

Castro, Fidel. *Bay of Pigs: 1961 Washington's First Military Defeat in the Americas.* Pathfinder Press, 2001

Castro, Fidel. *Che: A Memoir.* Ocean Press, 2006

Castro, Fidel. *My Early Years.* Ocean Press, 2005

Castro, Fidel. *My Life.* Allen Lane, 2007

Castro, Fidel. *The Prison Letters of Fidel Castro.* Nation Books, 1959

Castro, Fidel. *War, Racism and Economic Injustice: The Global Ravages of Capitalism.* Ocean Press, 2002

Chomsky, Aviva. *A History of the Cuban Revolution.* Wiley-Blackwell, 2011

Chomsky, Noam. *Hegemony or Survival: America's Quest For Global Dominance.* Penguin, 2003

Choy, Armando. *Our History Is Still Being Written: The Story of Three Chinese-Cuban Generals in the Cuban Revolution.* Pathfinder Press, 2005

Coltman, Leycester. *The Real Fidel Castro.* Yale University Press, 2003

De Toldedo, Lucia Alvarez. *The Story of Che Guevara.* Quercus, 2010

Dolgoff, Sam. *The Cuban Revolution: A Critical Perspective.* Black Rose Books Ltd, 1976

Dominguez, Jorge. *Cuban Economic and Social Development: Policy Reforms and Challenges in the 21st Century.* Havard University Press, 2012

Eire, Carlos. *Waiting for Snow in Havana.* Scribner, 2003

Elliston, Jon. *Psywar on Cuba: The Declassified History of U.S. anti-Castro Propaganda.* Ocean Press, 1999

English, T.J. *Havana Nocturne: How the Mob Owned Cuba... and Then Lost It to the Revolution.* William Morrow, 2008

Erikson, Daniel. *The Cuba Wars: The Fidel Castro, The United States, and the Next Revolution.* Bloomsbury Press, 2009

Escalante, Anibal. *Executive Action: 634 Ways to Kill Fidel Castro.* Ocean Press, 2006

Espin, Vilma. *Women in Cuba: The Making of a Revolution Within a Revolution.* Pathfinder Press, 2012

Esteban, Ángel. *Fidel & Gabo: A Portrait of the Legendary Friendship Between Fidel Castro and Gabriel García Márquez.* Pegasus Books LLCC, 2009

Estrada, Ulises. *Tania: Undercover with Che Guevara in Bolivia.* Ocean Press, 2005

Fernandez, Dr Rodolfo. *United States Vs. the Cuban Five: A Judicial Cover-up.* Editorial Capitán San Luis, 2006

Fitzgerald, Frank. *The Cuban Revolution In Crisis: From Managing Socialism to Managing Survival.* Monthly Review Press, 1994

Foss, Clive. *Fidel Castro.* Sutton Publishing, 2006

Geyer, Georgie Anne. *Guerilla Prince: The Untold Story of Fidel Castro.* Little Brown, 1991

Gleijeses, Piero. *Conflicting Missions.* Galago, 2003

Gonzalez, Mike. *Che Guevara and the Cuban Revolution.* Bookmarks, 2004

Gordon Nesbitt, Rebecca. *To Defend the Revolution Is to Defend Culture.* PM Press, 2015

Gott, Richard. *Cuba: A New History.* Yale University Press, 2004

Grando, Alberto. *Travelling With Che Guevara.* Pimlico, 2003

Guevara, Ernesto Che. *Che Guevara Speaks.* Pathfinder, 2000

Guevara, Ernesto Che. *Global Justice: Liberation and Socialism.* Ocean Press, 2002

Guevara, Ernesto Che. *Guerilla Warfare.* Pelican Books, 1969

Guevara, Ernesto Che. *Motorcycle Diaries: Notes On a Latin-American Journey.* Harper Perennial, 2007

Guevara, Ernesto Che. *Reminiscences of the Cuban Revolutionary War.* Harper Perennial, 2006.

Hansen, Joseph. *Dynamics of the Cuban Revolution: A Marxist Appreciation.* Pathfinder, 1994.

Hellinger, Daniel. Comparative *Politics of Latin America.* Routledge, 2011

Jones, Bart. *Hugo.* Bodley Head, 2008

Kapcia, Antoni. *Cuba: Island of Dreams.* Berg, 2000

Kapcia, Antoni. *Havana: The Making of Cuban Culture.* Berg, 2005

Kapcia, Antoni. *Leadership in the Cuban Revolution: The Unseen Story.* Zed Books, 2014

Kennedy, John F. *13 Days: The Cuban Missile Crisis.* Pan Books, 1969

Kennedy, Paul. *The Rise and Fall of the Great Powers: Economic Change and Military Conflict from 1500 to 2000.* Fontana Press, 1989

Lambie, George. *The Cuban Revolution in the 21st Century.* Pluto Press, 2010

Lamrani, Salim. *The Economic War Against Cuba: A Historical and Legal Perspective on the U.S. Blockade.* Monthly Review Books, 2013

Latell, Brian. *Castro's Secrets.* Palgrave Macmillan, 2012

Levine, Robert. *Secret Missions to Cuba.* Palgrave Press, 2001

Lister, John. *Cuba: Radical Face of Stalinism.* Left View Books, 1985

Lorenz, Marita. *The Spy Who Loved Castro. How I Was Recruited by the CIA to Assassinate Castro.* Ebury, 2017

Miller, Tom. *Trading with the Enemy: A Yankee Travels Through Castro's Cuba.* Atheneum, 1992.

Murphy, Dervla. *The Island That Dared: Journey's in Cuba.* Eland Press, 2008

Pavia, Peter. *The Cuba Project: Castro, Kennedy, and the FBI's Tamale Squad.* Palgrave Press, 2006

Perez, Louis. *Cuba: Between Reform and Revolution - 4th Edition.* Oxford University Press, 2011

Pineiro, Manuel. *Che Guevara and the Latin American Revolutionary Movements.* Ocean Press, 2001

Reid-Henry, S. *The Cuban Cure. Reason and Resistance in Global Science.* University of Chicago Press, 2010

Reid-Henry, Simon. *Fidel & Che: A Revolutionary Friendship.* Sceptre, 2009

Ripley, C. *Conversations with Cuba.* University of Georgia Press, 2001

Rodriguez, Juan Carlos. *The Bay of Pigs and the CIA.* Ocean Press 1999

Sanchez, Juan Reinaldo. *The Double Life of Fidel Castro: My 17 Years as Personal Bodyguard to El Líder Máximo.* St. Martin's Press, 2014

Saney, Isaac. *Cuba: A Revolution in Motion.* Zed Books, 2004

Santamaría, Haydée. *Rebel Lives: Haydée Santamaría.* Ocean Press, 2003

Schoultz, Lars. *That Infernal Little Cuban Republic: The United States and the Cuban Revolution.* The University of North Carolina Press, 2009

Skierka, Volker. *Fidel Castro.* Polity, 2004

Stout, Nancy. *One Day in September: Celia Sánchez and the Cuban Revolution.* Monthly Review Press, 2013

Sweig, Julia. *Cuba: What Everyone Needs to Know.* Oxford University Press, 2016

Szulc, Ted. *Fidel: A Critical Portrait.* Avon Books, 2000

Thomas, Hugh. *The Cuban Revolution.* Weidenfeld and Nicolson, 1996

Tovar, Carlos Méndez. *Democracy in Cuba?* Jose Marti Press, 1997

Villand, Michel. *My Business Partner Fidel Castro: Cuba, from the Dream to the Reality.* Roca Vicente-Franqueira, 2015

Von Tunzelman, Alex. *Red Heat: Conspiracy, Murder and the Cold War in the Caribbean.* Simon and Shcuster 2011

Walker, Steven. *Fidel Castro's Childhood: The Untold Story.* Matador 2012

Weinreb, Amelia Rosenberg. *Cuba in the Shadow of Change: Daily Life in the Twilight of the Revolution.* University Press of Florida, 2009

White, Mark. *Missiles in Cuba: Kennedy, Khrushchev, Castro and the 1962 Crisis.* Ivan R. Dee, 1997

Winter, Mick. *Cuba for the Misinformed: Facts from the Forbidden Island.* Westsong Publishing 2013.

Wright Mills, C. *Castro's Cuba.* Secker & Warburg, 1960

Yaffe, Helen. *Che Guevara: The Economics of Revolution.* Palgrave Press, 2009

Zayas, Luis Alfonso. *Soldier of the Cuban Revolution: From the Cane Fields of Oriente to General of the Revolutionary Armed Forces.* Pathfinder Press, 2011

For more information please email:

jamessheppard1981@gmail.com

25709788R00115

Printed in Poland
by Amazon Fulfillment
Poland Sp. z o.o., Wrocław